BUSINESS-DRIVEN COMPENSATION POLICIES

BUSINESS-DRIVEN COMPENSATION POLICIES

Integrating Compensation Systems with Corporate Strategies

Robert L. Heneman

AMACOM
American Management Association

New York • Atlanta • Boston • Chicago • Kansas City • San Francisco • Washington, D.C.
Brussels • Mexico City • Tokyo • Toronto

> *Special discounts on bulk quantities of AMACOM books are available to corporations, professional associations, and other organizations. For details, contact Special Sales Department, AMACOM, a division of American Management Association, 1601 Broadway, New York, NY 10019.*
> *Tel.: 212-903-8316. Fax: 212-903-8083.*
> *Web Site: amacombooks.org*

This publication is designed to provide accurate and authoritative information in regard to the subject matter covered. It is sold with the understanding that the publisher is not engaged in rendering legal, accounting, or other professional service. If legal advice or other expert assistance is required, the services of a competent professional person should be sought.

Library of Congress Cataloging-in-Publication Data

Heneman, Robert L.
  Business-driven compensation policies : integrating compensation systems with corporate business strategies / Robert L. Heneman.
    p. cm.
  Includes index.
  ISBN 0-8144-0541-X
  1. Compensation management. 2. Business planning. 3. Employees— Rating of. I. Title.
HF5549.5.C67 H4638 2000
658.3′22—dc21   *00-044172*

© 2001 Robert L. Heneman
All rights reserved.
Printed in the United States of America.

This publication may not be reproduced,
stored in a retrieval system,
or transmitted in whole or in part,
in any form or by any means, electronic,
mechanical, photocopying, recording, or otherwise,
without the prior written permission of AMACOM,
a division of American Management Association,
1601 Broadway, New York, NY 10019.

Printing number

10 9 8 7 6 5 4 3 2 1

To my wonderful children,
Mark Henry Heneman
and
Elizabeth Michelle Heneman

Contents

Preface	ix
Part 1: Strategic Pay Systems	**1**
Chapter 1: Overview and Model	5
Chapter 2: Corporate Business Strategies and Compensation Strategies	15
Part 2: Base Pay Systems	**41**
Chapter 3: Work Analysis	45
Chapter 4: Work Evaluation	71
Chapter 5: Market Surveys	95
Chapter 6: Pay Structures	137
Part 3: Performance Measurement and Rewards	**155**
Chapter 7: Individual Rewards	159
Chapter 8: Team Rewards	199
Chapter 9: Organizational Rewards	207
Part 4: Pay System Administration	**221**
Chapter 10: Strategic Pay Design	225
Chapter 11: Strategic Pay Implementation	235
Chapter 12: Strategic Pay Evaluation	253

Part 5: Checklist Summaries — 265

    Chapter 13: General Do's and Don'ts — 269

    Chapter 14: Business Strategy Checklist — 275

Appendix: Example Pay Communication — 293

Index — 317

About the Author — 325

Preface

Much has been written about the need to be strategic in compensation decision making in recent years. Compensation articles with a strategic focus have proliferated in trade magazines, books, and research journals. While we know about the importance of a strategic approach, in terms of both senior management desire for such an approach and the likely positive impact on organizational effectiveness, we unfortunately know much less about how to actually link compensation policies with corporate business strategies. This lack of "how-to" information is particularly problematic for practitioners who are charged with developing and administering strategic pay systems for their executives. My primary objective in writing this book is to show practitioners the how-to steps needed in strategic compensation decision making. My hope is that this book will be found on the desk of all human resources professionals and other practitioners involved in the design, administration, and evaluation of compensation systems.

A secondary objective is to help give life to compensation textbooks read by students in human resources classes. Compensation texts often do not contain the how-to instructions needed for students to learn to manage the vagaries involved in compensation decision making especially as they relate to business strategies. My hope is that this book will be used as a supplement to compensation textbooks to show students at an operational level how to be strategic regarding direct compensation decisions.

I would like to acknowledge the excellent assistance I received from four individuals in writing this book. Adrienne Hickey did a superb job of helping me develop this book in a meaningful format. Joan Evans did an outstanding job with the word processing associated with the book.

Preface

Amy Dooley did a great job of compiling the summaries at the back of the book. Brian Klaas shared many excellent insights that I have used to improve the content of the book.

Lastly, I would like to thank all those organizations and people that I have worked with in a consulting capacity over the years. The many important lessons that I have learned from them are shared throughout the book.

PART 1

STRATEGIC PAY SYSTEMS

Chapter 1: Overview and Model

Chapter 2: Corporate Business Strategies and Compensation Strategies

Strategic Pay Systems

A model of corporate business strategy and pay policy integration.

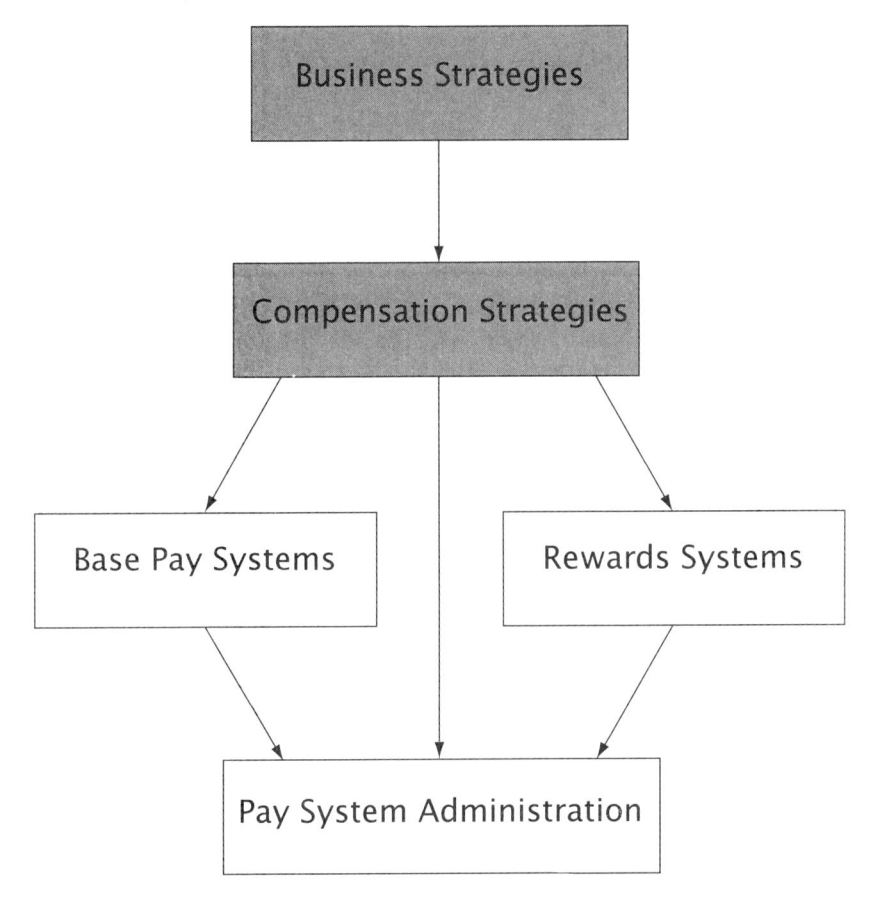

```
                    ┌──────────────────────┐
                    │  Business Strategies │
                    └──────────┬───────────┘
                               │
                               ▼
                  ┌────────────────────────┐
                  │ Compensation Strategies│
                  └───┬────────┬─────────┬─┘
                      │        │         │
           ┌──────────▼──┐     │    ┌────▼──────────┐
           │Base Pay     │     │    │Rewards Systems│
           │Systems      │     │    │               │
           └──────┬──────┘     │    └──────┬────────┘
                  │            │           │
                  └────────────▼───────────┘
                  ┌────────────────────────┐
                  │ Pay System Administration│
                  └────────────────────────┘
```

CHAPTER 1

Overview and Model

The ultimate goal of a pay system is to align the goals and interests of employees with the goals and interests of the organization. Organizations want to have their employees think and act like owners of the business. The reason for this desired alignment between employee and organizational goals can be captured in a phrase: "People don't wash rental cars." When employees feel as if they own the business, they are likely to do whatever it takes for the business to succeed. In the absence of a meaningful pay system, it is unlikely that employees will go the "extra mile" needed to make the organization successful. Conversely, with a meaningful pay system, employees are likely to go above and beyond the call of duty to take whatever actions are needed for the organization to be successful.

In order for employees to act like owners of the company, they need to know the goals of the company and be rewarded for the accomplishment of these goals. Two powerful tools are available to help make ownership happen. First, corporate business strategies help determine the goals toward which employees strive. Second, pay systems help channel employee efforts toward reaching those goals. The power of these two tools working in concert can be seen in a study of management by objectives (MBO) systems. In an MBO system, business goals are set with employees and rewards are provided for goal accomplishment. In a review of seventy studies of MBO systems, it was found that the average gain in productivity associated with an MBO intervention was 45 percent.[1] This is a very large gain in productivity for a human resource intervention.

Although the logic of combining goals and rewards to motivate performance is a straightforward proposition, the successful implementation of this proposition is a very complex process. It requires the merger of corporate business strategies with compensation policies. The objective of this book is to show a process that can be used to merge these two complicated systems in order to improve organizational effectiveness. Many books and articles write about the importance of integrating these two systems, but there is very little practical advice on how to best accomplish this undertaking. I will draw upon my twenty years of strategic planning and compensation consulting and research experiences to show how to effectively integrate corporate business strategies and compensation policies.

The Context for Integration

Before presenting a model on how to integrate corporate business strategies and compensation policies, a word of caution is needed. In order for compensation systems to be effective, they must not only be successfully integrated with corporate business strategies, but they must also be integrated with other business systems. These other systems include the laws and regulations of the larger society, the structure of the organization, business processes of the organization, the culture of the organization, and other human resources systems, including staffing and development. All of these systems need to "fit" together to form an integrated whole.

My reason for singling out one link, between corporate strategies and compensation policies, is the result of my experiences that this link is often the Achilles heel of compensation systems. Most pay system failures that I have observed took place because the pay system was a stand-alone program without a concrete foundation in the business plan. Be forewarned, however, that the link between corporate business strategies and compensation policies should not be emphasized to the exclusion of the link between compensation policies and other business systems. Accordingly, mention of these other business systems in relation to compensation policies will be made throughout the book.

An Integrative Model

Exhibit 1-1 presents a model to show the steps needed to integrate corporate business strategies and compensation policies in organizations. It also serves as a road map to the chapters covered in this book.

The premise of this model is that in most situations, the business strat-

Overview and Model

EXHIBIT 1-1

A model of corporate business strategy and pay policy integration.

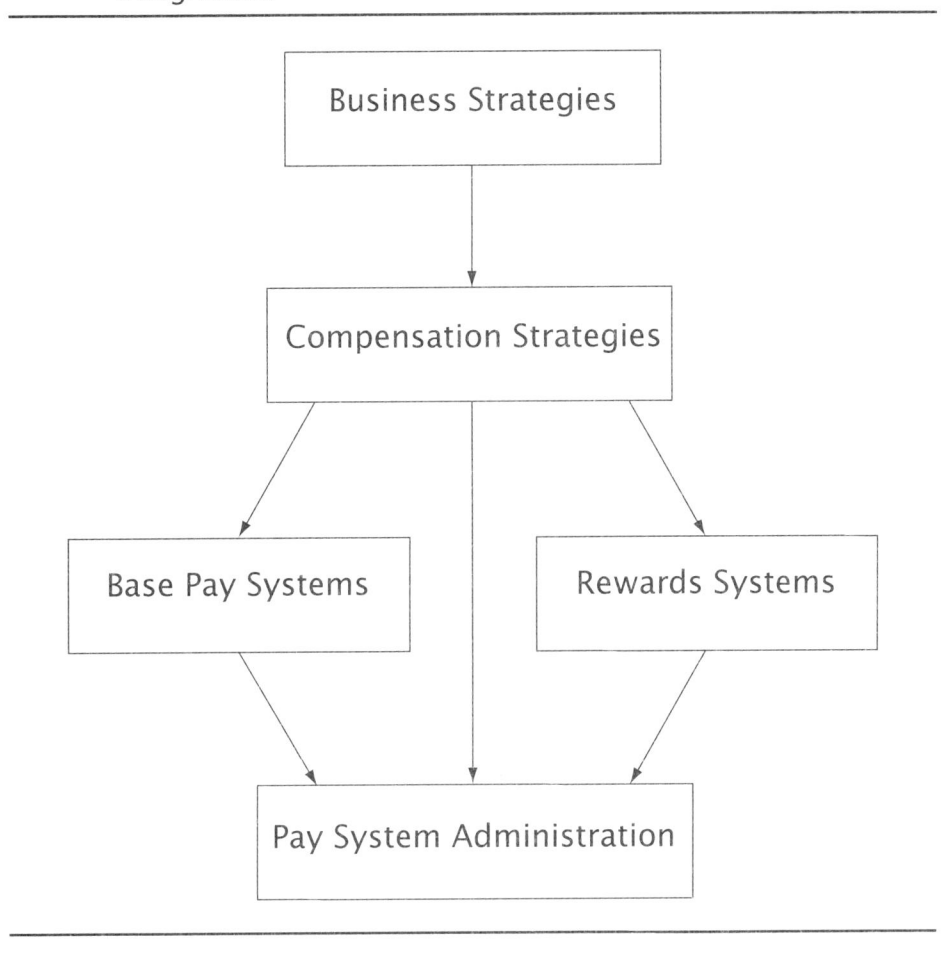

```
        ┌─────────────────────┐
        │ Business Strategies │
        └──────────┬──────────┘
                   │
                   ▼
        ┌───────────────────────┐
        │ Compensation Strategies│
        └──┬──────────┬─────────┬┘
           │          │         │
           ▼          ▼         ▼
  ┌────────────────┐      ┌────────────────┐
  │ Base Pay Systems│      │ Rewards Systems│
  └────────┬───────┘      └────────┬───────┘
           │         │             │
           ▼         ▼             ▼
        ┌─────────────────────────┐
        │ Pay System Administration│
        └─────────────────────────┘
```

egy must be formed prior to the development of the compensation system. That is, the compensation system should lag rather than lead business strategy. Hence, the corporate business strategy is the platform upon which compensation policies are developed and administered.

Both the formulation and administration of the compensation plan must be guided by the corporate business policy to ensure an alignment between the goals of the company and the goals of the workforce. Previous treatments of this topic focus on the need to integrate corporate business strategies with the formation of compensation policies, but, as will be shown in later chapters in this book, it is equally important to use the corporate business policy to guide the administration of the policy.

It should also be noted that there is no direct translation of the corporate business strategy into the formation and administration of compensation policies. To do so would ignore the larger business context in which the compensation system operates. Attention must also be paid in the compensation strategy to the laws and regulations of the larger society and the culture, business processes, and structure of the organization. All of these considerations are molded together in the compensation strategy, and, in turn, the compensation strategy results in the formulation and administration of pay policies.

The model shows that the corporate business strategy is a primary determinant of the compensation strategy. In turn, the compensation strategy determines the formation of base pay and incentive systems. It also determines the formation of benefit policies, but the focus in this book is on direct pay. Lastly, the model shows that both the pay systems themselves and the compensation strategy determine how the compensation policies are to be administered. The pay systems determine what needs to be administered and the compensation strategy determines how the compensation policies should be administered.

Case Studies

In order to demonstrate how the model works and to give a preview of the rest of the book, two case studies will be used to show how this model can be used as a basis for compensation decision making.

CASE 1

Cable Television

Meto Cable Communications (MCC) is a cable television company that operates in a large metropolitan area in the Midwest. It has been acquired by a national telecommunications company and is one of its most profitable companies since the acquisition. MCC has increased its subscriber base from 150,000 to 360,000. Total annual revenues have increased from $75 million to $210 million. MCC has been a leader in technology because all of its customers have fiber-optic cable running into their homes and businesses.

Business Strategy. The major source of competitive advantage for MCC has been its advanced technology. The early use of fiber-optic cable has opened the doors for many innovations in the cable industry, including the delivery of the Internet and interactive television. As others catch up with this state-of-the-art technology, they recognize that in order to sustain competitive advantage in the cable industry, they will also need to develop additional competencies. It is the belief of senior management at MCC that the competencies to be developed include: (1) an empowered workforce and (2) innovative products and services such as telephones, on-demand movies, interactive television, and Internet services. An empowered workforce is seen as critical because of the belief that it is likely to lead to high levels of satisfaction with work, which will lead to more satisfied customers. Innovative products and services are seen as another critical part of this business strategy because they will allow the subscriber to have all of their media needs satisfied by one provider rather than multiple providers.

These new competencies demanded that senior management follow a new operating paradigm. The old paradigm, based on a technology focus, follows:

- Many layers of management
- Rigid hierarchy
- Vertical orientation
- Top-down decision making
- Little upward communication
- Reporting relationships that interfere with service delivery
- Large amount of paperwork
- Many controls and approvals required
- Authoritarian supervision
- Small spans of control
- Little discretion and authority to perform

The new operating paradigm, based on employee empowerment and innovative products and services, follows:

- Few layers of management
- Flexible structure
- Horizontal orientation
- Shared decision making

- Upward communication
- Reporting relationships that emphasize service delivery
- Small amount of paperwork
- Few controls and approvals required
- Leadership emphasized
- Large spans of control
- Great discretion and authority to perform

Compensation Strategy. With the emphasis on technology as a business strategy, the organization used to employ a large number of technical personnel. The pay strategy was to pay above-market wages and to base pay increases on seniority in order to attract and retain talented technicians. Now that the fiber optics have been installed, far fewer technicians are needed, and, instead, MCC now employs a large number of customer service associates and a new set of research and development employees. The compensation strategy has shifted to a focus on paying for customer service and paying for bottom-line results. The previous pay system was formed by senior management, but the belief now is that employees should be empowered not only to make customer service decisions, but also to be involved in the design and delivery of pay systems. Finally, the development of new skill sets (i.e., customer service) needs to be rewarded to deploy former technicians to be customer service representatives.

Base Pay. The old pay system at MCC had a large number of pay grades with very narrow bands from the minimum to the maximum. Progression within the pay band was based upon seniority. The new pay system decreased the number of bands and increased the range between the pay minimums and pay maximums of each grade. These steps were taken to give all employees more discretion in performing their jobs and to be more responsive to customer concerns. Also, customer service teams were formed again to be more responsive to the customer. Team members were used as team leaders on a rotating basis. Base pay was upgraded for those months that a team member was upgraded to team leader.

Reward Systems. A number of new reward systems was implemented. A goal-sharing plan was put in place to reward associates for the accomplishment of targeted corporate goals such as cost savings and revenue enhancement goals such as customer service. This variable pay plan gradually substituted for above-market wages. In addition, a skill-based pay system was implemented. Previous technicians received pay bonuses, for mastering customer service and team skills (e.g., communications) while previous customer service representatives received bonuses for mastering technical skills (e.g., installations). By doing so, cross-functional skills were developed in the team, and the teams serviced a geographic area rather than a functional area. Seniority-based pay was eliminated and replaced with merit pay to reward the contribution of performance rather than time to the organization.

Pay System Administration. Previously, there was no director of compensation. A compensation director was hired to design and administer the new pay systems. Pay system design and implementation, previously done only by senior management, was now done by cross-functional task forces of high-potential employees along with the compensation director. The plans they developed were sent to senior management for approval. Input for pay plan development was solicited by the task forces by conducting focus groups with employees. An attitude survey was developed by a Ph.D. intern in industrial psychology to track employee reactions to the pay systems.

In short, this case illustrates how a change in strategic directions, from technology to empowerment and customer service, resulted in a shift in compensation philosophies, from time in grade to customer service and results. In turn, more flexibility was built into the base pay system with broadbanding, and rewards were provided for the delivery of new skills to the customer and heightened customer appreciation. Employees were empowered to develop new pay systems to support the new business strategy. As can be seen in this case, corporate business strategy is the force that guides pay policy formation and administration.

CASE 2

Computer Manufacturer

CDI is a multibillion-dollar computer manufacturer. Although it is profitable, CDI has lost market share in recent years to its competitors. Recent profitability of CDI is attributable primarily to cost cutting, but there is little budget left to trim. The company is now in the process of reorganizing itself to continue to be competitive in the new millennium.

Business Strategy. Originally, CDI had a corner on the market in terms of its technology. It provided state-of-the-art technology and was able to distribute its costs over multiple product lines. As a result, CDI built a loyal customer base and became a household name. In the process, it also built a very large and unwieldy bureaucracy and gradually reduced a large percentage of its research and development budget. In order to turn the company around, senior management has agreed upon the following business strategy to build up some newly needed capabilities in the company. First, managers are going to create a more flexible organization that is responsive to both customer and employee ideas. Second, cost containment will continue to be a major objective. Third, they plan to reinvigorate their major product line with the acquisition of new technology.

Compensation Strategy. A new compensation platform was built to support the new business strategy. Like many bureaucracies, the traditional model of pay used at CDI consisted of narrowly defined jobs slotted into narrow pay bands based on a job evaluation system developed in the 1970s. Movement within the pay structure was based on ratings of performance that yielded a merit pay increase. This traditional system of base pay plus merit was founded on a strategy of paying for the importance of the job title and an assessment of one's contribution to the job by an immediate supervisor. This traditional compensation strategy conflicts with the new business strategy in several ways. First, merit pay had become an entitlement and now conflicts with the goal of cost minimization. Second, the narrow job structure led to little flexibility in duties performed and little innovation through cross-functional orientation.

A compensation philosophy was developed to foster the new corporate business strategies. In particular, the number of pay bands was reduced and the pay ranges widened to build more flexibility into jobs. Greater attention was paid to the market than to merit ratings in the determination of pay in order to ensure that increases in labor costs were based on market value rather than on seniority in the company. The merit philosophy was retained, but the system was heavily weighted toward bottom-line results and skill acquisition by individual employees. A team-based structure was viewed as not consistent with the past and desired cultures of the organization. In short, the new compensation strategy was designed to make the new system more flexible, manage labor costs, and strengthen the link between individual performance objectives and the business strategy.

Base Pay Systems. Streamlined posting descriptions were created that emphasized the roles that people were expected to play, rather than emphasizing the duties and tasks that they were expected to perform. Skills required in the expected role were carefully defined. A broad-based classification system was used to group the jobs into bands, and the number of job grades was substantially reduced. Care was taken to ensure that the compensation strategy of managing labor costs was not compromised by building the control points to carefully tie each pay band to the market value of similar jobs.

Reward Systems. The merit pay plan was revamped to include new criteria for skill development and business performance results. Skills were emphasized in the merit pay system rather than through a skill-based pay system to recognize the large variety of jobs in the company, to minimize the large start-up costs associated with a skill-based pay system, and to preserve the individual merit culture. The merit pay plan was also revised to include business results for each position. A management by objectives type system was created in which each position had predetermined business goals to accomplish with measurable results. Categories of results given the greatest weight were those directly related to innovation, new product development, and cost minimization.

Pay System Administration. Previous pay communication efforts had been the sole responsibility of the human resources department. In order to better show the relationship between the business strategy and the compensation system, immediate supervisors were given the responsibility for communicating the plan to employees. Feedback was collected throughout the process by the human resources department to ensure that employees understood the relationship between their business objectives and the larger business strategy of the organization. This feedback was then used for ongoing changes to compensation policy formation and administration.

As with the previous case, it can be seen how the business strategy drove the formation of a new compensation strategy. In turn, that new compensation strategy set the stage for deciding which pay systems to include (e.g., revised merit pay plan) and which pay systems to exclude (e.g., skill-based pay). The detailed processes needed to make these steps take place are the topics of the rest of the book. This process will be broken down in a step-by-step fashion using the model framed in this first chapter.

Note

1. Robert Rodgers and John E. Hunter, "Impact of Management by Objectives on Organizational Productivity," *Journal of Applied Psychology* (1991): 76 (2), pp. 322–336.

CHAPTER 2

Corporate Business Strategies and Compensation Strategies

It is essential to have the corporate business strategy in hand before developing a new compensation system or revising an existing one. Most often, the corporate business strategy is readily available. Sometimes, however, while the corporate business strategy has been established, it may be difficult to locate. Other times, it may need to be formulated. Strategy formulation is especially likely to take place in lower levels of the organization. There may be a corporate plan, for example, that has little specific direction for a specific division or plant of the company. Under these circumstances, a local business strategy may need to be formulated prior to work on a compensation system. In this chapter, sources of strategies will be discussed along with strategy formulation.

Once the corporate business strategy has been formulated, it must be translated into a specific compensation strategy; this process will be shown in this chapter. Also, several case studies will be provided to show how this step is taken by organizations. An important point to bear in mind throughout the chapter is that generic compensation strategies, just like generic business strategies, are unlikely to be effective. They must be tailor-made to the needs of the business.

Business Strategy Types

Organizations seek to develop a unique approach to their product or service that competitors will have a difficult time imitating. If the strategic approach taken by a company is easily imitated by its competitors, then the strategy is not a source of competitive advantage because others can take the same steps.[1] Categories of business strategies whereby companies seek to develop unique capabilities follow.

Customer Service

Both service sector organizations and, increasingly, manufacturing sector companies are attempting to differentiate their services and products on the basis of customer service. Good customer service can be defined in terms of several factors.[2] One factor is a tangible outcome that customers receive from service agents, such as a timely response to customer concerns. Another dimension is reliability and the degree to which quality customer service is delivered on repeated business. Responsiveness refers to the extent to which customer demands are met. Empathy refers to the extent to which the service agent is empathetic toward the needs of the customers. Assurance refers to the extent to which promises made by the service agent to the customer are acted upon by the service agent.

Quality

Some organizations compete on the basis of the quality of their product or service. Often a total quality management program (TQM) is used to deliver high quality products and services.[3] In order to deliver high quality products and services, organizations rely on several sets of activities in a TQM program. First, statistical process control is used to measure the extent to which there are defects in the products and services being provided that need to be corrected. Second, constant contact is made with the customers to ensure that the product or service meets their specifications. Third, process reengineering often takes place to ensure that business processes are in alignment with the quality objectives. Fourth, decision making is pushed down in the organization. Employees are empowered to make decisions normally made by supervisors in order to be more responsive to the customer's specifications.

Innovation and Time to Market

Another way to differentiate oneself from the competition is to have innovative products and services that others would have a difficult time reverse engineering to produce a similar product or service. This requires that the organization be capable of learning how to be innovative on a repeatable basis. One innovation alone is unlikely to lead to competitive advantage over time. Moreover, good ideas must be brought to market quickly. In order for organizations to develop the learning capabilities needed for ongoing innovation, several key elements must be in place.[4] First, there must be a system in place to create new products or services. For example, cross-functional product development teams may be used. Second, there must be a knowledge transfer system. That is, learning in one part of the organization must be transferred to other parts of the organization. Some organizations, like General Electric, for example, have a Chief Learning Officer to make sure this transference of knowledge takes place. Third, knowledge must be institutionalized so that it can be used on a repeated basis. Expert systems are sometimes created to capture the knowledge base in an automated information system.

Productivity

By definition productivity refers to output divided by input. In order to be more productive than a competitor, one must increase output, decrease input, or do both. Output refers to the product or service provided, while input refers to the human capital used to deliver the product or service to the customer. Output can be increased by providing a high quality product or service. Input can be decreased by decreasing the number of people needed to produce a product or service. In order to accomplish a decrease in the number of employees needed, more qualified employees are needed to do more of the work and to develop more efficient ways to produce the product or service.

Cost

Perhaps the most obvious way to compete is to reduce costs, so that customers purchase from you rather than from a competitor with a higher price. Obviously, the approach is easy to imitate and may lead to "price warfare," eventually diminishing the quality of the product or service.

Financial

Another way to compete is by doing more with the capital in your organization than others do. The consulting firm of Stern Stewart uses an economic value-added (EVA) model to guide the corporate strategy of its clients. EVA is defined as the return to capital minus the cost of capital.

Essentially, it gauges the extent to which the company is generating returns on capital invested in the organization above and beyond alternative investments of the same amount of capital in some financial vehicle other than the organization.

Human Capital

Traditionally, labor has been viewed as a cost to the organization. Increasingly, however, labor is being viewed as a source of revenue generation as well. For example, Sears has shown that the employment relations climate at Sears is related to the bottom line of the business.[5] In particular, it has found that employee attitudes toward work are positively correlated with customer service ratings. In turn, customer service ratings are positively correlated with revenue growth at Sears.

Balanced Scorecard

Very few organizations have a pure business strategy of competing solely on the basis of customer service, quality, innovation, productivity, cost, financials, or human capital. Most organizations compete on multiple fronts and compete on the basis of more than one of these factors. Moreover, the "mix" of strategic factors that are emphasized by companies may shift over time in response to the market. An important concept that captures the actual complexities of business strategies just described is the balanced scorecard approach.[6]

A balanced scorecard approach implies that multiple strategies are pursued by firms at any one point in time and that the relative "balance" or weight of these strategies may change over time. Hence, a balanced scorecard approach to business strategy will list the strategies to be pursued over a period of time and also specify the relative weight of each strategy. Another way for an organization to be unique relative to its competitors is to have a unique blend of business strategies with synergy between the strategies.

Sources of Business Strategies

As previously indicated in this chapter, business strategies are often readily available in organizations. A brief description of business strategy documents follows.

Vision Statement

A vision statement is a statement of what the organization ultimately hopes to achieve. As such, it is sometimes called an "end-point" vision. Vision statements take various forms and lengths. Some vision statements are very broad, far-reaching philosophical statements. Others are very short with a specific measure of success (e.g., "be a $12 billion retailer by 2002"). A vision statement is sometimes referred to as an aspiration statement, as in "here is what we aspire to be."

Mission Statement

The mission statement describes the core capabilities of the company. Often embodied in the mission statement is the extent to which the company is "known" for customer service, quality, innovation, productivity, cost, financials, human capital, or some combination of these factors. For example, a company that views itself as "leaders in new product development" is likely to be pursuing a strategy of innovation. Other statements, such as "lowest cost manufacturer," may be much more self-evident.

Values

A values statement spells out the beliefs of senior management as to how business should be conducted by the business enterprise. Embodied in a values statement are likely to be beliefs about diversity, teamwork, customer service, ethics, and integrity. It is a guide to how business is to be conducted rather than what is to be achieved.

Critical Success Factors

Critical success factors list the events that must take place in order for the business to be successful. These events may include the development of core capabilities by the company as well as factors outside the company that need to take place (e.g., acquisitions).

Operational Plans

Operational plans are detailed action plans that spell out specific business goals for each unit in the business as they relate to the larger mission, vision, values, and critical success factors.

Cascading Goals in Business Planning

Not only may the corporate entity in a business have a vision, mission, values, critical success factors, and operational plans, but so too may each business unit within the organization. The business unit may be a division of the company, a department, a plant, a sector, a geographic region, or a work team. It is critical that these strategic plans at the business unit be in alignment with the strategic plans at the corporate level. That is, the strategic plans should naturally cascade down from one level to the next. Both corporate and business unit strategic documents need to be obtained prior to compensation strategy formulation. Discrepancies need to be resolved prior to compensation strategy formulation as well.

Strategy Formulation

Well-formulated business strategy is least likely to be found at the business unit level. In the absence of this information, the local business unit needs to go through a strategic planning process prior to the development of a new compensation system or the redesign of an existing system. The typical process followed is shown in Exhibit 2-1. This process is usually undertaken by senior management with the aid of a consultant.

The first step in the process is to conduct a SWOT analysis. Emphasis here is upon identifying strengths and weaknesses internal to the organization and identifying opportunities and threats external to the organization that are faced by the organization. This step usually requires amassing considerable internal and external data to make these assessments.

Based on this SWOT analysis, a path to the future is determined by focusing on facilitating forces (i.e., strengths and opportunities) and by avoiding or changing restraining forces (i.e., weaknesses and threats). This assessment of the facilitating and restraining forces in the SWOT analysis leads to a vision statement. If done properly, it is an honest assessment of what the organization can expect to deliver on given the forces shown in Exhibit 2-2 (on page 20).

The SWOT analysis, along with the vision, helps produce a mission statement. The mission statement describes the core capabilities that must be present in order to take advantage of strengths and opportunities and to counteract weaknesses and threats. The mission statement captures not

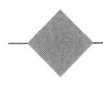

EXHIBIT 2-1

Business strategy formulation process.

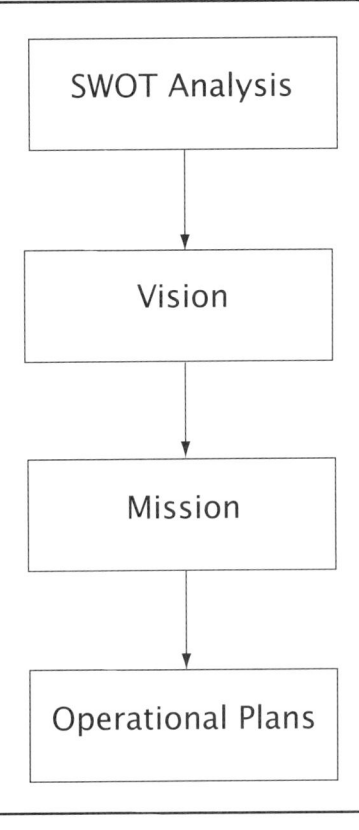

```
SWOT Analysis
      ↓
   Vision
      ↓
   Mission
      ↓
Operational Plans
```

only current capabilities, but also capabilities that can be realistically developed by the organization as a part of its balanced scorecard strategic portfolio.

Lastly, operational plans are developed to capitalize on current strengths and to develop new capabilities that can be used to exploit opportunities faced by the company and to thwart weaknesses and threats that may detour the accomplishment of the organizational mission. Operational plans are usually very detailed and lengthy relative to the other strategic planning documents and are most subject to change in the short run. As a result, designing compensation policies around this short-term document alone is likely to be a futile effort.

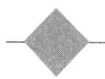

EXHIBIT 2-2
A SWOT analysis as the basis for vision and mission.

	Forces	
Location	Facilitating	Restraining
Internal	Strengths	Weaknesses
External	Opportunities	Threats

Compensation Strategy

As described in the previous chapter and shown in Exhibit 2-3, the formulation of compensation strategy is dependent upon business strategy and other forces. Given that the relationship between these other forces and compensation strategy is fairly well defined elsewhere in the literature, the focus here will be on the less well-defined link between business strategy and compensation strategy. Compensation strategy can be subdivided into five segments, as shown in Exhibit 2-4 (on page 24). A checklist of compensation strategy issues to consider is shown in Exhibit 2-5 (on page 25) for each segment. Each issue will be described in turn.

Pay Philosophy

The cornerstone to compensation strategy is the compensation philosophy of the company. This segment of the compensation strategy articulates fundamental beliefs about the goals of all components of the compensation system relative to the business strategy.

Internal vs. External Equity

The first fundamental issue to have a bearing on all compensation decision making is the extent to which internal versus external equity is to be

EXHIBIT 2-3
Forces influencing compensation strategy.

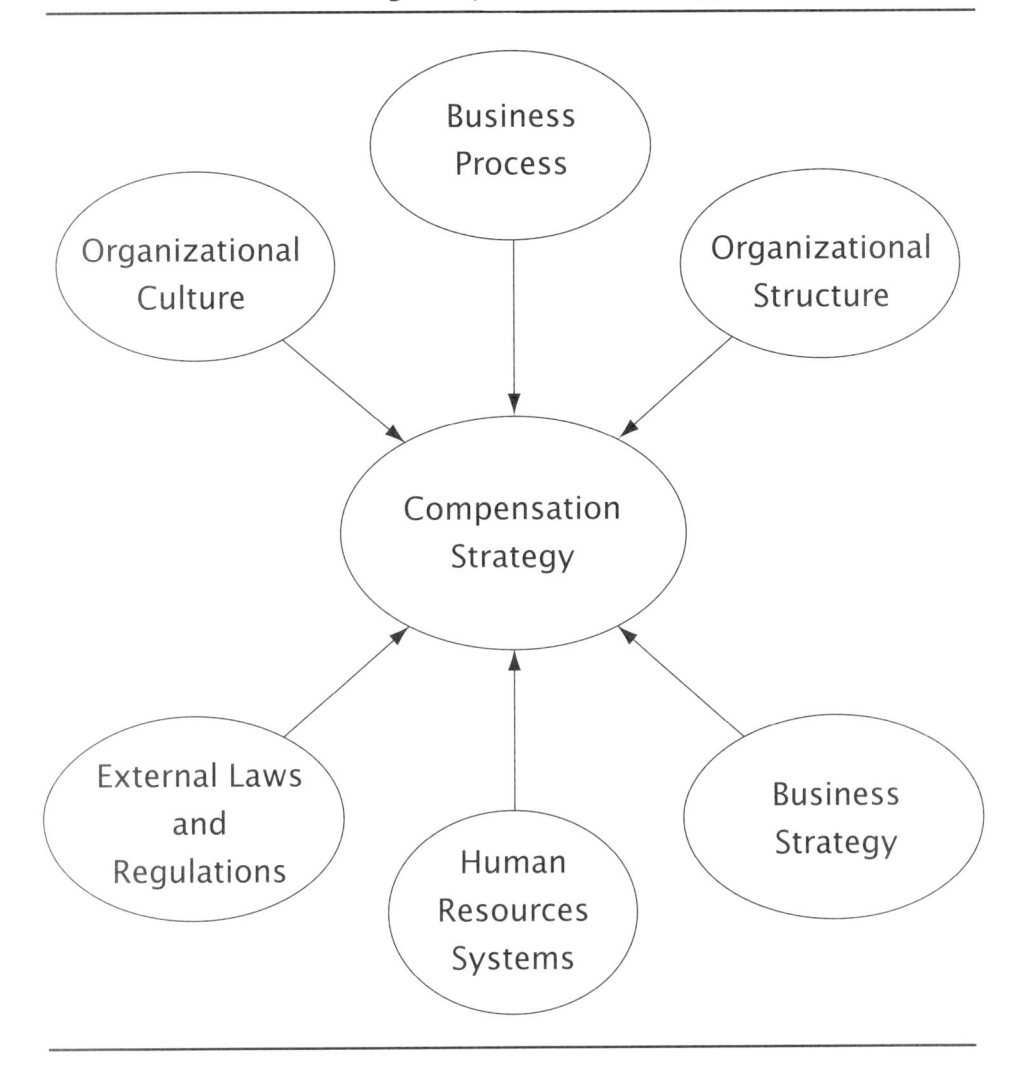

```
                    Business
                    Process
                       |
Organizational         v         Organizational
   Culture  ------> Compensation <------ Structure
                     Strategy
                    ^    ^    ^
                   /     |     \
                  /      |      \
       External Laws     |     Business
         and           Human    Strategy
       Regulations   Resources
                      Systems
```

stressed in the organization. In an ideal world, both internal and external equity would be emphasized and be in sync with one another. Frequently, however, internal equity and external equity strategies are not in perfect alignment with one another; thus, one or the other must be emphasized. An internal equity strategy determines the value of the job and/or person based on value added to the company as assessed by a job or person evaluation system. An external equity strategy determines the

EXHIBIT 2-4

Compensation strategy segments.

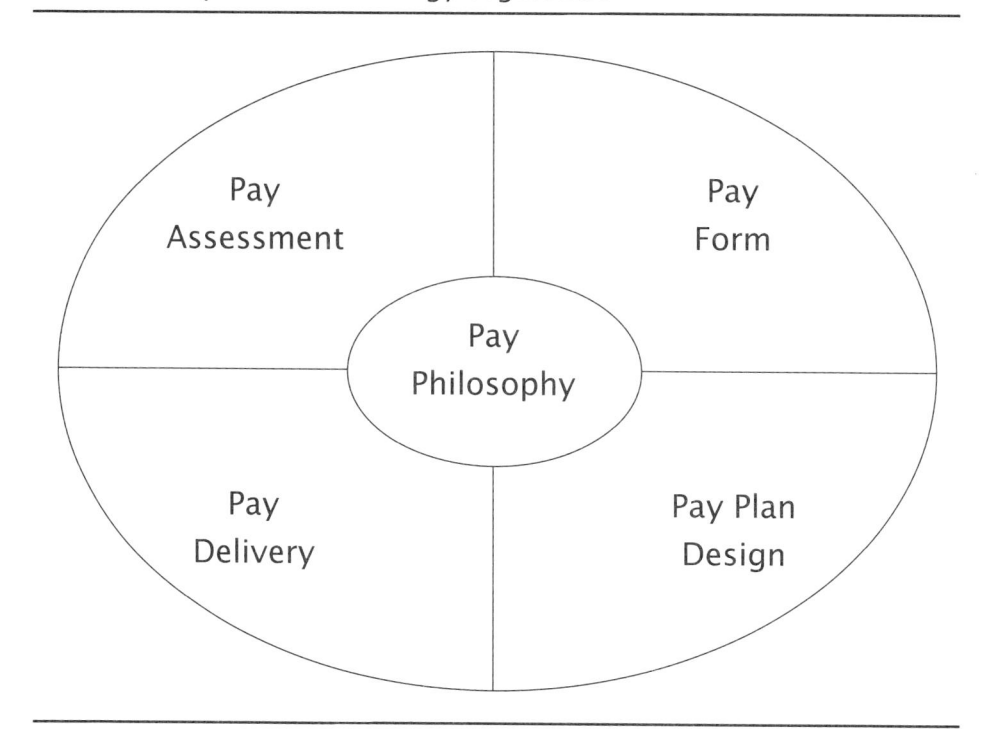

```
           Pay                    Pay
        Assessment                Form

                    Pay
                 Philosophy

           Pay                 Pay Plan
         Delivery               Design
```

value of the job or the person on the basis of the market as assessed by a market survey.

Organizations that place an emphasis on financials, cost, customers, or innovation as a business strategy are more likely to follow an external equity strategy because it is consistent with the business philosophy of setting product service prices at the market value. Organizations that emphasize quality are also more likely to use an external equity strategy because of the large administrative steps and costs associated with an internal equity strategy that may be inconsistent with a total quality management philosophy. Organizations that follow productivity as a human capital business strategy are likely to adopt an internal equity compensation strategy because of the intrinsic value of human capital to the company's business strategy.

A cautionary note is in order for companies that follow an external equity strategy. The assumption is that organizations have perfect market information. In many situations perfect market information is not avail-

EXHIBIT 2-5
Compensation strategy checklist.

Pay Philosophy
☐ Internal vs. External Equity
☐ Lead vs. Lag Market
☐ Attraction vs. Retention

Pay Assessment
☐ Job vs. Person
☐ Results vs. Behaviors
☐ Seniority vs. Performance
☐ Education vs. Skills

Pay Form
☐ Monetary vs. Nonmonetary
☐ Fixed vs. Variable
☐ Individual vs. Team

Pay Delivery
☐ Narrow vs. Broad Pay Bands
☐ Small vs. Large Pay Band Overlap
☐ Open vs. Closed Pay Communications

Pay Plan Design
☐ Participative vs. Nonparticipative
☐ Centralized vs. Decentralized
☐ Static vs. Dynamic
☐ Lead vs. Lag

---

able for reasons spelled out in Chapter 5 of this book. Hence, many companies opt to pursue both internal and external equity strategies.

Lead vs. Lag Market

When external equity is to be considered, as it most often is, a decision must be made whether to lead, lag, or match the market. The approach to be taken may be uniform for the entire company or vary by business unit or by occupation. By leading the market, the hope is that one can attract higher quality employees to the organization and retain existing staff. Attraction and retention are maximized because alternative employment opportunities in the market pay less. Although labor is more costly with a lead policy, the hope is that these additional costs will be paid for by more productivity from higher quality personnel attracted to the organization and by lower turnover costs. The philosophy of a lag policy is to pay less than the market average for labor in hopes of having lower labor costs and more profits. A compromise position is to match the market and compete on grounds other than labor costs.

Organizations with cost-driven business strategies are most likely to follow a lag policy for obvious reasons. Companies that place a premium on human capital with their business strategy are more likely to follow a lead policy to differentiate themselves from their competitors on the basis of labor quality. Organizations that emphasize total quality management (TQM) may also use a lead policy in order to attract talented people who do not need monitoring (e.g., performance appraisals). More efficient systems can be built without the administrative burden and cost associated with a performance monitoring system. Firms following the other business strategies are likely to follow a match the market philosophy.

Attraction vs. Retention

Organizations have a finite budget to be used for compensation. Tough decisions have to be made regarding the allocation of these dollars. One such decision is whether to devote more money to attracting the best talent available than to retaining current personnel. Customer- and quality-focused organizations must meet the demands of the customer immediately and don't have the luxury of waiting to attract better customer service-oriented employees so they are likely to emphasize retention. Innovative organizations are more likely to need to go to the outside market for employees with skill sets that are not available in-house. Cost-focused organizations are likely to put greater emphasis on attraction because there are usually fewer new entrants to the organization to be paid than there are current employees to be paid. Productivity-, financial-, and human capital–focused organizations are likely to maintain a balance between the two objectives.

Pay Assessment

In determining the amount to pay each employee, an assessment must be made of the value that the person adds to the organization. Both human capital and job characteristics can be used to make these assessments. Several hotly debated topics often accompany this segment of compensation strategy.

Corporate Business Strategies and Compensation Strategies

Job vs. Person

A very fundamental issue faced by compensation decision makers is how much emphasis to place on the job that the person holds versus how much emphasis to place on the different human capital characteristics that the person brings to the job in deciding rates of pay. Traditionally, major emphasis has been placed upon the job rather than the person. Elaborate job-based systems with job descriptions, job classifications, and job evaluation systems are commonplace in organizations. Increasingly, however, organizations are attempting to become more internally flexible to meet market demands, and, in doing so, some organizations are beginning to place more emphasis on the person than the job. Organizations with a person-based focus are more likely to have innovation, quality, and human capital as corporate business strategies. Flexibility is extremely important for the accomplishment of these business strategies. Organizations that are pursuing a low-cost or financial business strategy usually do not follow a person-based assessment strategy because the costs of this type of approach can be high. For example, the start-up costs of a skill-based pay system are quite large. Productivity-driven organizations are more likely to follow a job-based compensation strategy because it is easier and more relevant to build this kind of accounting system.

Results vs. Behaviors

Another decision-making point is whether to assess the results people achieve or to assess the behaviors expected to lead to the results. In organizations that emphasize productivity as a business strategy, usually both results and behaviors are emphasized. Results focus on the output side of the productivity ratio and behaviors on the input side of the productivity ratio. Financial- and cost-driven companies most often focus on a results-based compensation strategy so that people "pay for themselves." Organizations driven by customer service and human capital tend to favor behaviors because they are so crucial to the delivery of exemplary service. Quality-based organizations most often focus on results rather than on behaviors because this philosophy is consistent with the team philosophy of the importance of the overall system results rather than people's behavior within the system.

Seniority vs. Performance

Outside customer-driven organizations in the public and nonprofit sectors, it is becoming rare for an organization to emphasize seniority over performance. Whether performance is measured by behaviors or results is debatable, but the need to focus on performance is a part of most companies' compensation strategy regardless of the business strategy. The need to consider this issue in formulating a compensation strategy cannot be stressed enough. The importance of seniority versus performance needs to be clearly articulated rather than be implicit in the compensation policy because many employees still feel that the "fair" thing to do is to reward them for their years with the company. Action steps must be taken by companies to change that philosophy, and these steps are far more likely to be taken if the seniority versus performance tradeoff is explicitly addressed in the compensation strategy.

Education vs. Skills

A fundamental distinction exists between education and skills. Education refers to the mastery of declarative knowledge, while skills refers to the mastery of procedural knowledge. Education is usually obtained by taking courses in an educational setting, while skills are usually obtained through on-the-job experience. A low-cost business strategy is often associated with an education compensation strategy. To minimize costs, education is to be obtained off the job and paid for by the incumbent. Organizations that have a quality-based business strategy are likely to put more emphasis on skills that are specific to their business environment. In terms of business strategies other than quality or cost, organizations are likely to have a mix of education and skill assessment as part of their compensation philosophy. Increasingly, however, the emphasis is on education over skills, so that employees have the breadth of knowledge needed to add value to the firm as it changes over time. As with seniority, this is a very sensitive issue with employees and should be explicitly addressed in the compensation strategy.

Pay Form

Although the amount of money available for compensation in a company is finite, the form that pay merit takes can vary. Variance in pay form is also a function of the type of business strategy.

Monetary vs. Nonmonetary

Some forms of pay, such as recognition, are social in nature, cost the organization very little, and are labeled nonmonetary rewards. Other forms of pay are more direct, are very costly to the organization, and are referred to as monetary rewards. Obviously in a cost-driven business, emphasis is likely to be on nonmonetary rewards. Organizations driven by an innovation strategy are likely to place at least equal emphasis on nonmonetary versus monetary rewards in the spirit of providing creative rewards for creative people. Human capital–driven organizations are also likely to focus on both forms of compensation to emphasize the importance of human capital to the business strategy. Organizations with a focus on quality often stress nonmonetary rewards as a way to celebrate new process innovations that provide a higher quality product. Traditionally, customer service–driven organizations have used nonmonetary rewards to honor excellence in customer service (e.g., an employee of the month plaque displayed in the lobby). Finance-driven organizations tend to focus on monetary rewards given the importance of capital to their business strategy. Productivity-based organizations tend to focus on monetary rewards because this form of pay is consistent with their accounting and measurement systems.

Fixed vs. Variable

A fixed pay system implies that pay increases are across-the-board, based on membership in the organization, and/or built into base pay. A variable pay system implies that pay increases are based on performance and/or are in the form of a cash bonus. Increasingly, all organizations regardless of their business strategy are moving toward variable pay systems. Most likely to develop this philosophy are organizations with a cost- or finance-driven business strategy. Increased costs are to be incurred only if the business prospers. Other companies are also likely to follow a variable pay strategy, but for different reasons. Those that focus on innovation and human capital are more likely to provide pay in a variable form because of its motivational properties. Quality- and productivity-based organizations are also likely to use variable pay because the performance measures used often are based on the metrics used by the business to gauge business strategy success. Customer-driven organizations, especially in the public and nonprofit sectors, continue to rely upon fixed pay systems. These pay systems (e.g., across-the-board increases, cost-of-living increases, merit pay) are used to buy the loyalty of employees to the organization. Although they are usually not well paid relative to the market, they can always count on a pay increase each year. With this loyalty to a nonprofit organization, such as a nonprofit counseling agency, may come loyalty by the customer to the nonprofit service deliverer, such as a particular counselor.

Individual vs. Team

Pay can be given for individual accomplishments or for team (collective) accomplishments. Traditionally in the United States, pay has been allocated to individuals, rather than to teams. However, with the advent of team-based work systems like self-directed work teams in the United States, a part of compensation is increasingly being used for team pay rather than solely for individual pay. Team-based work systems are likely to be found in organizations with business strategies that emphasize quality and innovation. Hence, they are likely to have a team-based pay strategy. Firms pursuing other business strategies are less likely to have team-based pay systems.

Pay Delivery

Different forms of pay can be delivered using different vehicles. Different types of pay delivery vehicles need to be incorporated into the compensation strategy because they again vary by type of business strategy.

Narrow vs. Broad Pay Bands

The outside parameters of pay bands are defined by the minimum to be paid and the maximum to be paid for people who fall in a particular pay band. The maximum is usually set based on the maximum value of the job to the company as determined by a job evaluation system. Narrow pay bands help organizations minimize their costs. For example, someone in a clerical position in a university may have a Ph.D. but still be paid a low wage rate relative to professionals with a Ph.D. because the value of a clerical job to the university is low relative to the value of a professional job that actually requires a Ph.D. As a result, using narrow pay bands as a compensation strategy goes well with low-cost strategy employers. For similar reasons, narrow pay bands are prevalent with financially driven institutions. Because of the dampening motivational effects of narrow pay bands on bright people in low grades, organizations that pursue innovations, customer service, productivity, and human capital as business strategies tend to favor broad bands as a compensation strategy. Broad bands reward employees for performing outside the scope of their narrowly defined job duties, and they do not bump up against the maximum of the pay grade as quickly; hence broad bands may be more motivational as well as costly.

Small vs. Large Pay Band Overlap

The amount of overlap between pay bands has important implications for the development of human resources in organizations. A small amount of overlap communicates to employees in the organization that advancement is determined by developing new skills and acquiring more education so that they can move up to the next pay grade in the pay structure—one that requires a higher level of skill and/or education to receive higher levels of pay. In other words, a premium is placed upon promotion. On the other hand, a large amount of overlap between pay bands communicates the message that while one does not necessarily have the skills or education to advance, the person can nevertheless earn as much as or more than someone in adjacent pay grades by virtue of hard work and effort that result in solid business results.

Firms that emphasize quality, cost, financials, innovation, and productivity in their business strategy tend to have very flat organizations with fewer promotional opportunities. It is very difficult to retain quality personnel unless there is a large amount of overlap in pay grades. In order to successfully compete by quality, cost, financials, innovation, or productivity, human resources need to multitask for the organization to be effective; a large amount of overlap allows employees the room to be rewarded for the effort required to perform multiple tasks with the same level of value to the organization. Companies that compensate on the basis of human capital are more likely to have less overlap in pay grades in order to motivate upward movement in the pay structure. Employees are motivated to acquire new skills so that they can do higher structured work rather than do more tasks at the same level of complexity. A similar objective can also be achieved by having a large amount of pay band overlap along with a skill band pay system.

Open vs. Closed Pay Communications

The amount of detail about the compensation system revealed to employees can also vary by business strategy. A very closed system might, for example, reveal to each employee only his or her own pay and discipline employees for talking with other employees about the pay levels. A very open system would be one in which each employee knows every other employee's pay amounts. Traditionally, most compensation systems have been more closed than open. Increasingly, however, organizations are opening up the pay systems. More openness is especially likely to be found in companies with a human capital business strategy. In order to retain highly talented employees, no secrets are kept so that turnover does not take place as a result of hearsay. Closed compensation systems are most common in firms with a low-cost business strategy. The hope here is to minimize turnover by keeping employees ignorant about just how low their pay levels are. Organizations following business strategies other than cost or human capital are likely to pursue a midrange strategy that is neither too open nor too closed. Under this type of compensation strategy, data are not released about individual pay levels. However, pay ranges are made public as well as averages within the pay range.

Pay Plan Design

Compensation strategy includes not only the amount and process to be paid, but also the processes that were used to reach these decisions. Processes that need to be considered in the compensation strategy follow.

Participative vs. Nonparticipative

In a participative pay plan design, both employees and managers become involved in the design of the system. It is a method of empowering employees to perform roles previously performed only by management. In a nonparticipative pay plan design, only senior management is involved in designing compensation programs. A participative pay plan design strategy requires that an empowered work force already be in place. Usually, this type of work design system is found in organizations that emphasize productivity, innovation, customer service, quality, and human capital. An empowered work force is seen as a means to each of these business strategy ends. One is less likely to find participative decision making being used with employees in cost- and financially-driven organizations. More emphasis is placed on capital than on people with these business strategies, and financial matters, including compensation, are treated at the senior management level.

Centralized vs. Decentralized

The design of compensation strategy can take place at the corporate level or at the business unit level. In recent times, more and more organizations have experimented with developing compensation strategy at the business unit level; historically, compensation strategy has been formulated at the corporate level. Decentralized systems seem to work well only under specific business strategies. In particular, they tend to work with companies focused on quality and innovation. Under these business strategies, other business strategies are also often localized, so it is logical to link the pay system as well to decentralized strategy formulation. In most organizations, however, especially in cost- and financially-driven ones, most finances including compensation are controlled at the corporate level. Also, in many organizations, labor migrates from business unit to business unit, and different pay plans at different locations for the same work performed may be perplexing to employees. Organizations with productivity, human capital, and customer-driven business strategies are likely to develop strategic compensation plans at both the corporate and business unit levels. To do so allows for standardization across plans while allowing modifications for local circumstances. This compromise approach is sometimes referred to as "mass customization" and is likely to be used more often by companies in the future.[7]

Static vs. Dynamic

Temporal aspects of pay systems are important to compensation strategy as well as to the content of the pay system.[8] Organizations change their business strategies more frequently than ever before, and the question becomes how often should the compensation system change to reflect these changes? Too frequent change may undermine the credibility of the compensation strategy, while too infrequent change may undermine the business strategy. Experience suggests that significant business changes must occur for the compensation system to change. These changes in business strategy are most likely to take place in organizations pursuing an innovation strategy.

Lead vs. Lag

Compensation strategies can either lead or lag the business strategy.[9] A lead compensation strategy is used to show to employees the importance of subsequent business strategy changes. A lag compensation strategy is designed to reinforce the change in business strategy. As with very dynamic compensation strategies, lead compensation systems seem to work in very limited circumstances. Once again, organizations with a very innovative business strategy might use a lead compensation strategy to make the impending business strategy change more salient to employees.

Contingency Factors

The matching of business strategy to compensation strategy is a delicate task. Some general observations were made in the previous section on which compensation strategies seem to be the most logical for various business strategies. These are simply observations based on personal experiences of the author and are not grounded in research data because the data to substantiate these observations remains to be collected. Moreover, the relationship is often more complex than the pure strategies match portrayed. In particular, other contingencies must be considered along with business strategy in the formulation of compensation strategy, as they may modify the relationship between business strategy and compensation strategy. These contingency factors are shown in Exhibit 2-6, along with a summary of business and compensation strategies.

An example will help point out the importance of these contingencies in strategic compensation decision making. Take the case of the observation that participation in decision making is often used with quality-based business strategies. Although in general this may be true, it is only a starting point for compensation strategy discussions. Consideration must also be given to the contingency factors. A participative compensation strategy may not fit in a quality-based organization that is very hierarchical in terms of structure, that has a command and control cultural orientation, is very statistically driven in terms of business process, and is subject to unfair labor practice charges under the National Labor Relations Act for the use of company organized teams to decide benefits to be offered. Performance-based pay plans do not work well when staffing decisions are based upon seniority rather than performance. Business strategy should weigh heavily in compensation strategy formulation, but certainly it cannot be used independently of these contingency factors.

Case Studies

There is no mechanical algorithm to decide the compensation strategies on the basis of business strategy. The process is as much, or maybe even more, art than science. To solidify some of the points in this chapter, several cases will be presented to show the link between business strategy and compensation strategy.

EXHIBIT 2-6
Contingency factors to consider.

Business Strategy	Compensation Strategy	Contingencies
Customer Service		
Quality	Pay Philosophy	Human Resources Systems
Innovation and Time to Market	Pay Assessment	Organizational Structure
Productivity	Pay Form	Business Processes
Cost	Pay Delivery	Organizational Culture
Financial	Pay Plan Design	Laws and Regulations
Human Capital		

CASE 1

Law Firm

H, L, and C is a full-service law firm located in the Midwest and southeast. It started as a very small law firm twenty-five years ago and has now grown to be the eighteenth largest firm in the country. In order to successfully compete, small law firms are becoming very specialized boutiques or are being merged and acquired by other firms to become full-service law firms, as is the case with H, L, and C.

H, L, and C aspires to be a nationally recognized firm offering full service to large clients. Currently, it is regional in scope. The business strategy of H, L, and C is multifaceted and as such has a balanced scorecard emphasis to it. One facet of the firm's business strategy is to be very active in the communities at large that it serves. The firm wants to have a very visible presence so that people are aware of its services and reputation by word of mouth rather than by media. As a result, members of the firm are very active in professional associations, employer associations, and community service boards. A second facet of the business strategy is to have a highly talented staff in each practice area. No location has a resident expert in each practice area, but there must be a highly regarded expert in the firm available to provide guidance in all geographic areas. A third facet of the firm's strategy is to be very well managed and make extensive use of virtual technology to coordinate services across regions.

The compensation strategy was developed in response to the business strategy. While billable hours serve as the common denominator for determining value of the attorneys, monetary value is also placed on community involvement, firm management, professional development, teamwork, and the development of new clients. Community involvement is seen as a long-term performance strategy, while the development of new clients is seen as a short-term performance strategy. Professional development is important to reward in order to develop in-house expertise. Teamwork and firm management are needed to coordinate services in a virtual environment. Compensation decision making is kept at the equity partner level, and profits are shared with all associates, including nonattorneys. Profits are shared to facilitate shared services, and decision making is retained at the equity partner level to be consistent with the previous cultures at the firms acquired over time to form H, L, and C.

Corporate Business Strategies and Compensation Strategies

CASE 2

Implement Dealer

The Jacobs companies are located in Ohio and Arizona. They have a dealership network in each state and provide and service heavy operating equipment for road construction. They are family owned and have been in business for more than 100 years. The vision of the family is to become the largest dealership in both Ohio and Arizona. To achieve this vision will be difficult, because in recent years there has been a large influx of foreign competition in the market. Margins on products have been drastically reduced from about 20 percent to 6 percent, making cost issues a major concern. The Jacobs family believes that its major source of competitive advantage is its people, many of whom have been with the company for more than thirty years. The company takes great pride in the values developed over the years with the family and believes that this has fostered a feeling of loyalty by the workforce. In order to continue to grow, new skills (e.g., customer service, technical expertise) will need to be developed in the workforce, and work will need to be organized in a more efficient manner to reduce costs.

The business strategy is based upon a set of core values. One set of core values emphasizes high performance as defined by being creative and proactive, providing legendary service, developing superior skills, and routinely accomplishing business objectives. Another set of core values emphasizes business ethics and includes honesty, integrity, and fairness in all business relationships, including the employment relationship. A final set of core values is labeled commitment and includes having a caring attitude, sharing wealth with employees, and being loyal to the company.

The compensation strategy draws directly upon these core values. One important current objective to be met as a part of the high performance value is the reduction of cost. Pay supplemental to base pay is offered for cost minimization at the business unit level. Also, supplemental pay is part of the compensation strategy for improvements in product and service quality objectives. In order to foster loyalty to the company, there has never been a layoff at the Jacobs Family Company. In order to avoid layoffs, staffing levels are kept low and base wages are targeted below the market. Variable pay is used to make up the difference in market levels, and base wage savings are researched for downturns in the economy so that layoffs do not need to take place. Many nonmonetary rewards are used to recognize the importance of the "extended family members" to the organization. Tuition reimbursement is provided to reward loyalty to the company and to build new skills in the workforce.

CASE 3

Gourmet Rice Meal Manufacturer

Mealsolutions is a billion-dollar manufacturer of gourmet rice meals. It has developed many types of packaged meals that can be served with rice. The market is a very competitive one, and the company has decided to specialize in the high end of the market and hopes to become the number-one seller of gourmet meal solutions.

In order to accomplish this mission, Mealsolutions has had to undertake a massive restructuring of the business. Low-margin products have been discontinued and the labor force has been reduced. A new senior executive team has been assembled to guide the company back to profitability.

Several strategic directives were formed by the new senior executives to guide the transformation of Mealsolutions. First, they would create a vast knowledge base of customer preferences. Second, they would create an integrated business to deliver value to the customer. Third, they would grow a highly talented workforce that was committed to continuous improvement. Fourth, they would share the business results with employees. Fifth, they would meet the highest possible quality standards.

As can be seen from the business strategy, the business strategic focus is on a blend of customer service, quality, and human capital. As a result, the compensation strategy developed to support this strategy. One strategy was to share financial success with employees as shareholders in the company. Another was to ensure that the compensation system was equitable, open, and understood by all associates. In addition, employees were to receive compensation commensurate with their level of responsibility and contribution to the company. Rewards were to be based on business results. Lastly, employees were to be given choices from a compensation "menu."

Notes

1. J. Barney, *Gaining and Sustaining Competitive Advantage* (Reading, MA: Addison-Wesley, 1997).
2. B. Schneider and D. E. Bowen, *Winning the Service Game* (Boston: Harvard Business School Press, 1995); P. Parasuam, V. A. Zeitmal, and L. L. Berry, "SERVQUAL: A Multiple Item Scale for Measuring Consumer Perceptions of Service Quality," *Journal of Retailing*, (1998): 64, pp. 13–37.
3. E. E. Lawler, III, S. A. Mohrman, and G. E. Ledford, Jr., *Strategies for High Performance Organizations* (San Francisco: Jossey-Bass, 1998).
4. S. A. Snell, M. A. Youndt, and P. M. Wright. "Establishing a Framework for Research in Strategic Human Resource Management: Merging Resource Theory in Organizational Learning," in G. R. Ferris and K. M. Rowland (eds.) *Research in Personnel and Human Resources Management* (Greenwich, CT: JAF Press, 1996), pp. 61–90.
5. A. Rucci, S. Kirn, and R. Quinn, "The Employee-Customer-Profit Chain at Sears," *Harvard Business Review* (1998): January–February, pp. 82–97.
6. R. S. Kaplan and D. P. Norton, *The Balanced Scorecard* (Boston: Harvard Business School Press, 1996).
7. P. V. LeBlanc, "Mass Customization: A Rewards Mosaic for the Future?," *ACA Journal* (1997): Spring, pp. 16–32.
8. G. E. Ledford, Jr., "Designing Nimble Reward Systems," *Compensation and Benefits Review* (1995): July–August, pp. 46–54.
9. G. E. Ledford, Jr. and R. L. Heneman, "Compensation: A Troublesome Lead System in Organizational Change," in *Breaking the Code of Change*, edited by M. Beer and N. Noria (Cambridge, MA: Harvard Business School Press, In Press).

PART 2

BASE PAY SYSTEMS

Chapter 3: Work Analysis

Chapter 4: Work Evaluation

Chapter 5: Market Surveys

Chapter 6: Pay Structures

A model of corporate business strategy and pay policy integration.

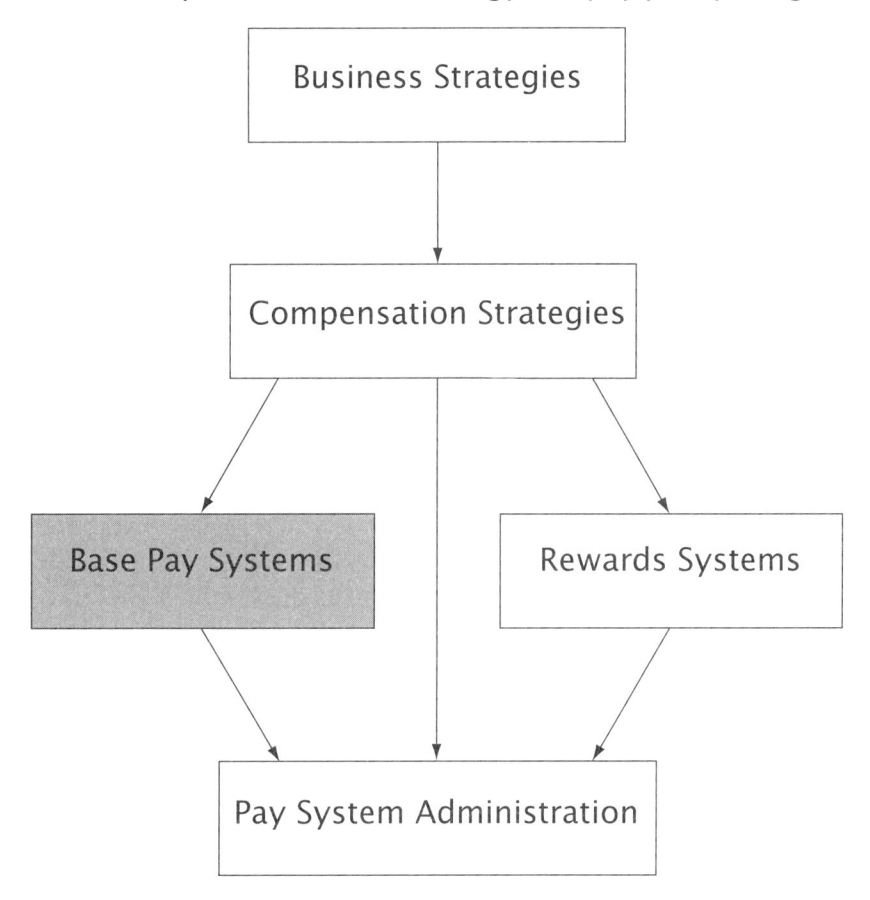

```
        ┌──────────────────────┐
        │  Business Strategies │
        └──────────┬───────────┘
                   ↓
        ┌──────────────────────┐
        │ Compensation Strategies │
        └────┬─────────┬───────┘
             ↓         ↓
   ┌─────────────────┐ ┌─────────────────┐
   │ Base Pay Systems│ │ Rewards Systems │
   └────────┬────────┘ └────────┬────────┘
            ↓                   ↓
        ┌──────────────────────────┐
        │ Pay System Administration│
        └──────────────────────────┘
```

CHAPTER 3

Work Analysis

The process of integrating compensation policies with corporate business strategies requires one to drill down further than the compensation strategy in order to be successful. In particular, this process requires an integration of the compensation strategy with all of the elements of a total compensation system. One such element is job analysis, which will be covered in this chapter in detail. The process of job analysis will be described, a recommended approach will be offered, and case studies will be provided.

The Need for Work Analysis

It has become fashionable in some human resources circles to suggest that job descriptions are dead. The argument goes that in order for an organization to be flexible, people in the organization must do whatever it takes to get the work done. That the "miscellaneous duties as assigned" box found on the last line of traditional job descriptions has become the job is the joke to accompany this philosophy.

The elimination of job descriptions is a critical mistake in human resources decision making, especially when it comes to compensation decisions. One reason that we need a clear description of the job is that job titles in and of themselves are not sufficient to make sound decisions. Consider the following job titles, for example:

Title	Actual Job
Vision control coordinator	Window washer
Environmental pollution control engineer	Street sweeper
Stage manager	Bouncer for *Jerry Springer*

The titles of coordinator, engineer, and manager have become aggrandized over the years in some cases. Imagine these job titles being matched up with coordinator, engineer, and manager jobs in a market survey when these jobs in the survey may require a B.A., B.S., and M.B.A., respectively.

Another reason job descriptions are not obsolete is related to the psychology of people at work. In the absence of clear expectations regarding work, people may feel role overload, role conflict, and role ambiguity. In turn, these feelings are related to stress, which may lead to absenteeism, turnover, and other dysfunctional consequences at work.

Along with avoidance of misleading job titles and stress, another reason for continuing to use job descriptions is the law. Equal employment laws and the courts' interpretation of these laws clearly require job analyses to be performed. There are literally thousands of court cases that make this point. In the absence of the job-related criteria found in job descriptions to make human resources decisions including compensation decisions, supervisors may fall victim to stereotypes about protected classes under the law.

Work Analysis Components

As shown in Exhibit 3-1, there are three layers to job analysis: the person, the job, and the context in which the person and job reside. All three of these components will be described.

Person

Characteristics of the person are often referred to as competencies and relate to the knowledge, skill, abilities, and other factors needed by the employee to successfully perform job duties in a particular work organization. Other factors refer to attitudes, beliefs, and values held by the person.

It is essential that these competencies be very precisely defined. Traditional shorthand labels may not sufficiently define the qualifications

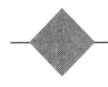

EXHIBIT 3-1

Layers of work analysis.

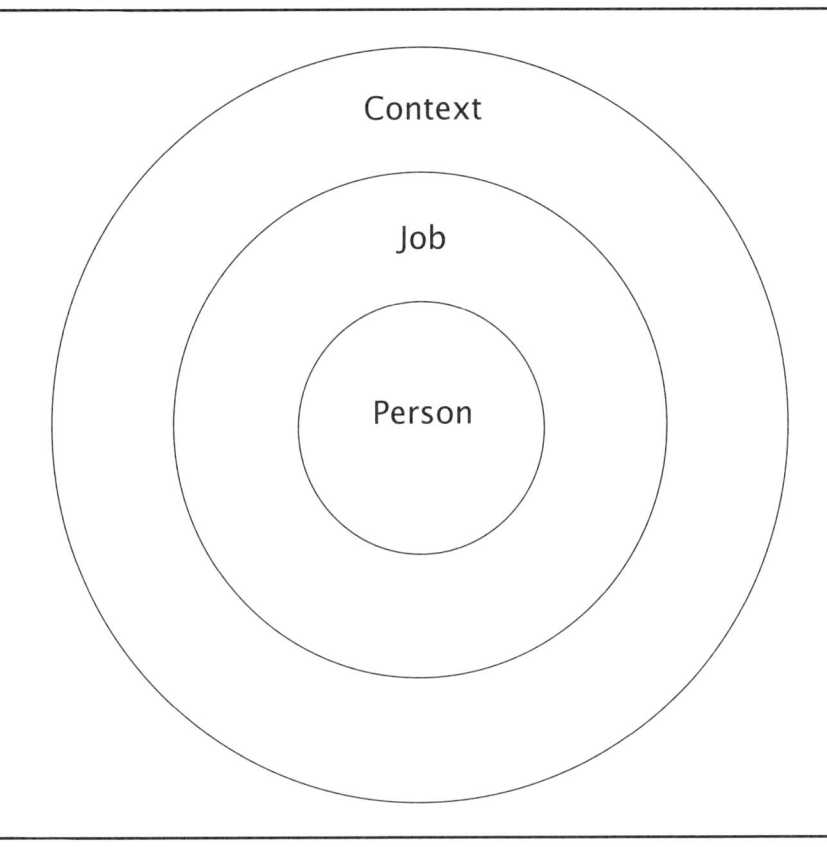

Concentric circles: outer "Context", middle "Job", inner "Person".

needed for the job. For example, a high school diploma does not always guarantee that one can read and write at a certain level. A certain number of years' experience in a particular job may no longer mean much given the aggrandizement of job titles previously discussed. Very basic abilities, including reading, writing, mathematical, speaking, and physical skills, need to be precisely defined.

An important consideration in the measurement of competencies is the need to make them specific to the business strategy of the organization. If, for example, self-directed work teams are going to be used, then the qualifications should clearly list characteristics needed to be a successful team member (e.g., interpersonal competence). While generic competency sets are available to companies, they are not to be encouraged. Generic competencies are unlikely to be related to company-specific business strategies and thus are not likely to be a source of competitive advantage because everyone has access to these generic competency sets. In short, qualifications or competencies that define the person for the job must be both very precise (i.e., reliable) and related to the business strategy of the organization (i.e., valid).

Job

The job defines what the organization expects people to do. Traditionally, duties, responsibilities, and sometimes even tasks have been listed for each job. It has become increasingly difficult to define work at the task level because many jobs are in a state of flux. Nevertheless, the law and sound compensation strategy still require a clearly understood definition of work that is expected to be performed. Rather than defining all the minute tasks associated with a job, there are higher order levels of work units than tasks that can be used.

In particular, jobs can be defined by the major areas of responsibility that people are expected to perform. These major areas of responsibility spell out the chunks, or segments, of work that people are responsible for. The major duties (behaviors) and/or role expectations (results) can then be precisely defined for each major area of responsibility.

Context

The valuation of the person and the job for compensation decisions can be made only if one knows the context in which they take place. The context of work includes several components. One component is working conditions, which include environmental circumstances such as travel required and exposure to hazardous situations.

Another important component of the context is the work process flow. This component, shown in Exhibit 3-2, describes how one job is related to other jobs, people, and processes inside and outside the organization. Input refers to where the work comes from; throughput refers to what the job incumbent does with the input once received; output refers to where the work goes once the job incumbent has completed it; and feedback refers to where feedback is received in the process. A network analysis also describes the context in which work is performed. It details interaction with superiors, external customers and vendors, teams, and departments.

Components of the work context might be used in the following manner in making compensation decisions. Organizations may wish to pro-

EXHIBIT 3-2
Work process flow.

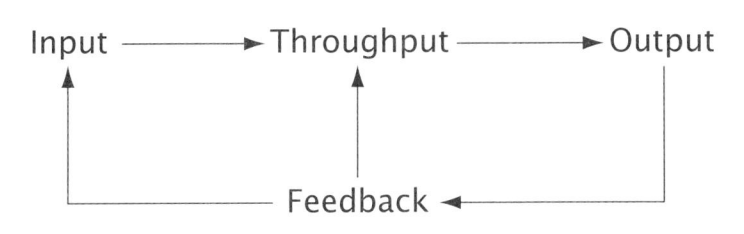

Input ⟶ Throughput ⟶ Output, with Feedback loop from Output back to Input and Throughput.

vide a compensation differential for hazardous working conditions. The working conditions component allows this data to be available to make the assessment as to which jobs qualify and which do not. An organization's business and compensation strategy may place high value on customer service. The network analysis component helps the organization assess which jobs have the most important interactions with the customer. An organization may emphasize teamwork in its business strategy and may need to know which jobs require extensive interaction in a team. The work process analysis provides this information.

The amount of information gathered in each of these categories (person, job, and context) will vary by type of business strategy, for example:

Business Strategy	*Job Analysis Emphasis*
Customer Service	Job
Quality	Context
Innovation	Person
Productivity	Job
Cost	Job
Financial	Job
Human Capital	Person

Some business strategies require that jobs be performed routinely in order to deliver consistent products and services. Business strategies requiring consistently performed jobs are often found in organizations with a focus on customer service, productivity, cost, and financial gain. In these organizations, emphasis is placed on the job more than on the person or the context.

Other business strategies require that organizations be very responsive to the changing nature of the market. Companies that focus on innovation and human capital are of this nature and need very flexible job assignments to meet the changing nature of the market. Hence, the emphasis is on the person more than the job or context.

Lastly, organizations that focus their business strategy on quality place a greater emphasis on the work context than on the job or person. Emphasis is placed upon developing systems of work organization rather than individuals in the organization in order to ensure quality products and services.

Work Analysis Measurement

Data Sources

In order to gather accurate job analysis information, multiple sources must be used. By having more than one source, a more comprehensive picture of the job is obtained and a system of checks and balances is created to minimize sources of bias. Sources to be used include documents, the job incumbent, the immediate supervisor, and job analysts.

Documents often contain information about the strategic importance of the job. These documents may include policy and procedure manuals, business planning documents, safety manuals, and operations manuals. The supervisor of the position is also likely to have knowledge of how the job fits in from a strategic perspective and should be consulted because this information may not yet be put into a document or is not one that is available to all.

The immediate supervisor may be too removed from the job to be knowledgeable about day-to-day details or the job. The job incumbent is a very insightful source here. While the supervisor provides a "top-down" perspective, the employee provides a "bottom-up" perspective. Both perspectives are needed for an accurate portrayal of the job.

The job analyst provides yet a third essential perspective, namely, that of someone outside the immediate work situation. This person tends to be less prone to biasing factors (e.g., personality conflicts) than are the job incumbent and supervisor in the immediate job situation. While perhaps being somewhat more "objective," the analyst's opinions are certainly not sufficient in and of themselves because the analyst usually does not have the familiarity with the job that the incumbent and supervisor have.

Data Collection Techniques

Whenever possible, multiple data collection techniques should be used. Any one method is subject to sampling error and measurement error. Multiple data collection techniques help minimize these errors through a system of checks and balances. Also, as will be described later, some sources provide in-depth information while others provide more breadth of information. Both breadth and depth are needed to develop a complete analysis of the job.

Questionnaires serve as the most efficient method of data collection. The cost to transmit them electronically or by mail is far less than the cost of face-to-face interviews. A questionnaire is likely to provide a great breadth of information on aspects of the job that may be overlooked by the job analyst. A more comprehensive view of work is also likely to be obtained when a questionnaire is used.

Interviews are less efficient but may provide much more in-depth information. They are of critical importance from a strategic perspective because they allow the analyst to better understand how the various job functions relate to the business strategy. Although time consuming and, hence, costly to do, interviews provide a much more detailed assessment of work. Cost can be minimized by using systematic sampling techniques to ensure that a sample smaller than the entire population of employees is used that is representative of the larger population of all employees. It should be noted that while focus groups can also be used to minimize costs, sampling error is just as big an issue as with individual interviews, and office politics during the focus group may bias the information obtained.

Many things that we do at work become habitual. Thus, job incumbents and previous job incumbents (supervisors) may inadvertently overlook important components of the job. Observation can be used to counteract this weakness. Moreover, an observer may be able to suggest new ways that the job can be described to be in greater alignment with the business strategy.

The Responsibility Summary Method

Over the years, I have developed a method of job analysis that has been helpful in my compensation projects. This method is summarized in the Responsibility Summary Questionnaire (RSQ) shown in Exhibit 3-3. A

(text continues on page 64)

EXHIBIT 3-3
Responsibility summary questionnaire.

PART 1—GENERAL INFORMATION

Title _____

Supervisor _____

Department or Team _____

Approval _____ Date _____

PART 2—WORK CONTENT

A. Basic Responsibility Overview

   Provide a short description of the overall responsibilities required while at work.

   _____
   _____
   _____
   _____
   _____
   _____
   _____
   _____
   _____
   _____

B. Major Areas of Responsibility

   Major areas of responsibility are major functions, categories, or dimensions for which an individual is responsible while at work. A major area of responsibility can also be described as a summary label for a collection of *work activities*. Most employees are usually responsible for somewhere between two and eight major areas of responsibility. For help on how to fill out this section, use the example of a completed responsibility summary in Exhibit 3-4 on page 65.

C. Major Areas of Responsibility—*Work Activities*

Work activities describe specific tasks that are needed to complete each major area of responsibility. In the following spaces, please write down each major area of responsibility indicated in Section B above, followed by five to ten specific work activities that make up each major area of responsibility. Refer to the attached example of a completed responsibility summary for more information on how to fill out this section.

Major Area of Responsibility: _____

Specific Work Activities for Major Area of Responsibility:

Base Pay Systems

EXHIBIT 3-3 (cont.)

_____

_____

_____

D. Major Areas of Responsibility—*Importance Rating*

List below the major areas of responsibility mentioned in Section B and indicate on a scale of 0 to 100 how important each major area of responsibility is to the overall effectiveness of the position. Make sure that the total number of points indicating importance adds up to 100 at the bottom of the page. Keep in mind that although an activity such as budgeting may take little time, its importance rating might be high. For more information on how to fill out this section, refer to the attached example of a completed responsibility summary.

Major Area of Responsibility #1: _____

Importance Rating: _____

Major Area of Responsibility #2: _____

Importance Rating: _____

Major Area of Responsibility #3: _____

Importance Rating: _____

Major Area of Responsibility #4: _____

Importance Rating: _____

Major Area of Responsibility #5: _____

Importance Rating: _____

Major Area of Responsibility #6: _____

Importance Rating: _____

Major Area of Responsibility #7: _____

Importance Rating: _____

Work Analysis

Major Area of Responsibility #8: _____

                              Importance Rating: _____

TOTAL IMPORTANCE POINTS (should equal 100)   _____

E. Major Areas of Responsibility—*Percent of Time*

List below the major areas of responsibility mentioned in Section B and indicate what percent of time, from 0 percent to 100 percent, each major area of responsibility requires. Make sure that the total number of percentage points adds up to 100 at the bottom of the page. Keep in mind, as mentioned on the previous page, that an activity such as budgeting may have a high importance rating but take a small percent of time compared with other activities required for the position. For more information on how to fill out this section, refer to the attached example of a completed responsibility summary.

Major Areas of Responsibility #1: _____

                              Percent of Time Spent: _____

Major Areas of Responsibility #2: _____

                              Percent of Time Spent: _____

Major Areas of Responsibility #3: _____

                              Percent of Time Spent: _____

Major Areas of Responsibility #4: _____

                              Percent of Time Spent: _____

Major Areas of Responsibility #5: _____

                              Percent of Time Spent: _____

Major Areas of Responsibility #6: _____

                              Percent of Time Spent: _____

Major Areas of Responsibility #7: _____

                              Percent of Time Spent: _____

Base Pay Systems

EXHIBIT 3-3 (cont.)

Major Areas of Responsibility #8: _____

Percent of Time Spent: _____

TOTAL PERCENT OF TIME SPENT (should equal 100)   _____

PART 3—QUALIFICATIONS

A. Knowledge

Check any of the types of knowledge below needed to perform the work responsibilities and provide additional details on the activities that make up each item. For example, a policy/procedure (item #1 below) might include safety procedures, inventory-integrity procedures, or HR policy.

_____ 1. Policies/procedures (describe below).

_____ 2. Computer systems, such as J. D. Edwards, M2M (describe below).

_____ 3. Personal computer systems, such as Lotus, WordPerfect, or Excel (describe below).

Work Analysis

_____ 4. Training required (describe below).

_____
_____
_____

_____ 5. Tools and equipment (describe below).

_____
_____
_____

_____ 6. Other (describe below).

_____
_____
_____

B. Experience

Indicate below the type of specific skills necessary to complete work responsibilities.

Skill Required: _____
_____

Skill Required: _____
_____

Skill Required: _____
_____

Skill Required: _____
_____

Skill Required: _____
_____

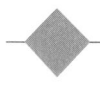

EXHIBIT 3-3 (cont.)

Skill Required: _____

_____

Skill Required: _____

_____

Skill Required: _____

_____

Skill Required: _____

_____

Skill Required: _____

_____

Skill Required: _____

_____

C. Education

Check any of the types of education, licenses, and certificates necessary to acquire the knowledge and skills to perform the responsibilities of the position and indicate any specific courses or areas of specialization when necessary. Please list the types of education, licenses, and certificates that are "basic requirements," rather than what might be on a "wish list" of education requirements.

_____ 1. Grade school education of ability to pass basic math and literacy tests at the eighth-grade level.

_____ 2. Some high school course work.

Specific courses: _____

_____ 3. Completion of high school education or GED.

Specific courses: _____

Work Analysis

____ 4. Some vocational training.

    Area of specialization: _____

____ 5. One-year job-related vocational program.

    Area of specialization: _____

____ 6. Two-year job-related vocational program.

    Area of specialization: _____

____ 7. Some job-related college course work.

    Specific courses: _____

____ 8. Associate degree:

    Major(s): _____

____ 9. Bachelor's degree:

    Major(s): _____

____ 10. Machinery/equipment certification.

    Specific types: _____

____ 11. Other (define below).

    _____

    _____

D. Basic Skills and Abilities

   Reading. List types of materials read on the job.

   _____

   _____

   _____

   _____

EXHIBIT 3-3 (cont.)

Writing. List the type of writing done on the job.

_____
_____
_____
_____

Speaking. List the type of conversation conducted on the job.

_____
_____
_____
_____

Mathematical. List the type of calculations performed on the job.

_____
_____
_____
_____

Physical. List the type of activity, amount that activity takes place, and amount moved.

_____
_____
_____
_____

PART 4—WORKING CONDITIONS

Working conditions are those that make up or are a part of the surroundings in which the work is performed. Indicate below any conditions that the position is exposed to in its work environment and indicate the average number of weekly hours of exposure per year.

Environmental conditions are those that affect the respiratory system or the skin. Some examples include extremely hot, cold, or humid work environments. Environmental conditions are important only if they are present to a degree or length of time that would cause discomfort or possible bodily injury. *Potentially hazardous conditions* are situations in which there is danger to life, health, or bodily injury. Examples include working conditions that require handling explosive material or equipment, pressurized equipment, and chemically toxic materials. *Travel,* another important working condition, is described as the amount of overnight travel required to complete the responsibilities of the job.

Environmental Conditions

Type of Environmental Condition: _____

_____ Average hours each week: _____

Type of Environmental Condition: _____

_____ Average hours each week: _____

Type of Environmental Condition: _____

_____ Average hours each week: _____

Type of Environmental Condition: _____

_____ Average hours each week: _____

Hazardous Conditions

Type of Hazardous Condition: _____

_____ Average hours each week: _____

Type of Hazardous Condition: _____

_____ Average hours each week: _____

EXHIBIT 3-3 (cont.)

Type of Hazardous Condition: _____

_____ Average hours each week: _____

Travel

Type of Travel: _____

_____ Average hours each month: _____

PART 5—WORK PROCESS FLOW

Indicate in very general terms below the type of work processes that are necessary to complete the responsibilities of the position.

1. Input processes. (Where does the work come from?)

   _____
   _____
   _____
   _____
   _____

2. Throughput processes. (Once you get the work, what do you do with it?)

   _____
   _____
   _____
   _____
   _____

Work Analysis

3. Output processes. (Once you complete the work, where does it go?)

_____
_____
_____
_____
_____

PART 6—NETWORK ANALYSIS

Check below the type of working interactions required and provide additional details describing the interactions.

_____ 1. Direct supervision of others (describe below).

_____
_____
_____
_____

_____ Number of associates supported

_____
_____
_____
_____

_____ 2. Interactions with external customers and vendors (describe below).

_____
_____
_____
_____

EXHIBIT 3-3 (cont.)

_____ 3. Interactions with own team/department (describe below).

_____
_____
_____

_____ 4. Interactions with other teams/departments (describe below).

_____
_____
_____
_____
_____

complete job description based on this approach is shown in Exhibit 3-4. It provides a starting point for gathering job analysis data. The data collected always need to be verified and supplemented by other sources and means as previously described.

Case Studies

I will show how the RSQ has been used in two cases. In each one, I will demonstrate how it was used to be consistent with and complementary to the business strategy and compensation strategy.

CASE 1

Educational Distributor

Educational Synergy, Inc. (ESI) is a Dallas-based distributor of educational products. Founded in 1965, it originally specialized in science products

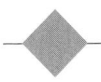

EXHIBIT 3-4
Responsibility summary.

GENERAL INFORMATION

TITLE: Department Supervisor
SUPPORTED BY: Assistant Manager
DEPARTMENT: Warehouse
DATE:

WORK CONTENT

Basic Responsibility Overview

To provide support to the shipping/receiving department. To ensure accurate receipt, storage, and shipment/transfer of product to and from the warehouse. To ensure accurate recordkeeping and documentation of warehouse inventory.

Major Areas of Responsibility

1. Participates in group projects aside from required work assignments.
   —Works with group to develop action plans and make recommendations on implementing activities.
   —Coordinates group activities with other departments.
   —Represents warehouse perspective on various projects.
   Percent of time spent: 5%   **Importance to position: 20**

2. Supports staff (i.e., assists with decisions regarding hiring and terminations; provides orientation, training, work direction, and discipline; and conducts performance reviews and makes salary recommendations) for fewer than ten associates.
   —Screens and conducts first interview and refers final applicants to managers.
   —Prepares work schedule for department and determines daily staffing levels to control labor costs and meet department labor budget.
   —Observes and documents associate behavior and advises managers of associate performance.
   —Monitors usage of equipment, ensuring only certified associates are utilizing equipment. Monitors compliance with safety measures.
   —Delegates and follows up on work assignments.
   Percent of time spent: 15%   **Importance to position: 40**

3. Provides support regarding the shipment and receipt of products to/from the warehouse.
   —Accurately logs in drivers, breaks truck seal, and records information in log.
   —Removes product from truck; checks it in against the packing list.
   —Applies security tags to product and moves it to the warehouse.

Base Pay Systems

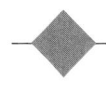

EXHIBIT 3-4 (cont.)

—Operates equipment according to company safety standards to assist in moving products.
—Inputs product transfer information into the computer.
—Packages product for shipment and completes bill for transfers.
—Enters product received via dropship into the computer.
Percent of time spent: 45%   **Importance to position: 25**

4. Ensures accurate recordkeeping and documentation of warehouse inventory.
   —Maintains appropriate forms and records to ensure inventory integrity.
   —Organizes and maintains supply of products.
   —Processes defective and overstock merchandise.
   —Performs routine housekeeping of warehouse products.
   Percent of time spent: 35%   **Importance to position: 15**

QUALIFICATIONS

Knowledge

1. Adheres to company's equal employment opportunity policy in all hiring, promotions, training, and termination activities related to the position.
2. Adheres to company policy on maintaining an environment free of sexual harassment.
3. Adheres to company's alcohol, drugs, and controlled substance policy.
4. Uses company safety procedures to supervise and assist in moving products in the warehouse.
5. Applies company inventory integrity procedures.
6. Utilizes company computer system to document receipt and shipment of products.
7. Applies company supervisor training and evaluation of associates.
8. Complies with Department of Transportation standards.

Skills

1. Has two to three years of general warehouse/inventory control experience.
2. Determines future staffing levels through use of planning skills.
3. Identifies department needs and adapts to changing environment.
4. Manages conflict effectively.
5. Influences activities of others through leadership skills.
6. Coordinates and integrates associates' work assignments.
7. Uses problem-solving skills.
8. Coaches and counsels associates.

9. Uses effective delegation and follow-up skills.
10. Exhibits and encourages team-building skills.

Education

Completion of high school education or GED.

Basic Skills and Abilities

1. Ability to read company materials, including policy and procedures manuals.
2. Legibility of writing and thoroughness in completing forms and paperwork.
3. Ability to express self and give specific responses. Ability to participate in one-on-one or small group discussions.
4. Ability to perform more complex mathematical operations for maintaining and processing budgets for inventory department.
5. Bends and kneels on a daily basis for five minutes each time to survey inventory shipments.
6. Sits on an hourly basis for more than sixty minutes at a time.
7. Reaches on a daily basis above shoulder height to retrieve, place, or sort objects weighing in excess of twenty-five pounds.
8. Lifts on a daily basis up to seventy-five pounds to a height of six feet. Carries products five minutes at a time.
9. Stands on an hourly basis on a hard surface for one hour or more without rest.
10. Walks on an hourly basis on a hard surface over a flat terrain, wearing steel-toe shoes on a smooth surface.

WORKING CONDITIONS

Environmental conditions include:
1. Hot, cold, or sometimes humid conditions in the warehouse (forty hours/week).
2. Regular lifting of inventory (eight hours/week).
3. Standing on hard surfaces (fifteen hours/week).
4. Noisy and dirty/dusty work environment on a constant basis (forty hours/week).
5. Low lighting and outdoors on a daily basis (thirty hours/week).

WORK PROCESS FLOW

1. Input processes include receiving shipments of product via distribution people, and relating product discrepancies to vendors and suppliers.
2. Throughput processes include accurate recordkeeping, documentation, and maintenance of warehouse inventory.
3. Output processes include shipping inventory from the warehouse to organizations.

EXHIBIT 3-4 (cont.)

NETWORK ANALYSIS

1. Directly provides support to fewer than ten warehouse employees.
2. Interacts with external distribution people, including truckers and express mail delivery people. Also interacts with vendors regarding product disparities.
3. Interacts with inventory team, other team supervisors in the department, and assistant manager.
4. Interacts with other departments, including human resources, accounting, and marketing.

Approvals: _____ Date: _____
               Manager

---

used in art and physical education as well as equipment like office furniture. Currently, the company is organized into cross-functional teams based on product lines. The organization has grown very rapidly in size, and it has distribution sites in three other geographic areas of the United States.

Business Strategy. A new president was recently named, and he has led the organization, with the help of a consultant, in developing a new strategic plan for the organization. The goal is to be the largest educational products distributor in the United States in the next five years. This will be a difficult goal to accomplish because the industry has become very competitive. To accomplish this goal, senior management has identified several critical success factors as part of the corporate business strategy:

1. A strategy of vertical integration is needed. Some products (e.g., science kits) should be assembled by ESI to minimize costs.
2. Quality needs to be improved. Even with a new information system, the number of returns and shipping errors is too high.
3. New product development is needed so that teachers see creative ways of combining products for educational purposes (e.g., factory simulations).
4. The adaptation of high-performance work systems is needed to reduce head count and to increase output. Team efforts will replace individual efforts.

Compensation Strategy. The compensation strategy closely mirrors the business strategy. Two components of the compensation strategy have relevance for the job analysis process. First, high-performance work systems with an emphasis on participation in decision making was to be used for all compensation system design. Second, total quality management principles were to be used in the design of the compensation system.

Other goals of the compensation strategy, which also drive other parts of the compensation plan to be shown in later chapters, include the following:

- Pay is an important component of our success in attracting, retaining, and motivating a high-quality work force.
- Pay is both a reward for demonstrated performance and an investment in future quality and productivity.
- Pay growth of individuals is ultimately a function of company performance and profitability.
- A pay structure should place a fair and appropriate value on each job's responsibilities relative to other jobs in the organization.
- A pay structure should be designed to be clearly communicated, easily understood, and consistently administered.

Job Analysis. The Responsibility Summary Questionnaire was used to collect data to develop job descriptions. Parts 5 (Work Process Flow) and 6 (Network Analysis) were very important in the process because they provided valuable data on redesigning jobs to be more efficient and consistent with the business strategy. In the spirit of the business and compensation strategies, a cross-functional team was formed to develop the job descriptions. The Responsibility Summary Questionnaire was first sent to all the teams for the completion of a questionnaire for each team position by the entire team. The completed Responsibility Summary Questionnaires were written into job descriptions by the consultant. As the consultant was writing up job descriptions, interviews were periodically conducted along with observations to clarify and expand upon the information listed in the Responsibility Summary Questionnaire.

Interestingly, all employees were expected to serve on cross-functional task forces designed to work on special projects such as job analysis, to improve organizational effectiveness. This was in addition to the normal team or functional responsibilities. As a result, a major area of responsibility listed on all employees' Responsibility Summary Questionnaires was project involvement. While the percent of time and the importance of this major area of responsibility varied, all employees were expected to be involved in decision making, and the major area of responsibility for project involvement reinforced this point in the business and compensation strategies.

CASE 2

County Engineers Office

The County Engineers Office (CEO) is responsible for road and bridge maintenance in a county that covers a large metropolitan area. It employs a staff of engineers to oversee bridge design, repair, and maintenance and employs a staff of maintenance workers to maintain the roads. Actual bridge and road construction is outsourced using a bidding process. Although a public sector organization, it faces private sector competition because the engineering and maintenance functions could be outsourced as well.

Business Strategy. The goal of CEO is to provide value-added road and bridge services to the public at a reasonable cost. In order to do so, CEO has been working on upgrading the skill levels of their engineers and maintenance workers while reducing the head count. Also, more harmonious relations with the union were to be promoted.

Compensation Strategy. In order to upgrade skills to be more productive as a result of a reduced head count, the compensation strategy emphasized high-performance work systems, especially participation in decision making. Also, emphasis was to be placed on merit rather than seniority in making pay increase decisions, as had traditionally been the case. Given a somewhat turbulent relationship in the past, with the union that represented the maintenance workers, the compensation strategy emphasized cooperation with labor management.

Job Analysis. A task force was set up to conduct the entire compensation project; it included members from most functions and levels in the organization. The local union president and a staff person from the national union were full voting members on the committee. The Responsibility Summary Questionnaire was used to update and expand upon brief job descriptions developed by the Civil Service Commission. Surveys were completed by all supervisors and their employees working together. An internal job analyst was used to coordinate the procedure and to write job descriptions. Inconsistencies were resolved by bringing in internal "job experts" to clarify inconsistencies across jobs. Final approvals for each job description were obtained by the committee, senior management, the local union leadership, and the national union leadership. Several jobs were redesigned as a result of this process.

CHAPTER 4

Work Evaluation

It has become popular in some compensation circles to label job evaluation an anachronism. As with job analysis, the logic is that if organizations are to become flexible and responsive to rapidly changing business conditions, then job hierarchies should not be created based on job evaluation systems. This line of logic is flawed for four reasons.

First, current laws and regulations make it clear that if a job evaluation system is not used to make internal equity decisions, then the courts will. A review of court cases clearly shows that in the absence of a job evaluation system, the courts will implicitly develop their own system to assess if discrimination has taken place.[1] Rational employers do not want to have job evaluation decisions imposed by a judge who may not be familiar with their business. Job evaluation is likely to continue to be an important legal issue as the U.S. Department of Labor continues to scrutinize carefully employer practices that may create a glass ceiling for minorities and women.[2]

Second, in the absence of a job evaluation system, employers resort to methods that may not be viewed as "fair" by employees.[3] It has become popular in recent times to group together jobs on the basis of occupation, market value, or some undefined criteria in the absence of a job evaluation system to determine the value of the job to the organization. To have very vague and general criteria for pay band decisions is likely to lead people to view the system as unfair because they do not know or understand the rules that are being applied. In turn, employees who view the system as unfair are likely to be dissatisfied with their pay and vent their frustration through absenteeism, turnover, or union vote.[4]

Third, it is also argued that market forces are "fair" to minorities and women. Sometimes this is not the case either. Systematic employer practices of discrimination are captured in market data and to the extent that an employer overemphasizes market data, the employer may be using data that contain bias based upon discriminatory practices by other employers.

Fourth, job evaluation plays a critical role in deciding market rates of pay for employees. When job evaluation actually captures the business strategies of the organization, jobs likely to have more of an impact on the company will be higher in the pay hierarchy, even if the pay level for the job is not justified by market wages. And the reverse holds true as well for jobs with less of an impact on the company. They may have pay levels less than the market wage. In summary, job evaluation offers a mechanism for organizations to decide which jobs to pay above the market and which to pay below the market. In order for this mechanism to work, organizations must carefully develop job evaluation standards that are closely related to their business strategies.

As can be seen from these four points, job evaluation systems should not be rejected outright. Moreover, as will be shown in this chapter, job evaluation can and should be crafted to meet the flexible nature of organizations. Job evaluation systems can serve as a powerful method of reinforcing the business and compensation strategies for employees.

Types of Job Evaluation Systems

Given the problems associated with ranking procedures just described and market pricing, they will not be reviewed as viable methods of job evaluation. As pointed out, often they do not assess the value of the job to the organization using meaningful criteria. Three types of job evaluation systems use much better defined criteria than ranking and market pricing systems: classification, factor systems, and competencies.

Classification Systems

Classification systems have been traditionally employed in the public sector, with the U.S. government being the largest user of this method of job evaluation. Interestingly, some larger private sector organizations such as IBM are now using classification systems as a method to streamline their job evaluation procedures.

With a classification system, written standards are created to assess

Work Evaluation

the value of the job to the organization. Jobs are then slotted into categories of value based on the written criteria for each category. For example, the lowest level classification may be for those jobs in which there is very little discretion to perform and no supervisory responsibilities. A mid-level classification may be for those jobs with either a moderate amount of discretion to perform or some supervisory responsibilities. A high-level classification may be a job in which there is a large amount of discretion required to perform the job and supervisory responsibilities.

In order to "slot" jobs into the appropriate classification, the manager and analyst view the job description and place the job in the closest matched classification category. Although this approach is straightforward from an administrative perspective, it will generate sound internal equity decisions only if the classification categories and the job descriptions are well defined.

Factor Systems

A factor system takes each job and evaluates it against multiple criteria one criterion at a time. Ratings can be done either on the basis of points (point factor system) or on the basis of ranking each job relative to each criterion (factor comparison systems). An example of the most often used method, the point factor system, is shown in Table 4-1. The result of evaluating each job against each criterion (factor) is a job hierarchy, shown in Table 4-2.

TABLE 4-1
A point factor job evaluation system.

Factor	Weight	Degrees 1	2	3	4	5
		Points				
Complexity	25	5	10	15	20	25
Knowledge	20	4	8	12	16	20
Difficulty	20	4	8	12	16	20
Impact	15	3	6	9	12	15
Skills	15	3	6	9	12	15
Contacts	5	1	2	3	4	5
Totals	100	20	40	60	80	100

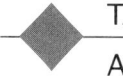

TABLE 4-2
A job hierarchy.

	Points			
Factor	Job A	Job B	Job C	Job D
Complexity	20	25	25	5
Knowledge	12	20	20	4
Difficulty	12	16	20	4
Impact	9	12	15	3
Skills	6	12	15	3
Contacts	3	4	5	1
Totals	62	89	100	20

Factors are units of compensable value or worth to the organization. Each factor is defined by degrees, which have written definitions for each degree and show the level of each degree. Each factor is weighted by its importance in determining value to the organization, and the weights are used to set up point values for each degree.

Descriptions of factors to use are not always easy to find. Organizations and consulting firms treat them as proprietary information. This may be a good thing, because it may force some organizations to develop their own factors rather than benchmark others. The custom-development of factors is to be preferred because it makes them specific to the business and compensation strategy of the company, which in turn makes it difficult for the company's competitors to use them.

Competencies

The latest approach to job evaluation requires the organization to evaluate people rather than jobs to predefined human capital criteria. These criteria are known as competencies and are described in detail in Chapter 3. People can be substituted for jobs and competencies substituted for factors in Tables 4-1 and 4-2 in order to create a competency matrix and person hierarchy, respectively, as shown in Tables 4-3 and 4-4. Notice how factors and competencies can be very similar or identical in some cases (e.g., knowledge). Usually, however, the factor approach places greater emphasis on the job than on the person, while the competency approach usually places more emphasis on the person than on the job.

TABLE 4-3
A competency-based system.

Competency	Weight	Degrees 1	2	3	4	5
Supervision	25	5	10	15	20	25
Leadership	20	4	8	12	16	20
Communications	20	4	8	12	16	20
Knowledge	15	3	6	9	12	15
Technical Skills	15	3	6	9	12	15
Ability	05	1	2	3	4	5
Totals	100	20	40	60	80	100

TABLE 4-4
A person hierarchy.

Competency	Person A	Person B	Person C	Person D
Supervision	25	20	25	5
Leadership	20	12	20	4
Communications	16	12	20	4
Knowledge	12	9	15	3
Technical Skills	12	6	15	3
Ability	4	3	5	1
Totals	89	89	100	20

Linking Job Evaluation to Compensation and Business Strategies

The selection and use of a particular job evaluation policy should be governed by the compensation and business strategy. This will now be shown for each job evaluation type.

Plan Selection

The decision as to which job evaluation method to use should be based upon the compensation and business strategies of the organization. Classification systems are usually associated with a low-cost strategy because they are easy to develop and administer. Factor systems lend themselves well to organizations that have cost, financial, and quality strategies because of the precision with these systems. Firms that pursue a strategy of innovation and customer service are more likely to use a competency system because of the flexibility allowed. Traditional productivity-driven organizations are likely to use a factor system, while greenfield start-up sites with a productivity emphasis are likely to use a competency-based system, a difference attributable to the different cultures in the two types of organizations.

Factor Selection

In selecting factors, there are a couple of general rules that apply irrespective of business and compensation strategies. There are also some rules issues to cover depending upon the company's specific compensation and business strategies. Both sets of rules will be covered.

A job evaluation system can easily become very complex and unwieldy. As a result, parsimony is needed in the selection of factors. That is, enough factors should be selected such that the factors encompass all-important aspects of the business and compensation strategies. As few factors as possible should be selected so that the factors do not overlap with one another and become redundant. As a general rule, one factor is probably not enough to capture the complexity of most compensation and business strategies, while nine or more are likely to lead to redundant factors.

Another general rule is that factors should always be weighted. By doing so, a very powerful message is sent to employees as to what is the most important portion of a multifaceted business strategy. The weight of factors not only points out the importance of portions of the business strategy, but also what it takes for employees to have upward mobility into higher level jobs in the organization (i.e., career mobility).

Specific types of factors to be used for different business strategies are shown in Table 4-5.

Competency Selection

The general rules regarding the number of factors and weighting of factors also apply to competencies. Also, some competencies seem to be better suited to certain business strategies, as shown in Table 4-6. As with factors, competencies specific to the specific strategy of the organization need to be developed.

TABLE 4-5
Typical factors listed by business strategy.

Business Strategy	Factors
Customer Service	• Customer service • Problem solving • Contacts
Quality	• Know-how • Leadership • Problem solving
Innovation and Time to Market	• Knowledge • Autonomy • Research
Productivity	• Effort • Responsibility • Economic impact
Cost	• Working conditions • Experience • Responsibility
Human Capital	• Knowledge • Skills • Ability

Competencies can be measured at different levels of the organization, and need to be considered. Competencies can be general or specific. General competencies are generic in orientation and apply to a large number of organizations. Specific competencies are tailor-made to the compensation and business strategies of the organization. Competencies can also be basic or advanced. Basic competencies are the ones needed for a person to perform in a satisfactory manner. Advanced competencies are needed for someone to be highly effective. Competencies can also be organizational or role based. Organizational competencies are cross-functional in orientation and are used for people across business functions. Role-based competencies refer to competencies required to perform specific assignments. An example of the different types of competencies as applied to an express mail delivery truck driver is shown in Table 4-7.

In general, organizations use basic competencies as a basis for screening people in selection decisions rather than as a basis for pay. The logic here is to not invest in these basic skills because they can be transferred to

TABLE 4-6
Typical competencies listed by business strategy.

Business Strategy	Competencies
Customer Service	• Communication skills • Interpersonal skills • Product knowledge
Quality	• Teamwork • Quality training • Leadership
Innovation and Time to Market	• Analytical skills • Motivation • Judgment
Productivity	• Management skills • Finance knowledge • Accounting skills
Cost	• Finance knowledge • Accounting skills • Product knowledge
Human Capital	• Skills • Personality • Leadership

TABLE 4-7
Sample competency types for an express mail driver.

Competency Level	Basic Competencies	Advanced Competencies Organizational-Based	Role-Based
General	Reading	Customer Service	Geographic Area
Specific	Driving a truck	Product Knowledge	Accounting Procedures

other employers and because these basic skills are, it is to be hoped, readily available in the market. Unfortunately, this is not always the case (e.g., illiteracy), and sometimes employers must pay for basic competencies. Employers are more likely to pay for advanced competencies because they are more difficult to find in the market. A similar logic is applied to general versus specific competencies. Companies are more likely to invest in paying for specific competencies because they are less transferable to other employers. On the other hand, more general competencies are usually used for screening decisions in selection because they are more readily available in the market. Finally, most organizations require the mastery of both organizational- and role-based competencies and tie both to pay. Pay for role-based competencies provides immediate returns to the organization, while pay for organizational-based competencies provides more long-term returns to the organization.

Case Studies

CASE 1

Educational Distributor

The compensation and business strategies and job analysis procedures were viewed in the case at the end of Chapter 3 for the educational distributor in this case. Consistent with this strategy, the following compensable factors were used: strategic impact, scope of responsibility, knowledge, skills, and physical demands. Given the importance of financial results to the company as spelled out in both the business and compensation strategies, the strategic impact factor and scope of responsibility factor were weighted most heavily by point values. Skills and knowledge received the next highest factor weightings because of the improved human capital required in jobs in order to develop new, creative, and high-quality products as spelled out in the business strategy. Because participation in decision making was an important component of the business strategy and important to fairness perceptions required by the compensation strategy, physical demands were used as a factor because it was recommended to the design team by employees. However, while included, it received a lower number of points than other factors because of the higher importance placed upon financial and product success by the organization relative to working conditions.

Strategic Impact

Definition: Degree to which the position can influence the economic goals of the organization (i.e., budgeting, customer satisfaction, revenue generation). Focus is on individual action/initiative required, the level and extent of input into plans and goals, as well as the level and extent of execution responsibilities. Cost, impact of success, or error is also a consideration.

Degree Points Benchmark Descriptions

Degree	Points	Benchmark Descriptions
(1)	5	• Execution of routine transactions with limited direct impact on economic goals • Little or no independent action or initiative required to carry out assigned duties
(2)	11	• Execution of routine economic transactions with some impact on economic goals • Primarily follows prescribed procedures but may utilize some independent action or initiative within prescribed bounds
(3)	16	• Execution of nonroutine activities having moderate impact on economic goals • Moderate level of individual action or initiative required in implementing economic goals through work activities of self and others
(4)	22	• Provides input into operational plans impacting economic goals • Responsible for input to and execution of operational plan • Moderate- to high-level individual action or initiative required in implementing economic goals through work activities
(5)	27	• Involved in development of strategy to meet economic goals of the organization • Formulates operational plan to meet economic goals • High level of individual action/initiative required in implementing economic goals through work activities

Scope of Responsibility

Definition: Degree to which the position exercises management oversight of people, function, and/or organizational unit and is accountable for results. Focus is on contacts and the presence or absence and degree of leadership activities such as coaching, supervising, participating in the selection and development of associates, and involvement in performance management. Extent of supervisory control over the job (autonomy) is also a consideration.

Degree	Points	Benchmark Descriptions
(1)	5	• Accountability is limited to individual activities; little or no influence on the actions of other associates • Contact is limited to providing and/or receiving information, primarily within the work area
(2)	10	• Accountable for outcomes impacting a limited portion of a process; responsibility may include sharing of specific, technical expertise with other associates • Contact involves explanation and/or interpretation of information, primarily within the work area
(3)	15	• Accountable for others to the extent that instruction and follow-up are required, as well as the imparting of routine skills to other associates • Involved at an informal level in activities such as selection and development of associates • Contact involves explanation and/or interpretation of information across related work areas
(4)	20	• Accountable for functional or departmental results; influences a large number of associates and imparts operational and organizational skills necessary to achieve results • Responsible for coaching, supervising, selecting, and developing associates • Contact occurs across organizational areas and involves discussions and/or recommendations regarding policies, practices, etc.
(5)	25	• Accountable for results of business unit involving complex and multiple functions; imparts strategic skills to other associates • Responsible for leadership of others in supervisory positions; impacts the supervisory, selection, development, and performance management activities of others • Contact occurs across organizational areas and involves input to decision making regarding policies, practices, etc. having broad organizational impact

Skills

Definition: Capability needed to perform required responsibilities, including the extent to which the position requires learning as the result of unpredictability and change. Focus is on knowing how to do specific things in order to perform specific responsi-

Base Pay Systems

bilities required by the position. Skill sets of value include problem-solving skills (conceptual, analytical, innovation, and learning), technical skills, and communication skills. The degrees reflect the relative value of these skill sets being used in conjunction with one another.

Degree Points   Benchmark Descriptions

		Skill Sets: Problem-Solving Technical Communication
(1)	5	• Low levels of two or three of the skill sets (may have a moderate level of one skill set)
(2)	9	• Moderate levels of two of the skill sets and a low level of a third skill set
(3)	14	• Moderate levels of two or three skill sets (may have a high level of one skill set)
(4)	18	• High levels of two of the skill sets and a moderate level of a third skill set
(5)	23	• High levels of all three skill sets

Knowledge (Education and Experience Combined)

Definition: The basic knowledge required to successfully perform the responsibilities required by the position. Basic knowledge can be acquired by formal education, training, experience on the job, or a combination thereof. Focus is on general knowledge and knowing what to do.

Degree Points   Benchmark Descriptions

(1)	3	• No experience required
(2)	7	• One to three years' experience and a high school education or some vocational training
(3)	10	• One to three years' experience and an associate's degree or four or more years experience of and a high school education
(4)	14	• One to five years' experience and a bachelor's degree
(5)	17	• Six to ten years' experience and a bachelor's degree

Physical Demands

Definition: Assesses the degree of physical exertion required of the job incumbent in performing the responsibilities of the position. Physical exertion can include movement, lifting, and/or general mobility.

Degree	Points	Benchmark Descriptions
(1)	2	♦ Office setting with little or no physical exertion or travel
(2)	3	♦ Office setting with large amount of physical exertion and travel
(3)	4	♦ Warehouse setting with typical physical abilities required and typical environmental conditions
(4)	6	♦ Warehouse setting requiring high levels of physical ability
(5)	8	♦ Warehouse setting with extreme environmental conditions

CASE 2

Large Retailer

TEAR is a large retailer of women's fashions and accessories. It is a national chain with stores located in malls across the United States.

Business Strategy. The long-term corporate strategy for the organization is to develop a $10 billion portfolio of brands. To do so will require a straight focus on a balanced scorecard that emphasizes financial, customer service, and internal process objectives. At an operational level, the stores will be expanded to include all of North America, investments will be made in the enhancement of core internal processes, vertical integration of the business units to support the strategic business units will take place, and a new corporate governance structure will be implemented.

Compensation Strategy. TEAR clearly believes that organizational change must be made from the top down. This is true with the business directions just outlined and true with the compensation strategy as well. It is also recognized that the proposed changes to the business practices will require the acquisition and development of new competencies at the senior management level. Previously, compensation at the senior management level was based on financial results and a ranking of executive positions by value to the company. In order to foster the balanced scorecard concept of "learning and growth," base pay as well as base pay increases will be determined on the basis of the mastery and use of new competencies for the senior executives. Eventually, as part of the compensation strategy, this approach will be cascaded down to management at the store level as well.

Job Analysis. A well-known consulting firm was brought in to define and establish competencies for the senior executive level. The competencies developed were based on the competency model created by the consulting firm for its clients as well as the development of some company-specific competencies.

Job Evaluation. The competencies were used to set the pay level for senior level executives. Each competency was defined in very specific and observable terms. Each executive was rated using a 360-degree review process against the competencies. In addition, a development plan was formulated for each executive to bring his or her base pay up to the maximum overtime. The competencies used were leadership skills, analytical skills, change management skills, customer focus skills, strategic management skills, and fashion knowledge. Each competency was further broken down into subcategories. For example, strategic management skills included strategy formulation and strategy implementation. These competencies were selected because they were thought to be related to the balanced scorecard of the company. That is, to the extent that managers possessed these competencies, it was thought that performance in scorecard categories would be maximized. For example, in order to achieve effective results with customers, there would need to be good customer service (customer focus skills) and desired products (fashion knowledge competence). In this manner, the competency model used to evaluate people in managerial jobs was based on a model of the business. How managerial work was to be performed (competencies) was driven by what business results needed to be accomplished in each scorecard category.

CASE

3

Education Agency

StarNet is a small educational agency responsible for networking computers in the primary and secondary school systems in a midwestern state. It has an unusual governance structure in that through the passage of a law to accompany its funding, it is allowed to function almost as if it were a private company. In short, it can create its own financial, operational, and human resources systems independent of the state systems. It is overseen, however, by executives of other agencies in the state government who function much like a board of directors.

Business Strategy. Competition for StarNet comes from a variety of sources. If the products and services provided are not delivered to the satisfaction of the school districts, then the agency may be disbanded and its functions returned to the department of education in the state. Alternatively, the school districts may select their own private vendors. In order to compete in this environment, it is critical that StarNet deliver more than technology. Customer service is critical and so is educational design and training, so that the school districts know how to make effective use of the technology. A core set of values has been set forth by senior management to provide guidance at work without the need for rigid rules and procedures.

Compensation Strategy. StarNet must pay at a wage rate that is competitive with both the public and private sector in order to attract and retain the talent needed to deliver upon its business strategy. Strong leadership and coordination are needed for a staff consisting of technicians, educators, and support staff. A balanced scorecard approach is needed to focus people's efforts on both results and behaviors.

Job Evaluation. A factor system was created with the following compensable factors: decision making, nature of management, and scope of management. These factors were selected based on the nature of the work spelled out in the business and compensation strategies. Communications, a factor common to many job evaluations, was defined specifically in terms of customer service with a variety of customer interactions, ranging from routine inquiries to responding to state legislators. Because the business strategy allowed StarNet to operate almost as an independent state business, fiscal accountability was an important factor. Given the need to coordinate a diverse group of employees without rigid rules and procedures, as called for in the business strategy, the nature as well as scope of management required in jobs were critical. Finally, given the need to deliver products and services essential to student achievement, decision making was also deemed a critical factor.

Job Evaluation Manual

1. Decision Making (20 points)

This factor evaluates the amount of independent judgment required by the job. In addition, it evaluates the complexity of the decisions reached, the autonomy to make decisions, and the impact of those decisions.

Points

- 4 Decisions require some judgment. Understand and follow instructions and use equipment involving few decisions. Perform routine duties working from detailed instructions and under clearly defined policies.

8   Decisions require simple analytical judgment. Plan and perform a variety of duties requiring knowledge of a particular field and the use of a wide range of procedures. Involves the exercise of judgment in the analysis of facts or situations regarding individual problems or transactions to determine the next steps within the guidelines of standard practice.

12 Decisions require complex analytical judgment. Plan and perform a wide variety of duties requiring general knowledge of policies and procedures applicable within a project or area of the organization, including their application to cases not previously covered. Requires considerable judgment to work autonomously toward general results, create methods, modify or adapt standard procedures to meet different situations, and make decisions based on prior decisions and policies.

16 Decisions require advanced analytical judgment. Involves highly technical or involved projects, presenting new or constantly changing problems. Requires outstanding judgment and initiative in dealing with complex factors not easily assessed and also in making decisions for which there is little precedent.

20 Decisions require advanced judgment. Plan and perform complex work that involves new or constantly changing problems where there are few developed methods or procedures. Involves participation in the development and implementation of policies, objectives, and activities for a project or the organization. Considerable insight and exceptional judgment are required to deal with factors not easily assessed, to interpret results, and to make decisions having a great impact on the organization.

2. Communication (Nature of Interactions with Customers) (20 points)

This factor evaluates the nature/type of interactions that a job is required to have with either internal or external customers. Typical contacts should be used to determine the level of this factor rather than rare or extremely infrequent events.

Points

4   Responds to routine inquiries (e.g., calls)
8   Prepares documents or verbal contents for distribution for an informational purpose (e.g., brochure, newsletter, budget)
12 Responds verbally or in writing to questions of a technical nature

16 Organizes or facilitates meetings and prepares materials with external constituents

20 Communicates with legislators and policy makers of a high-level nature (e.g., negotiations, updates, discussion of next steps)

3. Knowledge (20 points)

This factor measures the level of formal experience, education, certification, and licensure required to perform the job.

Points

4 High school or GED

8 Associate of arts degree plus three years' experience or a bachelor's degree or five years of related experience

12 Bachelor's degree plus three years' experience or relevant industry certification/licensure plus two years of related experience or eight years of related experience

16 Master's plus three years' experience or relevant industry certification/licensure plus three years' related experience or ten years of related experience

20 Ph.D. plus three years' experience or relevant certification/licensure plus four years' related experience or fifteen years of related experience

4. Fiscal Accountability (20 points)

Points

4 No responsibility for appropriations. May prepare and/or monitor internal and external purchasing and expenditures for a specific program and/or fund

8 May allocate expenditures of funds $3 million and below for approval of higher management

12 May allocate expenditures of funds above $3 million for approval of higher management

16 Responsibility for appropriating, allocating, and requesting expenditures of funds $3 million and below at the agency level without approval of upper management OR processing expenditures for an agency ensuring accuracy and validity of payments, ensuring that all state policies and procedures are followed

20 Responsibility for appropriations, allocation, and approval of expenditure of funds above $3 million at the agency level

5. Nature of Management (10 points)

Points

- 2 Position does not necessitate providing assistance or training to other associates; accountability is based on individual performance
- 4 Position requires minimal technical assistance or guidance to other associates, specifically through explanation and interpretation of policies, procedures, or other pertinent work information; accountable for only the portion of the process impacted by the work
- 6 Position requires assistance and/or basic training of routine skills and the interpretation of information common to other associates serving in a similar or lower capacity; accountable for others to the extent that communication continues as feedback for the learning of skills and information
- 8 Position requires the supervision of other associates and involves developing and evaluating other associates, planning and scheduling the work of other associates, and enforcing policies and procedures of StarNet and the state; accountable for project/business unit results; work necessitates contact with others across projects/departments within StarNet and involves discussions and/or recommendations regarding policies and procedures
- 10 Position requires the supervision of other project or departmental managers; accountable for multiple projects/departmental units within StarNet and the work of those projects/units and for communicating progress/failure to a higher authority, such as the board of directors; impacts the supervisory, selection, development, and performance management of other managers; work necessitates contact across Starnet for decision making regarding strategic planning having broad impact

6. Scope of Management (10 points)

This factor examines the number of direct and indirect subordinates whom the manager supervises.

Points

- 2 1–3 employees
- 4 4–7 employees
- 6 8–14 employees
- 8 15–20 employees
- 10 more than 20 employees

Work Evaluation

CASE 4

County Engineers Office

The compensation and business strategy of this office was reviewed in Chapter 3. Consistent with the business and compensation strategies in this office, the following factors were used: mental demands, physical demands, working conditions, responsibility, scope of supervision, leadership, knowledge, and experience. Two of these factors are particularly noteworthy relative to the business and compensation strategies. First, physical demands and working conditions were both recommended by the union. Although the point values for these factors were low (5 and 10 points out of 100, respectively), they were included in order to promote harmonious relationships with the union. Second, both supervision and leadership were included as factors. Supervision was viewed as the ability of employees to influence other employees independent of position title (i.e., manager). Some jobs require more leadership than others, so it was included as a factor rather than a performance appraisal standard. In high-performance work organizations, which the organization pursued as a goal in the business strategy, leadership was needed as well as traditional supervision for the work teams to be effective. Supervision as a factor was defined as formal position power to influence the activities of employees and was measured as the number of full-time permanent employees supervised per the labor agreement.

Mental Demands. Measures the mental effort associated with performing the job and the degree of concentration needed, including alertness, attention, and coordination of manual dexterity with mental or visual attention.

Points

- 0 Job is very routine and can usually be performed while thinking about other matters
- 3 Job has intermittent periods that require alertness and attention to detail
- 6 Job requires continuous mental attention (40 percent or more of year) to ensure that mistakes do not occur
- 9 Job requires continuous mental attention (40 percent or more of year) and precise mental concentration (40 percent or more of year) to correctly perform the duties of the job

Base Pay Systems

   12   Job requires complex problem solving along with intense and precise mental concentration (40 percent or more of the year) to correctly perform the duties of the job

   15   Job requires multiple and varied complex problem solving along with intense and precise mental concentration (40 percent or more of the year) to correctly perform the duties of the job

Physical Demands. Measures the level of physical exertion associated with job demands.

Points

   0   Little or no physical exertion required
   1   Some physical exertion required
   1   Extensive standing or walking requirements (40 percent or more of year)
   2   Extensive standing, walking, lifting (50 lbs.), and/or flexibility requirements (40 percent or more of year)
   5   Extreme lifting (100 lbs.) and/or flexibility requirements (40 percent or more of year)

Working Conditions. Measures job surroundings and environmental influences such as atmosphere, ventilation, noise, and congestion.

Points

   0   Little exposure to uncomfortable job surroundings and/or environmental conditions
   2   Slight exposure to uncomfortable job surroundings and/or environmental influences
   4   Uncomfortable working conditions with potential for minor injuries; likely to be exposed to extreme temperature, dust, or traffic
   6   Occasional dangerous working conditions with potential for major injuries; some exposure to extreme temperature, dust, or traffic
   8   Hazardous working conditions 40 percent or more of year (potential for death or severe injury even when safety procedures are followed) to include working with hazardous chemicals or electricity **or** working in right of way adjacent to moving traffic) **or** working with heavy equipment*
   10   Hazardous working conditions 70 percent or more of year (potential for death or severe injury even when safety procedures are fol-

---

*Motorized equipment weighing over 2 tons requiring an operator or driver that is used in performing construction and/or roadway maintenance.

lowed) to include working in right of way adjacent to moving traffic **or** working with heavy equipment*

Responsibility. Measures the responsibilities under the direct control of the job incumbent in terms of freedom of action to perform the job, the level of decision making required to successfully perform the job, and accountability for equipment assigned, materials used, safety, communications, and public relations.

Points

- 0   Little room to exercise independent judgment due to close supervision and clearly defined policies
- 3   Some room to exercise independent judgment, but job incumbent is expected to get approval from immediate supervisor for deviation from policy
- 6   Job requires the planning of materials used, equipment assigned, safety, and public relations and communication activities or the solving of routine problems; approval of plans is required by immediate supervisor
- 9   Job requires planning and the solving of routine problems without consultation with the immediate supervisor
- 12 Job requires the planning of complex projects and the resolution of complex problems in which the nature of the project and problems is not clearly defined from policy, supervision, or previous experience
- 15 Job requires the planning of multiple and varied complex projects and the resolution of multiple and varied complex problems in which the nature of the project and problems is not clearly defined from policy, supervision, or previous experience

Scope of Supervision. Supervision of full-time permanent employees. Supervision is defined as the direct responsibility for the work of subordinates, including the planning and scheduling of work, performance appraisal, and policy and safety enforcement.

Points

- 0   0 employees supervised
- 2   1–2 employees supervised
- 4   3–4 employees supervised

---

*Motorized equipment weighing over 2 tons requiring an operator or driver that is used in performing construction and/or roadway maintenance.

Base Pay Systems

    6   5–6 employees supervised
    8   7–10 employees supervised
  10   11 or more employees supervised

Leadership. Leadership of full-time, permanent employees.

Points

    0   Does not provide guidance to lower level employees
    3   Assists in guiding lower level employees
    6   Provides immediate guidance to lower level employees while performing work of the same nature; may provide basic training in work-related operations
    9   Assists in guiding employees toward organizational goals and/or supervising subordinates by providing input into planning, scheduling, performance appraisal, and/or policy enforcement
  12   Directly responsible for the work of two or more subordinates, including the planning and scheduling of work, performance appraisal, and policy and safety enforcement
  15   Supervises the work of other supervisors

Knowledge. Measured as the amount of training and education required to successfully complete the duties of the job.

Points

    0   Completion of grade school
    3   High school degree/GED or licensure
    6   High school degree/GED and post–high school training and/or certification/licensure in job-related areas
  10   Relevant two-year college degree and/or education-related certification/licensure
  12   Relevant four-year college degree and/or education-related certification/licensure

Experience. Measures the amount of relevant work experience needed to perform job duties at a competent level.

Points

    0   No experience necessary
    3   Six months of job experience or less
    6   More than six months of experience up to one year
    9   More than one year of experience up to two years

12 More than two years of experience up to three years
15 More than three years of experience

Notes

1. E. A. Cooper and G. V. Barrett, "Equal Pay and Gender: Implications of Court Cases for Personnel Practices," *Academy of Management Review*, (1984): 9, pp. 84–94.
2. T. S. Bland, T. H. Nail, and D. P. Knox. "OFCCP, White House Push Comparable Worth," *HR News*, May 2000, pp. 22–23; C. Fay and H. Risher. "New OFCCP Survey: Comparable Worth Redux?" *Workspan*, July 2000, pp. 41–44; M. A. Prost, "EEOC Cracks Down on Pay Discrimination Cases," *Human Resources Executive*, July 2000, p. 14.
3. J. Greenberg and C. McCarty, "Comparable Worth: A Matter of Justice," in *Research in Personnel and Human Resource Management*, Vol. 8, edited by G. R. Ferris and K. M. Rowland (Greenwich, CT: JAI Press, 1990) pp. 265–301.
4. R. Folger and M. A. Konovsky, "Effects of Procedural and Distributive Justice on Reactions to Pay Raise Decisions," *Academy of Management Journal*, (1989): 32, pp. 115–130; H. G. Heneman III, "Pay Satisfaction," in *Research in Personnel and Human Resource Management*, Vol. 3, edited by G. R. Ferris and K. M. Rowland (Greenwich, CT: JAI Press, 1985), pp. 115–140.

CHAPTER 5

Market Surveys

Increasingly, organizations are relying upon an external equity pay philosophy. That is, base wages and salaries are heavily weighted according to market value. Organizations are drawn to this approach for several reasons. First, in the case of a pure market pay strategy it makes the administration of the compensation system less complex. There is no need to merge internal equity data (i.e., job evaluation points) with external data. Second, it minimizes some of the emotional reactions to pay decisions. Pay decisions are attributed to neutral market forces rather than to decisions made by external decision makers. Third, organizations increasingly view their human capital as a source of competitive advantage. Organizations with a human capital strategy must be very sensitive to market forces in order to attract, retain, and motivate the best and brightest. Fourth, a hallmark of capitalism is to price goods and services relative to market values. Wages and salaries are derived from product and service prices and so too must reflect market forces.

Although market forces are very important to base pay decisions, market survey data are often biased by both sampling error and measurement error.[1] In terms of sampling error, it is usually not possible to gather complete data on the population to which the organization wishes to compare itself. Among the reasons for this sampling bias is that when conducting market surveys, not all organizations in the population participate. Some are too busy and others prefer not to. Also, there may be a lack of information about all firms in the population to which the organization wishes to make comparisons. Addresses may be difficult to obtain.

In terms of measurement error, the matching of survey jobs to company jobs is an inexact science at best. Often, job titles alone are used, and, as shown in Chapter 3, job titles in and of themselves may be very misleading. Also, even jobs with a similar job description by the company conducting the survey may not be perfectly matched. At the margin, job duties may differ along important dimensions not reflected in an abbreviated job description used as a reference point in a market survey.

The point being made here is not that market data shouldn't be used. They are and should be, regardless of the balance of an internal versus external equity philosophy regarding pay. In either event, and especially in the case of a pure market-based pay strategy, great care needs to be taken in the survey process to minimize sampling error and measurement error as much as possible. Techniques to do so will be discussed in this chapter.

Market Survey Steps

The steps to gather and analyze market survey data are shown in Exhibit 5-1. Each step will be viewed in turn.

Consider Strategy and Job Analysis

The guiding lights in the market survey process are the strategies of the organization (business and compensation) and the job analysis. In the absence of these critical guide lights, explained in Chapters 2 and 3, respectively, the process of conducting a market survey becomes overwhelming, especially in this electronic age when so much potential data exists. Also, the data collected have no meaning absent the context set by the strategy and job analysis. These two processes are crucial for the valid interpretation of market survey data by organizations. Exactly how these two guiding lights should be used will be covered in each of the next steps in the market survey process.

Establish Benchmark Jobs

Although it would be desirable from a sampling perspective to have survey data on all jobs in surveyed companies, it is often not possible to do for two reasons. First, it is time-consuming to fill out surveys. The more lengthy the survey, the less likely it is to be filled out. Hence, only a sample of jobs can be surveyed. Second, some jobs are unique to a specific organization, so others may not have them. Thus, the sample of jobs selected to be surveyed must be representative of jobs in the population.

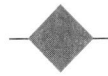

EXHIBIT 5-1
Market survey steps.

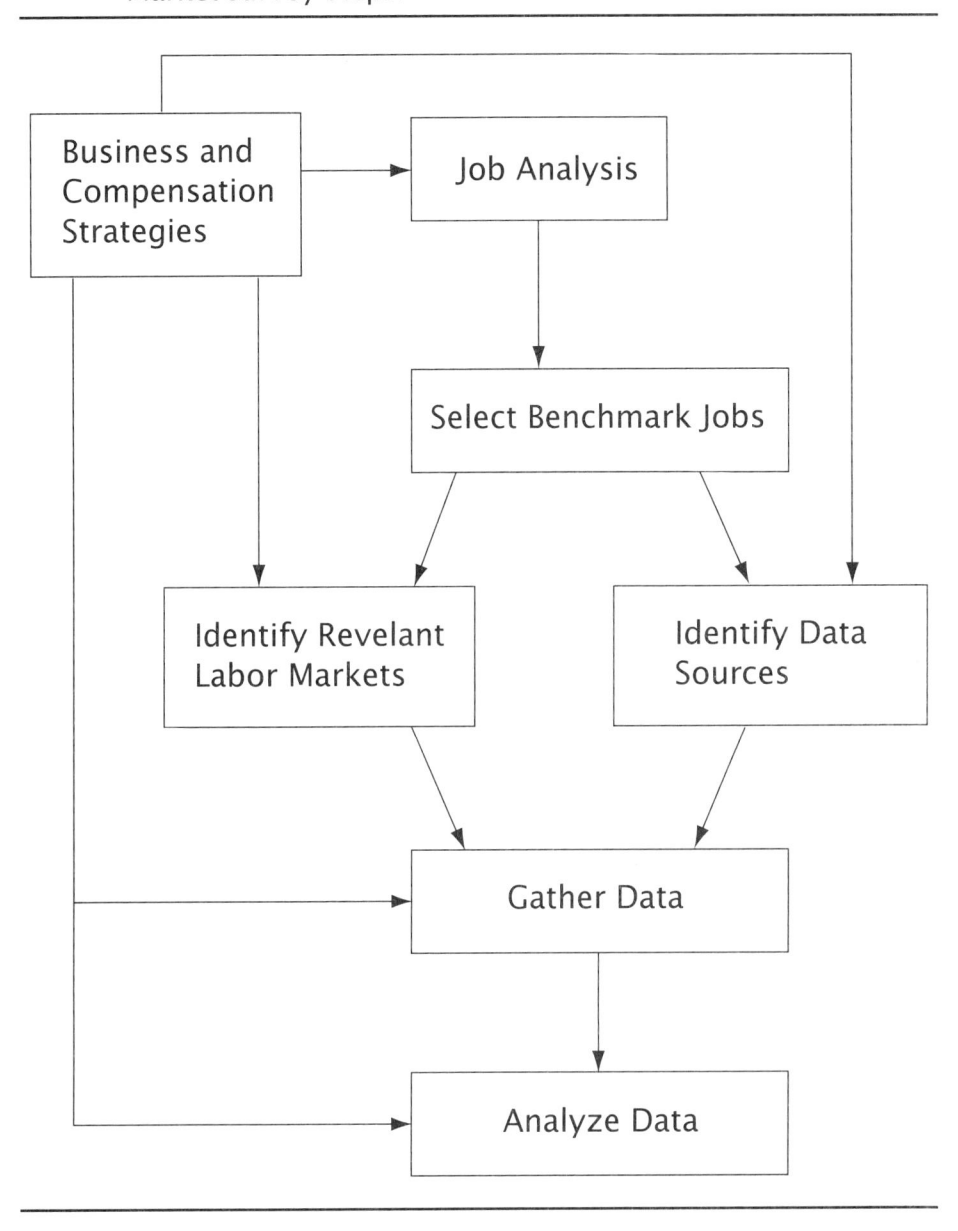

```
Business and Compensation Strategies
    → Job Analysis
    → Select Benchmark Jobs
    → Identify Relevant Labor Markets
    → Identify Data Sources
    → Gather Data
    → Analyze Data
```

In order to create a representative sample of benchmark jobs to be surveyed, a list of characteristics for benchmark jobs can be used.

- [ ] Well known
- [ ] Employs large number of people
- [ ] Job contents stable

The jobs to be selected need to be easily recognizable to other companies, likely to employ a large number of people, and be stable in content over time. A brief description of the benchmark jobs being surveyed should be attached to the survey to ensure that comparable data is being collected.

Benchmark jobs should be selected from all levels of the organization. By doing so, nonbenchmark jobs can be slotted relative to benchmark jobs to establish pay rates. For example, benchmark jobs might be a manager position and a supervisory position. In between these two positions in terms of job worth to company may be a scientific position as established by a job evaluation procedure. If the manager and supervisor market salaries can be assessed, then the salary to be paid the scientific position can be interpolated from the other two.

Determine Relevant Labor Market Characteristics

Just as it is impossible to survey all jobs, it is also impossible to survey all companies. Here are the characteristics used to determine the relevant labor market to survey.

- [ ] Region
- [ ] Industry
- [ ] Size
- [ ] Union/nonunion
- [ ] Financials
- [ ] Business strategy

The business and compensation strategy pursued by an organization influences the weight placed on each of these factors in deciding which companies to survey. Companies with a cost-driven strategy are likely to define the relevant labor market more locally in order not to incur the added costs of recruiting people at a national level and relocating them.

Market Surveys

On the other hand, a company with a human capital–driven strategy is more likely to recruit at a national level to ensure it has the most talented workforce possible. Organizations with a finance-driven business strategy are more likely to survey organizations with a familiar financial portfolio. Cost-conscious firms are likely to survey nonunion organizations because on average nonunion employees make less than unionized employees. Innovative companies may have distinct occupations internally and look to survey firms with other distinct occupations. Most organizations survey in the same industries for higher-level jobs and in multiple industries for lower-level jobs. Innovators may survey for higher-level jobs across industries because they may seek to attract talented people outside their industry. Firms with a human capital business strategy may also look outside their industry to attract the best talent. Organizations that have a compensation policy of leading the market are more likely to survey financially successful firms.

Identify Data Sources

A wide variety of data sources exists, some of which are listed here. More extensive lists along with addresses can be found elsewhere.[2]

- ☐ Government (federal, state, local)
- ☐ Consulting firms
- ☐ Survey firms
- ☐ Professional associations
- ☐ Trade associations
- ☐ Industry associations
- ☐ Labor unions
- ☐ Popular periodicals

Publicly available data are available for free or for a nominal charge through the government. Important sources here include the Bureau of Labor Statistics in the U.S. Department of Labor, Bureau of Labor Statistics at the state level, and local chambers of commerce. Usually, these sources are somewhat comprehensive but may be dated. Also, they are likely to include lower-level jobs rather than higher-level jobs. Consulting firms can offer more specific and up-to-date data, but they are much more expensive than government data. Survey firms' data also are more likely to be specific, up-to-date, and costly. Associations are excellent sources of data especially for professional positions, and the cost is usually less than the consulting and survey firm sources if the company conducting the survey is a member of the association and participates in the survey. National labor unions usually collect data from their own locals. Obviously, these data are only for bargaining unit positions. To the extent that they can be secured prior to actual negotiations, they can be very helpful in preparing to bargain. Lastly, periodicals such as *Business Week* report data on pay rates for executive level positions.

Because of the uniqueness of jobs as reflected in the job analysis and because of the uniqueness of business strategy, many organizations must gather their own data using procedures discussed in the next section.

Gather Data

Many sources of data can be collected in a survey. In conducting a survey, it is best to view compensation from a total compensation perspective:

Wages and salaries
- Actual
- Pay grade parameters

Benefits
- Health insurance
- Time off
- Pension

Rewards
- Incentives
- Recognition
- Development

Merit pay
- Actual

Pay practices
- Performance standards
- Reward systems
- Reward system effectiveness
- Number of pay grades

Market Surveys

Care must be taken to develop a survey that is long enough to provide important strategic data, but short enough to encourage participation. With the advent of electronic technology, companies are flooded with surveys. In order to be responded to, one must gather data that are valuable to the respondent, provide data that can't be found elsewhere (e.g., pay practices), or use surveys that are short in length. Other suggestions to improve the response rate of market surveys are:

- Fax rather than mail
- Call before faxing
- Make follow-up calls
- Keep length short
- Carefully select benchmark jobs
- Share the results with respondents
- Participate in other organizations' surveys
- Attach summary job descriptions for benchmark jobs

The use of person-based rather than job-based pay is a special case of survey collection. It is much more difficult to collect these data if for no other reason than that most organizations still have job-based systems. However, as pointed out in Chapter 4, some business strategies do lend themselves to person-based systems, and these data must be collected. Two approaches can be used. One approach is to use data from person-based surveys where data have been collected for competencies rather than for jobs. Unfortunately, competency-based market surveys are only in their infancy and difficult to locate. A second approach is to use a synthetic market-value approach. This procedure first requires the identification of competencies for a particular position. For example, 30 percent of the team leader position may require managerial competencies, while 70 percent may require technical competencies. Next, job-based survey data is examined to find the market value of jobs with similar managerial competencies and technical competencies. Lastly, the market value of the team leader is the sum of the average of the market value for jobs with similar managerial competencies multiplied by 30 percent plus the average market value for jobs with similar technical competencies multiplied by 70 percent.

Analyze the Data

Data collected from surveys are analyzed using various statistics. Those data analysis parameters include:

Base Pay Systems

- ☐ Minimum
- ☐ Midpoint
- ☐ Maximum
- ☐ Mean
- ☐ Median
- ☐ Mode
- ☐ Standard Deviation
- ☐ Weights
- ☐ Regression Line

Data of interest include both policy data and actual pay values for people. Policy data of interest usually include the minimum, midpoint, and maximum amounts to be paid by policy for each pay grade.

Survey data can be summarized using the mean, median, and mode. The mean is the simple average of figures and is a satisfactory measure when there are no extreme (high or low) values in the simple average being calculated. The median is the middle value in the distribution of numbers being averaged and is a better measure to use when these are extreme values in the average being calculated. The mode represents the numerical value most often reported.

An important distinction must be made for the proper collection and analysis of survey data. The average amount paid to people in a pay grade is not always equal to the midpoint of the pay grade. The midpoint is the company's stated policy as to the average it desires to pay people in this pay range. The average is the actual amount paid to people in the pay grade. If the midpoint and averages are treated in a synonymous fashion, faulty compensation decisions will be made. The standard deviation (SD) shows the amount of dispersion around the mean. It is a very helpful summary statistic but is often omitted from surveys. It can be used to assess the extent to which there is variability in pay policy across companies and is a good starting point for discussing where in the array of values the company wants to position itself.

The mean, median, mode, and SD should be used to analyze policy data collected in surveys (pay range minimums, maxims, and midpoints) as well as the actual market data (minimums, maximums, and averages), as shown in Exhibit 5-2.

In calculating averages, weighted averages can be used to weight the data points by strategic information value. For example, a company that desires to position itself as a leader in human capital may weight national

EXHIBIT 5-2
Important parameter combinations.

	Jobs			
	A	B	C	D
Pay Range Minimum				
Mean				
Median				
Mode				
SD				
Pay Range Midpoint				
Mean				
Median				
Mode				
SD				
Pay Range Maximum				
Mean				
Median				
Mode				
SD				
Actual Minimum				
Mean				
Median				
Mode				
SD				
Actual Average				
Mean				
Median				
Mode				
SD				
Actual Maximum				
Mean				
Median				
Mode				
SD				

survey data more heavily than local data in order to be able to attract the best talent per its strategy.

Averages are created for each pay grade. It is also useful to have an average of the averages to assess the overall market pay line. As shown in Exhibit 5-3, an average of the averages can be calculated in two ways. The

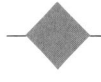

EXHIBIT 5-3

Handplot versus regression lines.

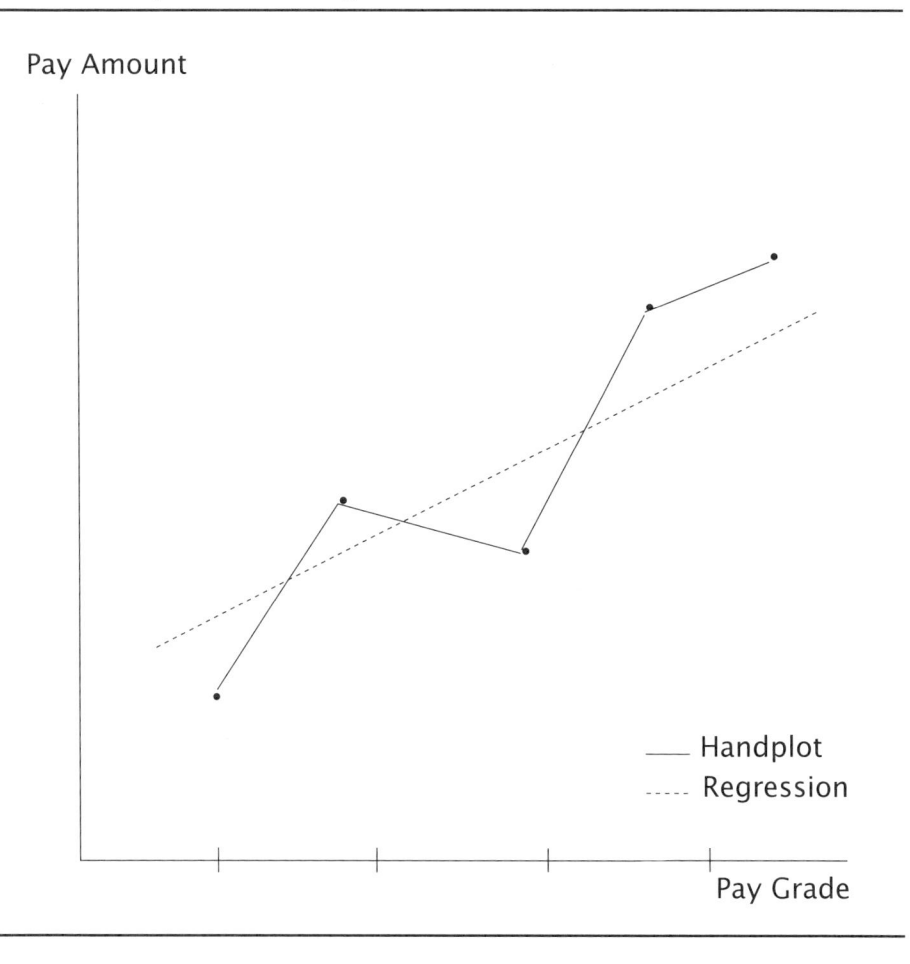

[Chart: Pay Amount vs. Pay Grade, showing Handplot (solid line) and Regression (dashed line)]

first way is to simply plot the average for each pay grade and connect the averages with a line. This approach is helpful in showing where there are possible conflicts between internal and external equity. That is, the market may value a pay grade more or less than the company. A decision must be made based on the compensation strategy whether to emphasize the internal data on pay grade formation or the external market data in setting actual pay levels. The regression line is the best fitting line of the data, as it minimizes the distance between the market line and the surveyed data points. Although it is a more precise measure of the market line, it is unstable with a small number of survey respondents.

Case Studies

CASE 1

Appliance Manufacturer

McDial is an international manufacturer of appliances for the home. Its largest and most profitable manufacturing plant is located in a small town in the Midwest. Geographically, it is located in the middle of a triangle between three major metropolitan areas. Each metropolitan area is about ninety minutes away from the manufacturing plant.

Business and Compensation Strategy. The McDial manufacturing plant has always been a technological leader in the appliances that it manufactures. As a result, it has a household name and excellent sales and margins over the years. Recently, the market has changed. Several international entrants have come into the market, and another major manufacturer has developed more sophisticated technology. Sales and margins have declined appreciably in both domestic and international markets.

Senior executives at McDial are very concerned and want to return this manufacturing plant to its status as the flagship of the company and industry. To do so, they have decided to close down two new product lines and redevote themselves to the appliances manufactured at this plant. Until sales at the plant rebound, as a result of new technology being developed at corporate headquarters, labor costs at the plant are a major concern.

Prior to the downturn in sales, very little attention was paid to market wages. Given the high levels of seniority and low turnover rates, it was generally assumed that the pay package was considerably above the local labor market. The compensation strategy shifted from one of leading the market to matching the market in order to manage labor costs. Incentives were considered for the first time to make up the difference between leading versus matching the market. It was also essential that the organization continue to remain union free.

Market Survey. As a result of the new emphasis on reduced labor costs, the organization conducted a market survey for the first time in years. Prior to conducting the survey, several important strategic decisions were made. First, the survey would be for the bulk of the manufacturing jobs rather than all jobs because the bulk of the labor costs resided in these positions. Second, the relevant labor market would not only include the immediate area for these jobs, but also the suburbs of the three major metropolitan areas nearest the plant. Attention had not been given previously to the metropolitan areas because of the commuting distance. But with the new philosophy of matching the market, there was concern that current employees would endure the commute because the market wage would be higher in the metropolitan suburbs than in the local area surrounding the plant. Third, the survey would not include items about wages, but rather items on incentive pay practices. It was also decided to include some items about benefits in order to interpret the wage results in the context of total compensation. Fourth, in order to remain nonunion, surveys were sent to both union and nonunion manufacturing plants. Fifth, the survey results of three automobile manufacturing plants were analyzed separately because of their very high pay rates relative to the market. The cover letter and survey are shown in Exhibit 5-4.

CASE 2

County Children Services Agency

Wright County Children Services (WCCS) is located in a large metropolitan area. It offers protective services for children, develops programs aimed at preventing abuse or neglect, and places children in homes. It draws upon a large volunteer base as well as full-time employees who cover a gamut of jobs, including social workers, attorneys, and office personnel. WCCS is about to enter a new round of negotiations with the union that represents its nonexempt employees and has conducted a market survey.

Business and Compensation Strategy. The overriding vision of the organization is to provide a safe environment for children to grow and develop. In order to do so, WCCS has core capabilities of technical services, care, and fund-raising. The overriding compensation philosophy is one that emphasizes matching the market, making the pay system a fair one, and making nonunion increases comparable to union increases. Most recently, emphasis has also been placed on developing a pay for performance system at the agency level. The executive director does not believe in individ-

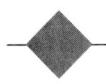

EXHIBIT 5-4
Appliance manufacturer market survey.

Dear Area Manufacturer:

The divisions of the appliance manufacturer have retained The Scioto Group, a compensation-consulting group, to conduct a very brief compensation survey of regional manufacturers.

We would like you to participate in this survey. It will take only about five minutes of your time to complete. Three (3) jobs are of interest: assembler, press room operator, and mechanic/millwright.

As a thank you for your time and effort in completing this survey, we asked The Scioto Group to send you a complimentary composite of the results. We hope this data will be of value to you. One of the more interesting pieces of information you will receive in this survey, which you may not have received in other regional surveys, is a summary of pay for performance practices by manufacturers in our region.

Survey results need to be compiled in a very short time. Therefore, we request that you fax your completed survey back to the consulting group or call them with your responses by no later than Friday, September 8.

We appreciate your involvement and will be happy to participate in your future surveys. Should you have any questions, please contact me.

Many thanks,
Manager, Human Resources
Enclosures (2)

Benchmark Job	Start Rate per Hour	Top Rate per Hour	Avg. Hourly Rate	# of Months to Top Rate	Approx. # in Class
Assembler					
Press Room Operator					
Skilled Trades Mechanic/ Millwright					

	Holidays	Vacation	Medical Coverage	401(k)
# of Months before Eligibility Begins				

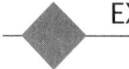

EXHIBIT 5-4 (cont.)

1. Do you have a 401(k) or savings and investment plan? (Circle one.)   Yes   No
   Does your company match? (Circle one.)   Yes   No
2. Do you offer a pension benefit? (Circle one.)   Yes   No
   If yes, is it a (Check one.) _____ Defined contribution? _____ Defined benefit?
3. Do you currently pay or anticipate in the future paying on the basis of performance? (Circle one.)   Yes   No
   If yes, which of the following measures of performance do you/will you base pay upon? (Check all that apply.)
   _____ Performance appraisals   _____ Profits
   _____ Accomplishment of team goals   _____ Skill acquisition
   _____ Cost control   _____ Attendance
   _____ Productivity   _____ Safety
   _____ Quality   Other: _____
   _____ Customer service
4. Please complete the following demographic information:
   - # of employees: _____   % of full-time employees: _____
   - Are you nonunion? (Check one.) _____ Yes   _____ No
   - Are you currently hiring? (Check one.) _____ Yes   _____ No. If yes, for what type of jobs: _____
   - Name _____ Telephone # _____
   - Company _____

The following job descriptions are for the three (3) key jobs covered by this survey. Please refer to these descriptions when answering the corresponding questions. Thank you.

Assembler/Production Operator

Operates various types of single-purpose machines, plastic molding, and expandable polystyrene molding machines, and all auxiliary equipment, plus performs a variety of assembly and disassembly operations. Works under the supervision of the departmental supervisor. Job does not exercise direction.

Press Room Operator

Operates all single- and double-action power presses, fabricating, spin rolling, and related equipment. Works under the supervision of the departmental supervisor. Job does not exercise direction.

Mechanic/Millwright

Inspects and tests all types of equipment to determine the potential for mechanical failure or the reason for these failures and makes corrections as required to prevent failure of the equipment or to restore normal operation. Operates all types of mechanical diagnostic equipment, uses standard mechanics' tools, mobile high-lift equipment, ladders, and miscellaneous hand and power tools. Works under the supervision of the departmental supervisor and occasionally receives directions from technicians, planners, engineers, and factory service representatives. Is often responsible for the safety of and work performed by an apprentice.

---

ual incentives, which he thinks lead to destructive competition between employees. Hence, payouts are to be based on agency accomplishments rather than on individual or departmental goals. A goal of the agency is to reduce the number of pay bands.

Market Survey. Given the wide array of jobs at WCCS, a wide array of survey sources were collected and consulted. These sources included other public sector agency surveys, the Bureau of Labor Statistics, and professional associations such as the National Association of Social Workers. Again, because of the diverse nature of the jobs, a fairly large number of benchmark jobs was selected. Data about benefits were not collected, because a recent survey of benefits had already been collected by the agency. Data were obtained on the number of pay grades, amount of overlap in pay grades, and incentive practices in order to have data to begin to reduce the number of pay bands and to develop an incentive system. In defining the relevant labor market, it was believed that the talent needed to fulfill the vision of the agency for nonexempt jobs could be found in the local labor market, while for exempt jobs, the talent needed was available at the state level. Other counties in the state of comparable size and mission were surveyed. The survey is shown in Exhibit 5-5.

EXHIBIT 5.5
County children services agency market survey.

PAY SURVEY

The following pay survey is being conducted on behalf of Wright County Children Services. The purpose is to determine the market rate for the following positions as benchmarks for the organization. The survey should take less than fifteen minutes to complete. All participants will receive anonymous data that is collected from this survey. All results will remain anonymous.

A. For the following positions, please indicate the number of individuals in the position and the minimum, average, and maximum **hourly** wage rate (exclude benefits and incentives) for each position. For reference, job descriptions are located in Appendix A.

1.	Accounting Clerk 3:	Number	Minimum	Average	Maximum
2.	Attorney 3:	Number	Minimum	Average	Maximum
3.	Attorney 4:	Number	Minimum	Average	Maximum
4.	Child Welfare Caseworker 2:	Number	Minimum	Average	Maximum
5.	Child Welfare Caseworker 3:	Number	Minimum	Average	Maximum
6.	Child Welfare Caseworker, Supervisor:	Number	Minimum	Average	Maximum
7.	Data Processor (Help Desk Technician):	Number	Minimum	Average	Maximum
8.	Director of Human Resources:	Number	Minimum	Average	Maximum
9.	Director of Information Systems:	Number	Minimum	Average	Maximum
10.	General Office Clerk:	Number	Minimum	Average	Maximum
11.	Investigator 2:	Number	Minimum	Average	Maximum
12.	Investigator 3, Supervisor:	Number	Minimum	Average	Maximum
13.	Lead General Office Clerk:	Number	Minimum	Average	Maximum
14.	Office Manager:	Number	Minimum	Average	Maximum
15.	Personnel Aide:	Number	Minimum	Average	Maximum

Market Surveys

16. Programmer/Analyst: Number   Minimum   Average   Maximum

17. Social Program Coordinator: Number   Minimum   Average   Maximum

B. The following information concerns pay structures, ranges, and measures.

1. Please indicate the number of pay ranges your organization currently has: _____
2. What is the average percent overlap between ranges: _____%

   $$**\text{Overlap} = 100 \times \frac{\text{Maximum rate grade A} - \text{Minimum rate grade B}}{\text{Maximum rate grade A} - \text{Minimum rate grade A}}$$

3. What is the average number of steps per pay grade? _____
4. Is step progression based on (Check all that apply.):
   ____Seniority
   ____Longevity
   ____Skill
   ____Performance
5. Do you have pay for performance plans? _____
6. If yes, what measures of performance do you have?
   ____Quality measures
   ____Quantity measures
   ____Customer service
   ____Financial measures
   ____Performance appraisal scales
   ____Other (Please list.): _____
7. Is performance measured at the agency level? ____Yes ____No
8. Is performance measured at the employee level? ____Yes ____No
9. Is performance measured at the department level? ____Yes ____No
10. If currently working under a labor contract, what are your negotiated wage increases for (Fill in all that are applicable.)
    2001: ____% 2002: ____% 2003: ____%
11. For nonbargaining positions, what are your estimated wage increases for:
    2001: ____% 2002: ____% 2003: ____%

C. Company or agency background information.

1. Total number of employees: _____
2. Total number of unionized employees: _____
3. Company or agency name and address: _____

Base Pay Systems

◆ EXHIBIT 5-5 (cont.)

4. Contact person to send results to: _____
_____
_____
_____

Thank you for your time.

Appendix A: Job Descriptions

Accounting Clerk 3: Under general supervision from section supervisor, employee analyzes expenditures and/or receipts, prepares reports for incorporation into agency financial statements, maintains general books of account (manually and/or automated); may act as lead worker. Education/Training Required: Ability to calculate fractions, decimals, and percentages; two courses of high school accounting or two college courses in accounting and six months' experience in comparable position. Prefer an associate degree in accounting or two years' relevant experience.

Attorney 3: Employee is under the general supervision of Attorney 4; prepares and presents court cases, conducts legal research, and offers legal advice; prepares for and conducts quasi-judicial hearings.
Education/Training Required: Law degree and at least three months' experience as legal aide, legal intern, or licensed attorney. Prefer three years' experience in child welfare or the practice of juvenile law.

Attorney 4: To proactively increase the agency's effective and efficient legal operation within Juvenile Court; to facilitate legal interaction with the Juvenile Court to help the agency fulfill its mission of reducing abuse and neglect within the community; to provide legal and administrative guidance to staff in order to protect children; to coordinate and supervise casework staff; to interact with collateral county and court entities to ensure cooperation.
Education/Training Required: Admission to state bar, twelve months' experience practicing as a lawyer, three management classes/three months' management experience.

Child Welfare Caseworker 2: Provides protective services and case management to abused, neglected, and/or unruly children; provides support and direction to families and coordinates with the court system and other community agencies for treatment.
Education/Training Required: Master's degree in social work or related area or bachelor's degree and a minimum of one year of post-degree related child welfare/social work.

Market Surveys

Child Welfare Caseworker 3: Provides protective services and case management to abused, neglected, and/or unruly children; provides support and direction to families and coordinates with the court system and other community agencies for treatment; assists in supervising and training other social workers; handles the most difficult or "sensitive" cases compared to lower-level social workers.
Education/Training Required: Master's degree in social work or related area and a minimum of one year of related child welfare/social work experience, or bachelor's degree and a minimum of two years' post-degree related child welfare/social work.

Child Welfare Caseworker, Supervisor: Employee coordinates and supervises unit of social workers and support staff; provides clinical and administrative guidance to staff in order to protect children.
Educational/Training Required: Master's degree in social work or related area and a minimum of three years' related child welfare/social work experience, or bachelor's degree and a minimum of four years' post-degree related child welfare/social work.

Data Processor (Help Desk Technician): Employee is under general supervision of office manager; controls data processing through coordination of program.
Education/Training Required: Ability to calculate fractions and one course in supervision; 1,000 hours of training in data processing. Prefer two years' experience with PC use and word processing.

Director of Human Resources: Under supervision of agency general counsel, directs and administers all agency human resources policies and programs affecting bargaining unit and exempt staff including personnel, labor relations, and all applicable state and federal regulations, as well as county practices and procedures. Directly supervises all personnel officers and clerical staff in division.
Education/Training Required: Minimum: Six months' experience as Personnel Officer 3 or comparable supervisor experience, or undergraduate course work and twelve months' supervisory personnel experience, or graduate degree in public or business administration.

Director of Information Systems: Manages and directs the information systems department, which coordinates agency-wide information systems. This incorporates the online computer system, which supports daily agency operations, provides management information, and provides required data for transmission to the agency.
Education/Training Required: Prefer a master's degree and several years' experience in related field.

General Office Clerk: Enters new material on clients and resources into the central computer service; performs other clerical-related duties.
Education/Training Required: Ability to add, subtract, multiply, and divide by whole numbers; 300 hours of experience with CRT or similar

EXHIBIT 5-5 (cont.)

video display equipment. Prefer minimum of two years' clerical experience and basic information systems knowledge.

Investigator 2: Independently investigates (researches and studies reports, records, and documents and verifies information given, conducts correspondence to request information) family situation to determine a child's program eligibility for Title IV-E or Medicaid; obtains Medicaid card; approves adoption subsidies; serves as liaison between clients and agency.
Education/Training Required: Ability to calculate fractions, decimals, and percentages; one course in investigative methods, practices, and procedures; one course in case preparation techniques; one course in effective oral communication; one course in technical writing or equivalent. Prefer an associate's degree plus relevant work experience.

Investigator 3, Supervisor: Provides supervision to investigators and/or clerical staff in obtaining funding from local, state, and federal revenue sources; assists the departmental supervisor in planning, developing, and directing the work flow of the department; acts as lead employee in developing eligibility determination systems to enhance the funding of the agency.
Education/Training Required: One course in investigative methods, practices, and procedures; one course in rules of evidence; one course in case preparation techniques; one course in effective oral communication; one course in technical writing, plus twelve months' paid experience as lower-level investigator for employing agency. Prefer bachelor's degree and two years' relevant work experience or associate's degree and five years' related work experience.

Lead General Office Clerk: Acts as lead general office clerk.

Office Manager: Provides direct supervision to office personnel in the region performing clerical functions, develops and implements routine and complex procedures for clerical function and work flow of assigned region, provides secretarial services to regional and associate director.
Education/Training Required: Ability to calculate fractions, decimals, and percentages. Prefer a minimum of four years' clerical experience.

Personnel Aide: Processes and types Personnel Actions (PAs) for agency regarding transfers, promotions, resignations, etc., including salary adjustments, annual increments, name changes, licensure, etc. for employees.
Education/Training Required: Ability to calculate fractions, decimals, and percentages; one course in typing or data entry; one course in public relations.

Programmer/Analyst: Employee writes large computer programs, performs analysis and systems design, maintains and modifies existing systems.
Education/Training Required: Prefer a bachelor's degree with major in information systems or related technical area, plus one year of post-degree experience in administrative systems.

Social Program Coordinator: Serves as a utilization/case reviewer under the supervision of the director of monitoring and quality assurance; assists in monitoring and evaluating services to families/children and program compliance; identifies additional services that may be required to meet identified treatment needs; reviews continued need for services; completes reports that advise clinical and administrative staff of current assessment, including potential problems related to length of stay, cost, and service delivery; collects and interprets data for use in analysis of program service delivery; identifies and reports issues targeted for system-wide improvement.
Education/Training Required: Completion of undergraduate major program core requirements in social or behavioral science and eighteen months' experience in delivery of social/human services. Prefer a master's degree and some related work experience or bachelor's degree and several years' related work experience.

CASE

◆ 3 ◆

County Engineers Office

The business strategy, compensation strategy, and compensation components for this organization have been described in Chapter 3. In terms of the market survey, several strategic issues arose. First, previous wage surveys had relied only upon public sector data. Given the mission of the office and the heightened competition between the public and private sector, the survey was sent to both public and private sector employers (e.g., contractors). Second, employees constantly pointed to the private sector as a source of higher wages. The survey asked about benefits as well as wages in order to show that while private sector wages were indeed higher, employees received less from a total compensation perspective when benefits were factored in. In order to minimize the length of the survey and to obtain the most important information, only those benefit items were surveyed that both labor and management agreed had been a source of strife and/or confusion for employees. Also, data on the number of hours were collected as well because in the private sector, some contractor jobs did not provide a full year of work and because this was a very important piece of information from a total compensation perspective. Third, the union had collected a large amount of its own data on wages in comparable public sector organizations. Because members of the union were involved in the redesign of the compensation system, they were glad to share these data prior to negotiations. Data from the union proved to be very valuable because, in at least one case, they were more accurate than the data management had available. At the tail end of the compensation project, management used the union data to upgrade the wages of the job with the largest number of employees in the office to a higher level than originally agreed upon by the labor-management compensation committee or by management. The survey used in this stage of the compensation project is shown in Exhibit 5-6.

CASE 4

Educational Distributor

The business strategy, compensation strategy, job analysis procedures, and job evaluation procedures have been described for this company in Chapter 4. The market survey, shown in Exhibit 5-7, was very similar to the others shown in this chapter. One interesting strategic element of this survey was the method used to identify the relevant labor market. In the spirit of participative management, employees were encouraged to submit the names of companies that they viewed as attractive alternative opportunities for themselves and others in their jobs and were also asked to identify places of likely talent for the educational distributor to attract labor. Before being used in the survey, the nominated companies were viewed by the compensation committee and senior management. Many of these companies were used and had not previously been considered. By using this approach, the company kept close to its business strategy of participation in decision making. In turn, employees voiced almost no concerns about external equity when the new pay structure was created. They had been given an opportunity to exercise their "voice" during the process.

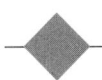

Market Surveys

EXHIBIT 5-6
County engineers office market survey.

Compensation Survey

Exempt Jobs (see attached descriptions)	Minimum Monthly Salary	Maximum Monthly Salary	Average Monthly Salary	Average Number of Months Worked per Year
1 Acct Clerk I				
2 Acct Clerk II				
3 Asst Hwy Maint Supt				
4 Bridge Supt				
5 Chief Engr Tech				
6 Dept Head/Engr				
7 Equip Maint Supt I				
8 Fiscal Officer				
9 Human Resources Dir				
10 Hwy Maint Supt				
11 MIS Coordinator				
12 Project Engr				
13 Prop Record Analyst				
14 Real Estate Admin				
15 Secretary				
16 Sr Survey Tech				

Nonexempt Jobs (see attached descriptions)	Minimum Wage Per Hour	Maximum Wage Per Hour	Average Wage Per Hour	Average Number of Months Worked per Year
17 Auto Mechanic I				
18 Bridge Worker I				
19 Bridge Worker III				
20 Engr Tech I				
21 Engr Tech II				
22 Equip Operator I				
23 Equip Operator III				

Base Pay Systems

EXHIBIT 5-6 (cont.)

24	Hwy Worker IV
25	Route & Sign Marker I
26	Route & Sign Marker II
27	Storekeeper I
28	Survey Tech I
29	Survey Tech II

Compensation Policy and Practices/Adjustment to Base Pay

1. How many pay bands (pay ranges) are currently in use in your company? _____
2. How many different job titles are currently in use in your company? _____
3. What was the percentage of increase in wages or salaries last year? _____%
   Percentage anticipated next year? _____%
4. When are "cash outs" (payment of unused portion) for vacation dispersed?
   _____ the end of each year _____ when the employee leaves the organization _____ employee loses unused portion
5. When are "cash outs" for sick leave dispersed?
   _____ the end of each year _____ when the employee leaves the organization _____ employee loses unused portion
6. When are "cash outs" for personal days dispersed?
   _____ the end of each year _____ when the employee leaves the organization _____ employee loses unused portion
7. Please list the maximum accruals for the following and the period of maximum accrual (in years):
   _____ days of sick leave, with a maximum accrual period of _____ years
   _____ personal days, with a maximum accrual period of _____ years
   _____ vacation days, with a maximum accrual period of _____ years

Benefits

1. What percentage of your employee health care insurance premium is paid for by the employee? _____% Individual coverage _____% Family coverage
2a. Please check which of the following benefits are offered to your employees. Also, please indicate the percentage of employee copayment (after deductible) for services.

Market Surveys

    ____Hospitalization   ____%   ____Medical   ____%
    ____Major medical   ____%   ____Managed health care   ____%
    ____Dental   ____%   ____Vision care   ____%
    ____Prescription drug   ____%   ____Paid disability leave   ____%

b. How much is the employee deductible? $_____

3a. Does your company provide term life insurance to the employee?
   ____Yes   ____No

b. Does your company subsidize the cost of term life insurance?
   ____Yes   ____No

c. If yes, what percentage of the life insurance cost does the company pay?
   ____%

4a. Does your company provide disability insurance to the employee?
   ____Yes   ____No

b. Does your company subsidize the cost of disability insurance?
   ____Yes   ____No

c. If yes, what percentage of the disability insurance cost does the company pay?
   ____%

5a. Does your company offer tuition reimbursement?
   ____Yes   ____No

b. If yes, what is your tuition reimbursement policy?
   ____% reimbursement after ____ month(s)/____year(s) of service

6a. Does your company provide uniforms to employees?____Yes____No

b. If yes, does the uniform include the following?
   shoes ____Yes ____No
   coat   ____Yes ____No
   shirt   ____Yes ____No
   pants ____Yes ____No
   other, please specify_____

7. Please indicate your company's number of paid days per year for the following:
   a. Number of paid holiday days per year: ____
   Please indicate which of the following holidays are paid days off for your employees:
      ____ New Year's Day   ____ Labor Day
      ____ Martin Luther King Day   ____ Columbus Day
      ____ Presidents' Day   ____ Veterans Day
      ____ Memorial Day   ____ Thanksgiving Day
      ____ Independence Day   ____ Christmas Day
   Please list any other holidays that are paid days off for your employees (also include the day after Thanksgiving, if applicable) _____

Base Pay Systems

EXHIBIT 5-6 (cont.)

    b. Number of paid sick days per year ____

    c. Number of paid personal leave days per year ____

8. Does your company offer deferred compensation?
   ____Yes ____No

9. Describe your company's vacation policy in terms of service requirements per amount of paid vacation time earned.
   Vacation during first year of service = _____
   ____Years of service = ____vacation days
   ____Years of service = ____vacation days
   ____Years of service = ____vacation days
   ____Years of service = ____vacation days
   ____Years of service = ____vacation days
   Maximum vacation possible = ____vacation days after ____ years of service

10a. What type of retirement plan does your company offer?
   ____PERS ____401(k) ____Other, please specify _____

    b. If PERS, does the employee pay into PERS, or does the company pay into it for them?
   ____employee pays   ____ company pays

Demographic Information

Please complete the following demographic questions.
- Total # of employees ____ # of full-time employees ____
- What percentage of your workforce is unionized? ____%
- Your company's two-digit code (see below) ____ ____. If other, please specify.
  _____
- Company name _____
- Company address _____

- Your name _____ Title _____
- Your telephone number _____
- Should the complimentary compilation of survey results be sent directly to you?
   ____ Yes ____ No, please forward the results to:

Company codes

Public
01 County
02 State
03 Municipality
04 City
05 Township
06 Other

Private
09 Engineering consultants
10 Building construction—general contractors and operative builders
11 Construction other than building construction—general contractors
12 Construction—special trade contractors
13 Other

BENCHMARK POSITION DESCRIPTIONS

1. Account Clerk I

Generally performs routine clerical, bookkeeping, and other financial record-keeping duties; posts and audits accounting data to books and ledgers; processes purchase invoices and vouchers; maintains financial and inventory records; has knowledge and ability to operate various business equipment; performs related work as required.

2. Account Clerk II

Generally performs bookkeeping and other financial record-keeping duties; prepares payroll records and submits to auditor for processing; records hours worked, etc.; prepares bank statements; performs related work as required.

3. Assistant Highway Maintenance Superintendent

Assists highway maintenance superintendent in supervision and planning of highway maintenance activities; supervises crew leaders in maintenance of highways (e.g., surface treatment, patching, asphalt surfacing, snow removal), bridges, signs, guardrails; inspects progress of projects or supervises special highway maintenance projects and/or work crews in district maintenance section; performs related work as required.

4. Bridge Superintendent

Plans, schedules, and supervises maintenance and repair of bridges, culverts, and guardrails in assigned area; performs related work as required.

EXHIBIT 5-6 (cont.)

5. Chief Engineer Technician

Acts as lead worker (i.e., trains and provides work direction) over lower-level engineer technicians in all phases of preparing and drafting design projects and/or acts as coordinator to ensure all interested parties are informed as to status of project and/or ensures that survey crews are furnished with pertinent data; performs final drafting work (e.g., checks for conformance with specifications and does final revisions); makes major plan revisions reviewed by engineers and designs details; performs related work as required.

6. Department Head/Engineer (e.g., Bridge Design, Highway Design, Survey, Traffic)

Functions as chief of the department and adviser on specialized problems that might arise; supervises operations and personnel within the department; formulates uniform policies for design, plan composition, specification preparation, etc.; coordinates with other departments to avoid overlap and delay; evaluates all phases of operation to increase efficiency and comply with departmental policy; reviews and approves all plans; advises staff on technical matters; performs related work as required.

7. Equipment Maintenance Superintendent I

Directly supervises auto mechanics in equipment maintenance and repair in garage or inspects equipment assigned to counties for condition and repair needed and maintenance; directly supervises assigned clerical and support personnel; performs related work as required.

8. Fiscal Officer

Plans, directs, manages, and coordinates fiscal program for agency; directly supervises professional and assigned clerical personnel involved in fiscal operation activities and assists in development of and/or develops policies and conducts financial planning regarding fiscal operations; performs related work as required.

9. Human Resources Director

Directly supervises personnel officers and administers personnel program in agency; may act as assistant to higher-level personnel administrator or deputy director in administering total personnel program; interprets Chapter 124 of State Revised Code, explains procedures to and advises administrators, personnel officers, and employees of same, ensuring compliance; performs related work as required.

Market Surveys

10. Highway Maintenance Superintendent

Plans, supervises, and coordinates work of highway maintenance superintendents and highway maintenance programs in multiple territories (headquarters); checks written reports and submits to higher authority; reviews requisitions and handles personnel and public relations functions; performs related work as required.

11. MIS Coordinator (Computer Coordinator)

Generally provides computer support for the engineering department. Evaluates hardware, software, and training. Is responsible for the overall operation of and security for the computer system. Creates programs, databases, spreadsheets, etc. Manipulates data and creates statistical reports. Ensures that proper backup and storage of data is maintained. Provides technical expertise as needed; performs related work as required.

12. Project Engineer

Surveys, checks calculations, and observes work to provide routine control, inspection, and supervision of contractors working on construction contracts; calculates, reviews, records, and generally completes all project field office work; keeps project diary, reviews plans, checks quantity calculations, checks various records, and maintains files; estimates costs for contract jobs; checks estimated costs submitted by contractors; analyzes technical reports; prepares for and assists in plan reviews; administers highway construction plans; interprets contract provisions and makes decisions; fills out all related forms; performs related work as required.

13. Property Records Analyst

Lays out, drafts, and plots maps; drafts illustrations for reports and/or displays; performs related work as required.

14. Real Estate Administrator

Oversees appraisal, negotiation, and purchase of property for right-of-way purposes; writes legal advertisements, invitations to bid, etc. for newspaper publications of road and bridge projects.

15. Secretary

Generally performs secretarial and clerical duties in the office; acts as telephone receptionist and receives visitors; schedules appointments; types correspondence, reports, and related documents; has knowledge and ability to operate various office machines as required; performs related work as required.

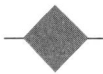

EXHIBIT 5-6 (cont.)

16. Senior Survey Technician

Oversees crew of survey technicians (e.g., coordinates daily activities; reviews work for completeness and accuracy), signs deeds, writes property descriptions, performs boundary surveys, solves routine mathematical problems, orders supplies, and maintains equipment; performs related work as required.

17. Auto Mechanic I

Generally performs routine and preventative maintenance and repairs of minor automotive equipment and vehicles under close supervision; assists in the rebuilding of engines, removing and replacing major and minor components of vehicles and equipment; has knowledge of and ability to use a wide variety of equipment and tools for making repairs, such as grinding wheel, chain hoists, presses, etc.; performs related work as required.

18. Bridge Worker I

Generally performs unskilled and semiskilled labor in the repair and construction of county bridges; has knowledge of and ability to use hand and power tools and various light equipment in the repair and construction of bridges; performs related work as required.

19. Bridge Worker III

Performs as working supervisor in construction, repair, and maintenance of bridges; interprets construction plans, plans work assignments, ensures proper equipment and materials are delivered to and secured at job site; performs general labor duties as required; performs related work as required.

20. Engineer Technician I (aka Draftsman I)

Generally performs subprofessional civil engineering work; draws designs and plans of roads and bridges; has knowledge of and ability to operate blueprint machine, white printer, and microfilm machine; performs related work as required.

21. Engineer Technician II (aka Draftsman II)

Generally performs difficult and complex subprofessional engineering work in the office and/or in the field; designs drainage structures, roads, and/or bridges; has knowledge of and ability to use skilled drafting equipment and techniques; performs related work as required.

22. Equipment Operator I

Under general supervision from equipment or maintenance superintendent or other administrative supervisor, operates motorized equipment to spread salt, plow snow, mow grass, clean streets, and perform other highway maintenance operations; performs related work as required.

23. Equipment Operator III

Under general supervision from equipment or maintenance superintendent, highway worker supervisor, or other administrative supervisor, operates heaviest types of construction equipment and performs minor maintenance and repair of equipment; performs related work as required.

24. Highway Worker IV

Generally operates moderately complex vehicles and equipment requiring specialized skill and/or training, such as backhoe, roller, carryall, distributor, chip box; may transport personnel, materials, and/or equipment in light or heavy trucks; may lead work crew activities; has knowledge of and ability to operate and use moderately complex equipment; performs related work as required.

25. Route and Sign Marker I

Assists in marking route signals on roads and highways (i.e., edge lines, centerlines, crosswalks, railroad warnings, school markings, parking lots, etc.); operates centerline machine and small paint-striping equipment, places warning signs, cones, and barrels as needed; maintains all equipment; performs related work as required.

26. Route and Sign Marker II

Acts as working supervisor in striping roads and highways, operates centerline striping machine, operates small paint-striping equipment; supervises maintenance of truck and striping equipment; performs related work as required.

27. Storekeeper I

Receives and distributes stock and supplies; receives shipments; unloads stock and checks for correct quantity and condition; issues and delivers supplies and equipment; maintains perpetual inventory; requisitions needed stock pending approval of supervisor; performs related work as required.

28. Survey Technician I

Assists in physically searching and locating legal documents that define road centerlines, property boundaries, section corners, and other bound-

EXHIBIT 5-6 (cont.)

aries; operates various surveying equipment (plumb bob, tapes, chains, prism and tripod setups, etc.); develops working knowledge of some survey instruments; performs related work as required.

29. Survey Technician II

Assists in physically searching and locating legal documents that define road centerlines, property boundaries, section corners, and other boundaries; operates various surveying equipment and some instruments; computes elevation differences; computes and checks antenna heights for GPS setups; performs related work as required.

EXHIBIT 5.7
Educational distributor market survey.

Wages and Salaries

Benchmark Job	Minimum Annual Salary	Maximum Annual Salary	Average Annual Salary	# Employees in Job Classification
Controller/Finance and Accounting Director				
Buyer				
General Accountant				
Purchasing Manager				
Programmer Analyst				
Safety Manager				
Manager of General Accounting				
MIS Manager				
Transportation Manager				
Computer Operator				

Market Surveys

Warehouse
Manager
_____

Human Resources
Director
_____

Compensation Policy and Practices/Adjustments to Base Pay
1. For which of the following shifts do you pay a shift premium? (Check all that apply.)
   _____ Second _____ Third _____ None _____ Other _____
2a. Do you currently make a cost-of-living adjustment (COLA)? (Check one.) _____ Yes _____ No (If no, skip to question 3)
   b. How was the COLA determined? _____

3a. Which of the following determines how your *salary structure* (the array of pay rates for different jobs within a single organization) shifts (Check all that apply.)
   _____ Cost of living
   _____ Competition in the labor market
   _____ Changes in wages and salaries in other companies
   _____ Our company's ability to pay
   _____ Other _____
   b. How frequently does your salary structure shift? (Check one.)
   _____ Every other year
   _____ Once a year
   _____ Twice a year
   _____ Other _____
4. What is the basis for progression through a salary range? (Check all that apply.)
   _____ Individual performance (merit pay)
   _____ Seniority
   _____ Skill-based review
   _____ Other _____
5a. What do you do if an employee is paid *under* the job's minimum rate?
   _____
   _____

   b. What do you do if an employee is paid *over* the job's maximum rate?
   _____
   _____

6. Organizationwide, which jobs are more difficult to fill? _____
   _____

7. What is your company's compensation practice relative to the labor market? (Check one.)
   _____ Above market   _____ Competitive with market
   _____ Below market   _____ Do not use market information

EXHIBIT 5-7 (cont.)

Benefits
1. What percentage of your employee health care insurance premium is paid for by the employee? ____% Individual coverage ____% Family coverage
2. Please check which of the following benefits are offered to your employees. Also, please indicate the percentage of employee copayment (after deductible) for services.
   ____ Hospitalization ____% ____ Medical ____%
   ____ Major medical ____% ____ Managed health care ____%
   ____ Dental ____% ____ Vision care ____%
   ____ Prescription drug ____%
3a. Does your company provide term life insurance to employees? ____ Yes ____ No
  b. Does your company subsidize the cost of the term life insurance? ____ Yes ____ No
  c. If yes, what percentage of the life insurance cost does the company pay? ____%
4a. Does your company provide a 401(k) or similar savings/investment plan to the employees? ____ Yes ____ No
  b. Does the company match any portion of the employees' contributions? ____ Yes ____ No
  c. If yes, what portion does the company match? _____
  d. Does the company add profits to its 401(k) plan? ____ Yes ____ No
5a. Does your company offer a pension benefit? ____ Yes ____ No
  b. If yes, is it a: ____ Defined contribution plan? ____ Defined benefit plan?
6. Please indicate your company's following forms of time off with pay:
   # of paid holidays per year: ____   # of paid sick days per year: ____
   # of paid personal leave days per year: ____
7. Describe your company's vacation policy in terms of service requirements per amount of paid vacation time earned.
   Vacation during first year of service = _____
   ____ Year(s) of service = _____ vacation
   ____ Year(s) of service = _____ vacation
   ____ Year(s) of service = _____ vacation
   ____ Year(s) of service = _____ vacation
   Maximum vacation possible = _____ vacation after _____ years of service

Incentive Pay Programs
1a. Does your company use any type of incentive pay plans, or do you anticipate using such plans in the future? ____ Yes ____ No (If no, skip the next section on Demographic Information.)

b. If yes, which employees are/will be eligible for incentive payments?
_____
_____

2. Which of the following measures of performance are used/will be used to determine incentive pay? (Check all that apply.)
   ___ Performance appraisals
   ___ Accomplishment of team goals
   ___ Cost control
   ___ Productivity
   ___ Quality
   ___ Customer service
   ___ Education
   ___ Profits
   ___ Skill acquisition
   ___ Attendance
   ___ Safety
   ___ Competencies
   ___ Other _____

3a. Do you/will you put any portion of *pay at risk* (that portion of employees' wages or salaries that are taken away to fund the incentive plan)? ___ Yes ___ No (If no, skip to question 4.)
 b. If yes, what percentage of pay is/will be at risk? ___%

4a. What is the total amount of incentive bonuses paid to employees as a percent of total payroll cost? ___%
 b. What was the average size of the bonus as a percent of salary in 2001? ___%
 c. How often are payouts for bonuses scheduled? ___ per year

5. How do you determine eligibility for an incentive pay bonus? (Check all that apply.)
   ___ Supervisory recommendation
   ___ Job title
   ___ Seniority
   ___ Job level
   ___ Minimum performance level
   ___ Other _____
   _____

Demographic Information

Please complete the following demographic questions.
- # of total employees _____ # of full-time employees _____
- Annual turnover rate _____%
- What percentage of your workforce is unionized? _____%
- Company's annual gross revenue: $_____
- Your company's two-digit industry code*_____
- Company name _____
- Company address _____
  _____
- Your name _____ Title _____
- Your telephone number _____
- Should the complimentary compilation of the survey results be sent directly to you?
   ___ Yes ___ No, please forward the results to: _____
   _____

*From the following list of industry codes, please use the one that best describes your company.

EXHIBIT 5-7 (cont.)

Agriculture, Forestry, and Fishing
01 Agricultural production—crops
02 Agricultural production—livestock
07 Agricultural services
08 Forestry
09 Fishing, hunting, trapping

Mining
10 Metal mining
11 Anthracite mining
12 Bituminous coal
13 Oil and gas extraction
14 Mining and quarrying of nonmetallic minerals, except fuels

Construction
15 Building construction—general contractors and operative builders
16 Construction other than building construction—general contractors
17 Construction—special trade contractors

Manufacturing
20 Food and kindred products
21 Tobacco manufacturers
22 Textile mill products
23 Apparel and other finished products made from fabrics and similar materials
24 Lumber and wood products, except furniture
25 Furniture and fixtures
26 Paper and allied products
27 Printing, publishing, and allied products
28 Chemicals and allied products
29 Petroleum refining and related industries

Manufacturing (Continued)
30 Rubber and miscellaneous plastic products
31 Leather and leather products
32 Stone, clay, glass, and concrete products
33 Primary metal industries
34 Fabricated metal products, except machinery and transportation products
35 Machinery, except electrical
36 Electrical and electronic machinery, equipment, and supplies
37 Transportation equipment
38 Measuring, analyzing, and controlling instruments; photographic, medical, and optical goods; watches and clocks
39 Miscellaneous manufacturing industries

Transportation, Communication, Electric, Gas, and Sanitary Services
40 Railroad transportation
41 Local and suburban transit and interurban highway passenger transportation
42 Motor freight transportation and warehousing
43 U.S. Postal Service
44 Water transportation
45 Transportation by air
46 Pipelines, except natural gas
47 Transportation services
48 Communication
49 Electric, gas, and sanitary services

Wholesale Trade
50 Wholesale trade—durable goods
51 Wholesale trade—nondurable goods

Retail Trade
52 Building materials, hardware, garden supply, and mobile homes
53 General merchandise stores
54 Food stores
55 Automotive dealers/gas service stations
56 Apparel and accessory stores
57 Furniture, home furnishings, and equipment stores
58 Eating and drinking places
59 Miscellaneous retail

Finance, Insurance, and Real Estate
60 Banking
61 Credit agencies, except banks

Finance, Insurance, and Real Estate
62 Security and commodity brokers, dealers exchanges, and services
63 Insurance
64 Insurance agents, brokers, and services
65 Real estate
66 Combinations of real estate, insurance, law offices
67 Holding and other investment offices

Services
70 Hotels, rooming houses, camps, and other lodging places
72 Personal services
73 Business services
75 Automotive repair services and garages
76 Miscellaneous repair services
78 Motion pictures
79 Amusement and recreation services, except motion pictures
80 Health services
81 Legal services
82 Educational services
83 Social services
84 Museums, art galleries, botanical and zoological gardens
86 Membership organizations
87 Research, engineering, and accounting services
89 Miscellaneous services

Public Administration
91 Executive, legislative, and general government, except finance
92 Justice, public order, and safety
93 Public finance, taxation, and monetary policy
94 Administration of human resources programs
95 Administration of environmental quality and housing programs
96 Administration of economic programs
97 National security and international affairs

Nonclassifiable Establishment
99 Nonclassifiable establishment

Controller/Director of Finance and Accounting

Responsibility Overview: This position directs the finance and accounting functions of the company and oversees financial reporting and statement preparation. This position is responsible for providing accurate financial data to be used for business planning and strategy purposes.

The controller typically has a bachelor's degree and at least ten years of accounting experience. This position directly supervises two accounting managers and two financial analysts and has indirect supervisory responsibility for the entire accounting area. The controller reports directly to the vice president and chief financial officer.

Base Pay Systems

EXHIBIT 5-7 (cont.)

Major Areas of Responsibility:
- Analyzes and interprets financial results and advises senior management regarding the financial ramifications of various initiatives and options
- Monitors and enhances financial controls and reporting procedures
- Acts as company liaison in communicating with external investors and banking partners

Director of Human Resources

Responsibility Overview: This position oversees the various functional areas of human resources (employment, training, benefits, safety). This position's primary responsibility is to ensure that all HR activities are in accordance with state and federal regulations, employee needs, and the company's strategic plan.

The director of human resources typically has a bachelor's degree and at least ten years of HR experience. This position supervises two to four functional managers. The director of HR reports to the vice president of HR.

Major Areas of Responsibility:
- Provides daily input on benefits, training, staffing, and safety issues
- Develops the departmental budget
- Maintains communication with senior management, management, and employees to ensure the coordination and appropriateness of HR initiatives and programs

Information Technologies (MIS) Manager

Responsibility Overview: This position plans, coordinates, and manages the activities of a functional area of the information technologies department (network systems, technical services, sales information support, etc.). This position's primary responsibility is to ensure that internal customers receive the technical support required to complete their tasks.

The information technologies manager typically has a bachelor's degree and at least five years of experience in management information systems. This position directly supervises five to seven programmer analysts. The information technologies manager reports to the vice president, information technologies.

Major Areas of Responsibility:
- Consults with clients regarding computer technology needs, problems, and other related issues
- Performs ongoing assessment of current technology and determines appropriate enhancements
- Develops the budget for hardware and software in the functional area of responsibility

Purchasing Manager

Responsibility Overview: This position oversees a purchasing department responsible for $15 million in inventory that includes 60,000 items. This position participates heavily in the development of standards for quality, price, and service and the plans required to meet those standards.

The purchasing manager typically has a bachelor's degree and at least five years of replenishment/procurement experience. This position directly supervises ten to twelve buyers and indirectly supervises twelve to fifteen purchasing assistants. The purchasing manager reports to the director of supply services.

Major Areas of Responsibility:
- Establishes and monitors purchasing policies, procedures, and process flows
- Certifies annual item costs and monitors system integrity
- Develops departmental budgets

Programmer Analyst

Responsibility Overview: This position writes computer programs required for various company operations. This position also installs, tests, and trains users on new and existing computer applications.

The programmer analyst typically has a bachelor's degree and at least three years of programming experience. This position has no formal supervisory responsibilities and reports directly to an MIS manager.

Major Areas of Responsibility:
- Maintains and enhances existing software applications by programming (OS/400, RPG/400, and CL languages), designing online help, and responding to user requests for assistance
- Assesses computer application needs and designs, tests, and installs new applications; trains users
- Maintains current computer system through performance tuning and data storage management

Safety Manager

Responsibility Overview: This position is responsible for programs and procedures intended to ensure a safe working environment. This position investigates accidents and administers workers' compensation claims.

The safety manager typically has a bachelor's degree and at least five years of safety experience. This position may have supervisory responsibility for one clerical support person. The safety manager reports to the director of HR.

Major Areas of Responsibility:
- Promotes safety awareness by conducting regular inspections and by creating safety awareness programs

EXHIBIT 5-7 (cont.)

- Conducts safety orientation and training
- Maintains compliance with state and federal safety regulations

Manager of General Accounting

Responsibility Overview: This position manages the general accounting area, which includes the accounts payable, accounts receivable, billing, and freight audit functions. This position's overall responsibility is to monitor and maintain the accuracy of day-to-day general accounting activities.

The manager of general accounting typically has a bachelor's degree and at least five years of accounting experience. This position directly supervises one staff accountant and eighteen to twenty accounting clerks. The manager of general accounting reports directly to the controller.

Major Areas of Responsibility:
- Analyzes company's cash position and communicates with banks to transfer funds as necessary
- Compiles a variety of reports/information on a monthly and annual basis (e.g., 5500 Report, year-end audit information) and coordinates the monthly closing for the four supervised functions
- Assists various departments with annual budget preparation and monthly budget reviews (budget vs. actual)
- Performs a variety of general accounting duties (maintains schedules, completes forms requiring company financial information, processes supplier credit applications, etc.)

General Accountant

Responsibility Overview: This position is involved in a variety of accounting activities, including general ledger accounting, financial statement and report preparation, and account reconciliation. This position also completes special accounting-related projects (e.g., problem research and resolution, system design).

The general accountant typically has a bachelor's degree and at least five years of accounting experience. This position has no direct supervisory responsibility and reports to the manager of financial reporting.

Major Areas of Responsibility:
- Performs general financial analysis and reporting duties
- Collects information and prepares financial statements; analyzes and resolves discrepancies between budgeted and actual expenditures
- Reconciles various accounts on a monthly basis (accounts receivable, accounts payable, etc.)

Transportation Manager

Responsibility Overview: This position is responsible for the efficient transit of company products to and from suppliers and customers. This position negotiates with carriers regarding inbound and outbound shipping.

The transportation manager typically has a high school education and at least five years of general transportation experience. This position supervises three to five transportation assistants. The transportation manager reports to the director of safety.

Major Areas of Responsibility:
- Maintains communication with carriers regarding rates, services, and competitive programs
- Develops departmental budget based on assessment of future transportation needs
- Works with customer services and shipping to resolve customer problems associated with shipped items

Warehouse Manager (Shipping or Receiving)

Responsibility Overview: This position is responsible for the accurate and timely flow of product into or out of the distribution center. This position oversees receiving and stocking activities or packing and shipping activities.

The warehouse manager typically has at least five years of warehouse experience, with at least three of those years in a supervisory capacity. This position directly supervises two supervisors and indirectly supervises twenty to forty warehouse employees. The warehouse manager reports to the director of distribution, who oversees all warehouse operations.

Major Areas of Responsibility:
- Monitors daily operations in the receiving or shipping areas of the warehouse and responds to problems that arise
- Assesses productivity and establishes productivity objectives for assigned area
- Develops departmental budget

Computer Operator

Responsibility Overview: This position carries out functions and maintains applications necessary for the operation of a computer system. This position runs and monitors various computer programs.

The computer operator typically has an associate's degree and one to three years of experience in computer operations. This position reports to an MIS manager. The computer operator has no supervisory responsibilities.

Major Areas of Responsibility:
- Performs daily, weekly, and monthly computer system backup procedures

EXHIBIT 5-7 (cont.)

- Operates and maintains system printers
- Analyzes and addresses cabling, terminal, and printer problems

Buyer

Responsibility Overview: This position makes product purchases based on the knowledge of corporate goals regarding inventory levels and cost. This position negotiates with suppliers to secure low-cost/high-quality product.

The buyer typically has at least two years of experience and a high school education, with some college course work preferred. The buyer supervises one assistant and has responsibility for managing the inventory levels of 5 to 15,000 products. This position reports directly to the purchasing manager.

Major Areas of Responsibility:
- Analyzes inventory levels, determines buying quantities, and locates new and lower-cost sources of product
- Replenishes product inventory by negotiating with suppliers and executing buys
- Maintains ongoing relationships and represents the company's interests with 200 to 400 suppliers

Notes

1. S. L. Rynes and G. T. Milkovich, "Wage Surveys: Dispelling Some Myths about the 'Market Wage,'" *Personnel Psychology* (1986): pp. 71–90.
2. R. Platt, ed. *Salary Survey Guidebook: Finding and Evaluating Compensation and Benefit Data* (New York: AMACOM, 1998).
3. R. L. Heneman and G. E. Ledford, "Competency Pay for Managers and Professionals: Implications for Teachers," *Journal of Personnel Evaluation in Education* (1998): pp. 103–121.

CHAPTER 6

Pay Structures

The pay structure is a policy guideline for the organization that shows allowable rates of pay. It portrays the compensation strategy of the organization in operational terms. The pay structure is formed by merging the results of the job evaluation, as shown in Exhibit 6-1.

A pay structure shows the parameters within which people are to be paid in the organization. As with any policy, there may occasionally be deviations from the pay structure, but to the greatest extent possible, a pay structure is adhered to in the organization because it supports the aims of the business and compensation strategies of the organization. Unless discipline is maintained with the pay structure, pay practices may break down in the organization and lead to a lack of integration of individual and corporate goals. Organizational effectiveness may be diminished as a result.

There are different types of pay structures. Some pay structures are better suited for some business strategies than others. The pay structures will now be reviewed in the context of business and compensation strategy.

Types of Pay Structures

In general, a pay structure shows the array of pay rates to be paid to people in various pay grades or bands. Differences in pay structures reflect differences in how the bands are constructed and how people progress within a pay band.

EXHIBIT 6-1
Pay structure formation.

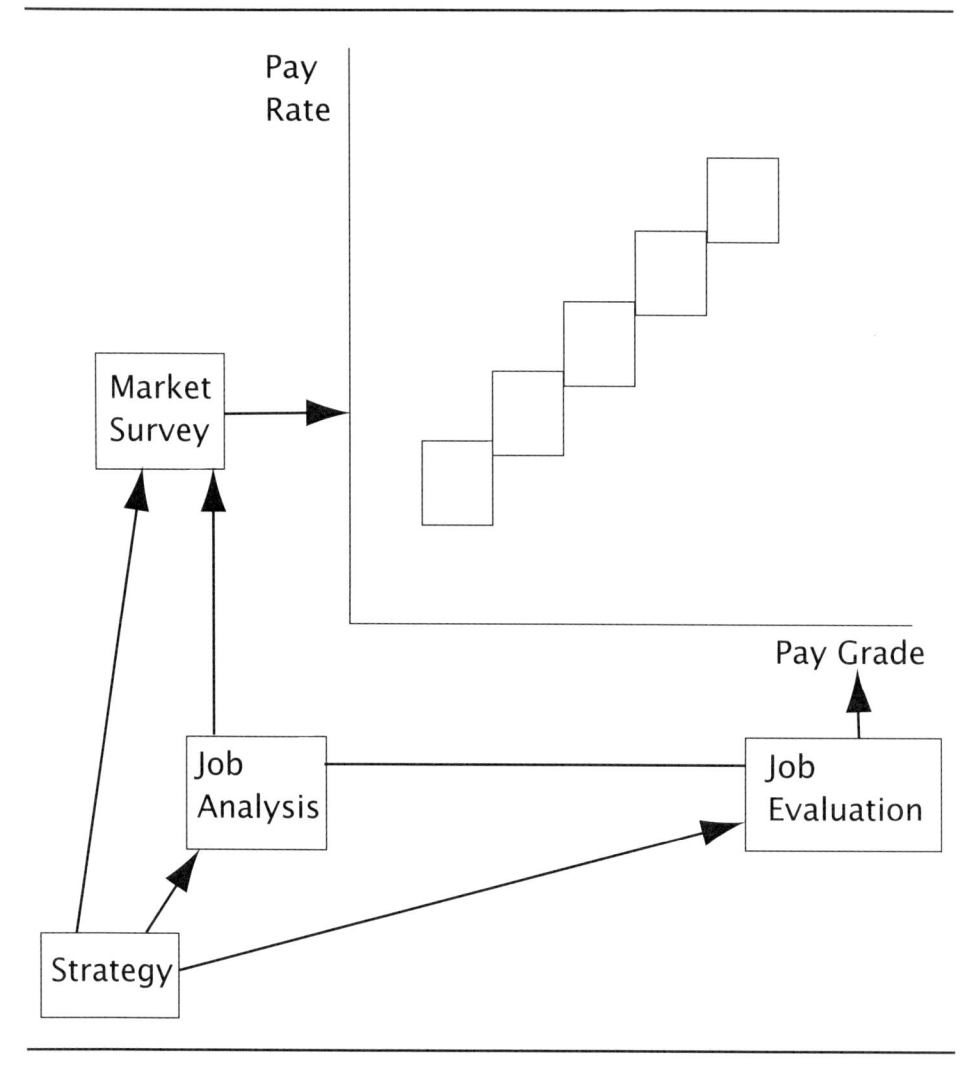

[Diagram: A flowchart showing "Strategy" at the bottom with arrows pointing to "Job Analysis", "Market Survey", and "Job Evaluation". "Job Analysis" connects to "Job Evaluation" and "Market Survey". "Market Survey" feeds into a graph with "Pay Rate" on the y-axis and "Pay Grade" on the x-axis, showing a stepped pattern of overlapping boxes ascending from lower-left to upper-right. "Job Evaluation" points up to "Pay Grade".]

Single Rate

The most straightforward type of pay structure is a single rate structure, shown in Table 6-1. Pay grades or bands are typically formed on the basis of job evaluation points and/or occupational similarity. Differences between pay grades reflect natural breaks in the distribution of point values as shown in Table 6-1 or are formed on the basis of a uniform spread in points (90–100, 80–89, etc.) or occupations (e.g., exempt vs. nonexempt).

TABLE 6-1
Single rate pay grade structure.

Job Evaluation Points	Pay Grade	Hourly Wage
92–100	4	$13.85
83–89	3	12.75
70–78	2	11.30
59–67	1	10.50

Pay rates are usually established by pay grades rather than by person or job for two reasons. First, the system is less complex to administer. Second, it reflects the less-than-perfect reliability of job evaluation systems. As a result, minute differences in pay between jobs may reflect measurement error more than actual value differences to the organization.

The unique aspect of single rate structures is that a single rate is paid for each grade. Regardless of seniority or performance, an employee is paid the same rate of pay when that job is slotted into the particular grade.

The major strength of a single rate structure is the ease of administration associated with this policy. The major downside is that it fails to differentiate between the specific contributions and accomplishments of the jobholder and the pay grade. In unionized companies, this weakness may actually be viewed as a strength from the perspective of the union because employees are not seen as being in competition with one another.

Increasingly, single rate structures are very difficult to find. The diminishing use of these systems is probably attributable to their failure to support many business strategies; if anything, they usually conflict with business strategies. A single rate structure can be advantageous if cost minimization is the driving business strategy in that the lack of complexity of the system translates into fewer dollars needed to administer the system.

Pay Ranges

Pay ranges are formed in the same manner as single rate structures. Unlike single rate structures, however, each pay grade is defined by a range of pay values, as shown in Exhibit 6-2. The reason for having pay ranges rather than a single rate is to provide flexibility to managers in rewarding employees for their individual contributions (e.g., seniority, performance,

Base Pay Systems

◆ **EXHIBIT 6-2**
Pay range pay structure.

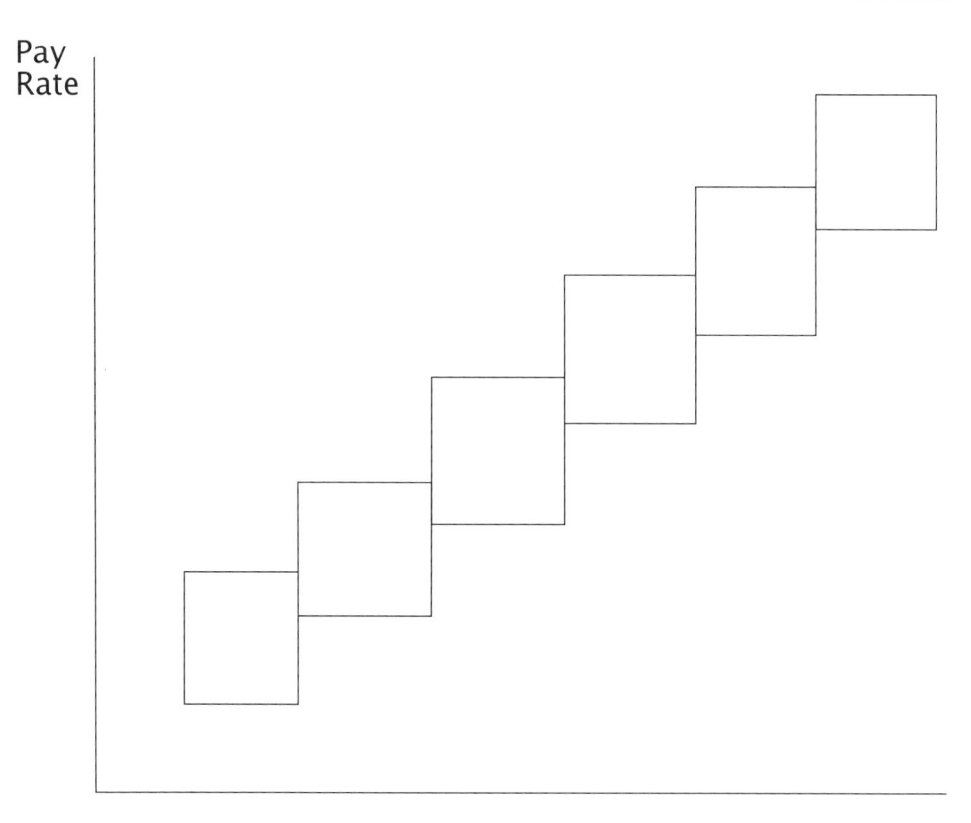

knowledge, skill) to the organization. Even though two job incumbents may hold jobs in the same pay grade, one incumbent may be paid more based on greater individual contributions to the organization in terms of years worked, performance ratings, degree, or skill certification.

Pay ranges are more difficult to administer than single rate structures. However, this weakness is counteracted by the major strength of the system—the flexibility that managers have to reward people for their accomplishments in order to motivate future accomplishments. Pay ranges certainly fit better with all the business strategies reviewed in this book other than cost. As will be shown later in this chapter, the number and width of pay ranges varies by business strategy.

Pay Structures

Locked Step

A locked step pay structure, often found in the public sector, is a compromise between a single rate structure and a pay range structure and is shown in Exhibit 6-3. It is a compromise in that it has a moderate level of complexity and allows for a moderate level of differentiation between employees on the basis of their contributions. It achieves these compromises in terms of complexity and flexibility in the following manner.

Like a pay range structure, and unlike a single rate structure, the locked step structure has ranges of pay to reward individual contributions. However, like a single rate structure and unlike a pay range structure, there are limits imposed on rewards for individual contributions. These limits, known as "locked" or "fixed" steps, determine the amount that an employee can progress in a pay band at any one time. An employee can progress by only a certain number of steps per pay review period based on the step progression policy. The step progression policy spells out the number of steps that can be advanced and the reasons for advancement in the pay guide. Reasons for advancement in the pay grade are usually seniority and/or performance.

An advantage to a locked step structure is that it provides some flexibility to managers in rewarding individual contributions. Another advantage is that it helps manage labor costs in the organization because employees can advance only a predefined number of steps in a pay review period. The downside to this approach is the restricted amount of discretion that a manager is given in differentiating employees on the basis of individual contributions.

As with a single rate pay structure, the locked step pay structure lends itself to cost-minimizing business and compensation strategies. It also lends itself to balanced scorecard approaches in which cost is a major

EXHIBIT 6-3
Locked step pay ranges.

Pay Grade	Step 1	2	3	4	5	6	7
4							
3							
2							
1							

Base Pay Systems

scorecard category. For example, an organization with a business strategy based on innovation may want to have the flexibility to reward employees for innovative contributions to the organization. On the other hand, the company may be limited in the amount that it can afford for recognition. Given these two business strategies reflected in the balanced scorecard, the organization may need to use a locked step system.

Broadbanding

A variation of the pay range pay structure is broadbanding. In essence, it reduces the number of pay grades and widens the pay ranges. Exhibit 6-4 depicts the collapse of nine pay grades into three pay grades. Although it is common to collapse existing pay grades into broad bands, broad bands can be created independent of an existing pay range structure (e.g., greenfield start-up site).

Several major advantages exist for broadbanding. First, it provides a large amount of discretion to managers in rewarding individual contributions. Using Exhibit 6-4, for example, a person in the lowest of the nine

EXHIBIT 6-4
Narrow versus broad bands.

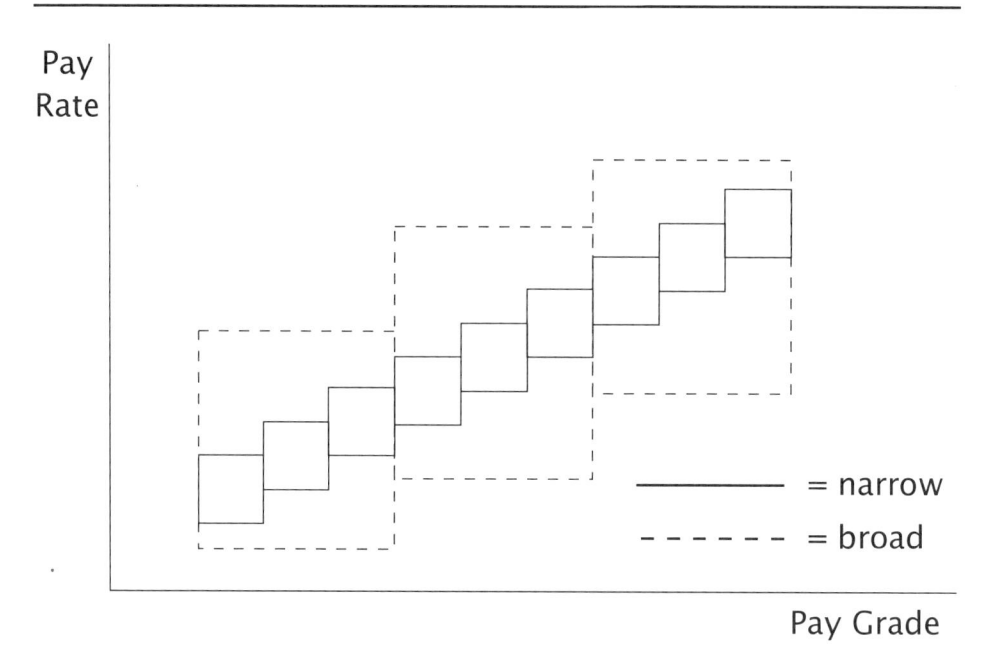

——— = narrow
- - - - - = broad

142

pay bands can earn as much as or more than the person in pay bands two or three in the nine-band structure because, under the three broadbands, people in pay bands one, two, and three of the nine-band structure are now in pay band one of the broadband structure. Second, more senior employees who may not have been eligible for a pay increase under the nine-band system because they were at the maximum level to be paid out for their pay band can now receive a pay increase because the maximum allowable under the three band system is higher. Third, and most important of all, broadbanding encourages employees to go beyond the bounds of their traditional job description and become multiskilled so that they can perform multiple tasks. That is, they no longer have to live within the confines of their narrowly defined jobs in the narrower nine-band pay structure.

A potential major disadvantage to broadbanding is cost. The number of people eligible for pay increases and the amount available may both increase. Hence, under this approach, individual contributions must be measured in a reliable and valid way to manage progression within the band. In the absence of an excellent measurement system for progression within the bands, runaway costs may result. Costs can also be managed by placing control points in each band based on market value. Taking this step, however, in essence reverts the broad bands back to narrow bands in a traditional pay range structure.

Broad bands work very well with a business strategy of innovation. People can be rewarded for what they contribute, more than for the type of job they hold. Broad bands work well with a customer service orientation because progression within the bands can be based on the mastery of customer service competencies. Broadbanding could be considered for cost-minimizing firms as well only if the strategy resulted in a head count reduction of value greater than increased salaries. Broad bands lend themselves less well to quality-driven business strategies because the person may override the system, and the system is the most important element in TQM settings. In organizations driven by productivity, broadbanding can work, but the accurate measurement of employee contribution is critical. Otherwise, input may increase in the form of increased pay faster than output rises.

Market Pricing

As mentioned in Chapter 5, under a strict market pricing arrangement, a very limited form of job evaluation, if any, takes place. Pay rates for jobs are pegged to jobs that have been benchmarked in the market survey. Jobs may be related to jobs with known market value by grouping them by occupation or type of job, for example:

- Exempt versus nonexempt
- Professional versus nonprofessional
- Union versus nonunion
- Key contributor versus non–key contributor
- Line versus staff
- Management versus nonmanagement
- Technical versus nontechnical
- Value added versus non–value added
- Classified versus nonclassified

Such an approach can produce pay ranges for each job grouping independent of more formal job evaluation procedures. The advantage of this approach is that external equity is almost exclusively emphasized. Such an approach may be optimal for organizations that place heavy strategic emphasis on managing costs. Organizations with an innovative business strategy may also emphasize this approach in order to free employees from the constraints imposed by an internal equity driven method of job evaluation. The disadvantages to market pricing include internal equity issues raised and the availability of solid market data.

Pay Structure Policy Issues and Strategy

When pay structures more complex than a single rate structure are used, there are a number of parameters that must be set. Often these parameters are set on history, convention, and/or rule of thumb. Additional consideration should be given to strategic considerations in setting these pay structure parameters.

Midpoint

The midpoint is usually set uniformly for all job grades at the average market wages in order to be "competitive." Such an approach is not always appropriate for strategic reasons. One issue that must be carefully considered is the extent to which the organization should lead or lag rather than match the market. The difference between these company pay lines is shown in Exhibit 6-5.

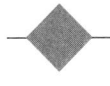

EXHIBIT 6-5
Uniform company pay line versus market.

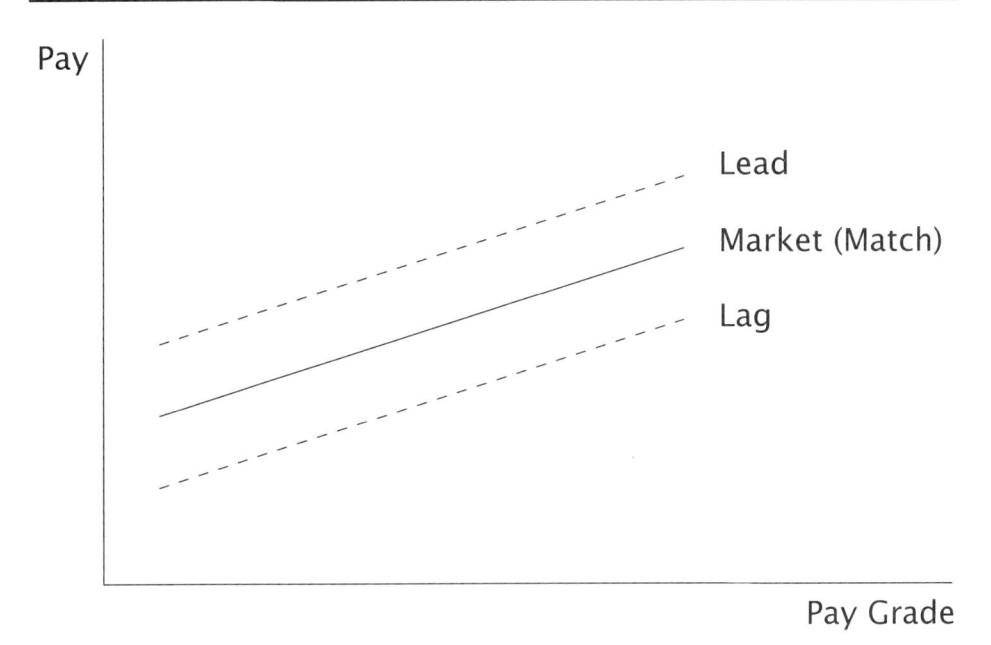

[Graph showing three parallel upward-sloping lines labeled "Lead" (top, dashed), "Market (Match)" (middle, solid), and "Lag" (bottom, dashed), with "Pay" on the y-axis and "Pay Grade" on the x-axis.]

When cost is a major strategic concern, then consideration may need to be given to a lag policy, paying less than the market. If there are a large number of jobs, lagging by even a small amount or for a part of a year may lead to substantial cost savings. To do so, however, may lead to attraction, retention, and motivation issues because better opportunities are plentiful in the labor market. The difference between the lag and market lines may be able to be made up for employees based on reward systems, which are covered in the next chapter.

A second issue that must be considered is whether a uniform lead/lag/match policy should be used for all jobs in the organization. If internal equity is not an overriding concern of the compensation strategy, then two or three of these approaches can be used for various job categories. For example, Exhibit 6-6 shows the somewhat common situation in which zn-higher-level jobs follow a lead the market policy while lower level jobs follow a lag the market policy within the same company. Organizations with an innovative business strategy may follow this approach to lead the market for those positions that add most value to the organization (e.g., research and development personnel). Organizations with a balanced

EXHIBIT 6-6
Nonuniform company pay line versus market.

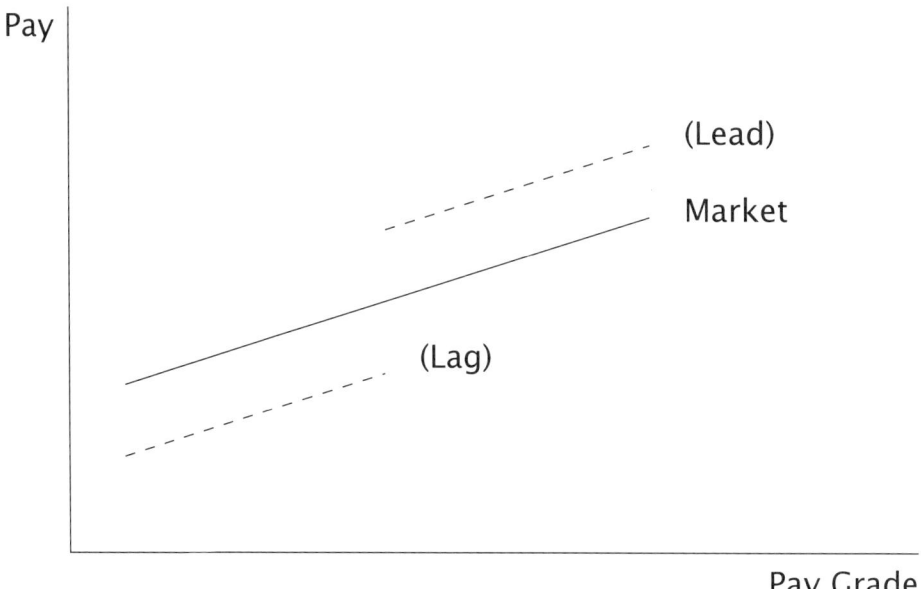

scorecard approach and cost as an important priority may need to pay below the market for some jobs to afford to pay for other more important jobs at the market rate.

Range Width

As shown in Exhibit 6-7, a pay range is defined by three parameters: minimum, midpoint, and maximum. The minimum is the lowest amount to be paid for a person in a pay grade. It is usually set at the minimum level needed to successfully attract, retain, and motivate people for jobs in a particular pay range. The maximum is the maximum amount the organization is willing to pay for people in a particular pay grade. In essence, the maximum becomes a "cap" to pay increases in pay grades in recognition of the fact that any one job adds only a finite amount of value to the organization.

The distance between the minimum and maximum is known as the width of the pay range. A traditional rule of thumb is that this distance should be 40 percent. This rule of thumb was created during a period

EXHIBIT 6-7
Pay range parameters.

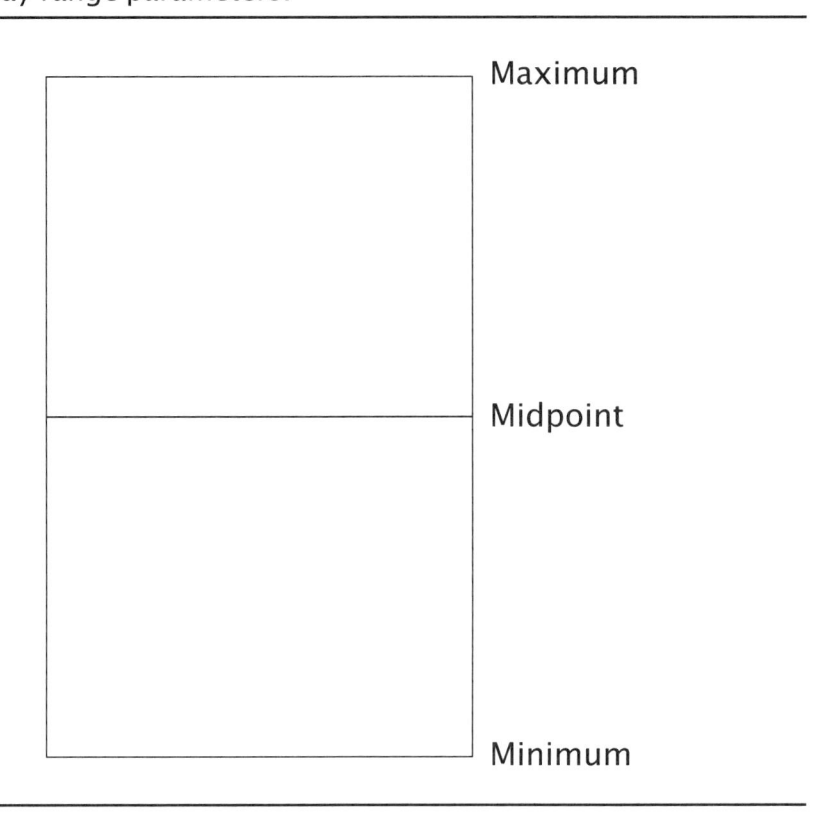

```
                                    ─ Maximum



                                    ─ Midpoint



                                    ─ Minimum
```

when many organizations were bureaucratic in structure with a large number of pay grades and ample opportunity for promotion up the pay grades. In recent times, the spread has increased in many organizations to 60 percent to 80 percent and, in organizations with broad bands, to a spread of over 100 percent in some cases. Organizations have become flatter with fewer promotional opportunities, and larger bands provide opportunity for pay growth without promotion. The general point to be made here is that larger spread allows for more flexibility in the organization and requires fewer pay ranges for pay advancement.

Cost- and production-driven organizations are more likely to have narrow bands to minimize labor cost and productivity input. The pay range is likely to be broadened in organizations where more flexibility is required as a result of the business strategy, such as in companies driven by customer service, quality, or innovation.

Just as a lead/lag/match policy may not be uniform across jobs, so too may pay range widths not be uniform across jobs. A larger spread may be used for some jobs (e.g., high-level jobs), while a smaller spread may be used for other jobs (e.g., lower-level jobs). As with a lead, the market policy for some select jobs, a wider pay range for some select jobs is a way to pay additional amounts to those jobs that add more value to the company. A problem with this approach of heterogeneous pay range widths is, of course, perceptions of internal inequity by those people in jobs with a smaller width to their pay range.

Number of Pay Grades

The larger the number of pay grades in the organization, the greater the number of promotional opportunities for employees. Some organizations prefer to have a large number of pay grades to reward employees for good performance with upward mobility and to encourage employees to develop the knowledge and skills needed to progress to the next pay level. Service-driven organizations such as banks, for example, have a large number of job titles, reflecting a large number of pay bands.

Even with a large number of pay grades, upward mobility is eventually thwarted due to the reduced number of jobs as one moves up the hierarchy. Fewer pay bands suggest to employees that they need to grow within their pay band rather than move up to higher pay bands. As a result, the number of pay bands is correlated with the width of pay ranges. As the number of pay bands is reduced, pay band width must be increased in order to provide upward mobility within pay bands.

Overlap between Pay Grades

Motivation for employees to expand their knowledge and skill sets is a function of the amount of overlap between pay grades. With a large amount of overlap, there is less incentive to acquire the skills and knowledge to progress to a higher level pay band because one can earn almost the same amount in a lower pay band. Cost conscious organizations may have large pay range overlap because there are fewer jobs available in higher pay bands. On the other hand, organizations with a strategic focus on human capital, quality, productivity, or innovation are more inclined to have less overlap in pay grades to motivate the improvement of human capital by employees. Even with a large amount of overlap, motivation to improve one's human capital can be increased by linking advancement

Pay Structures

within the pay grade to the mastery of specific skills or competencies defined for each pay grade. However, the level of human capital mastery is likely to be greater the more people have to advance to another pay grade because the human capital demands in higher-level jobs are likely to be greater. From a balanced scorecard perspective, both cost and human capital can be emphasized by having a small amount of overlap. The human capital strategy component is emphasized by the multiple skills mastered by employees, while the cost component of business strategy is emphasized by the reduction in cost that comes from the reduced head count needed with employees who can perform multiple tasks.

Case Studies

CASE 1

Educational Distributor

The pay system development for the educational distributor case has been covered in Chapters 3 and 4. The market data and job evaluation data were combined to form the pay structure shown in Table 6-2.

In order to minimize labor costs, the pay range widths were kept nar-

TABLE 6-2
Pay structure for educational distributor.

Pay Grade	Minimum	Maximum
1	$ 5.80/hr	$ 8.20/hr
2	6.80/hr	9.80/hr
3	8.20/hr	11.80/hr
4	9.70/hr	13.97/hr
5	24,500.00/yr	36,750.00/yr
6	32,000.00/yr	48,000.00/yr
7	38,400.00/yr	57,600.00/yr
8	47,166.00/yr	87,594.00/yr
9	70,000.00/yr	130,000.00/yr

Base Pay Systems

row for lower-level jobs, where the bulk of the positions resided in the organization. Pay range widths were widened for higher-level jobs to emphasize the importance of these jobs to the organization.

CASE 2

County Engineers Office

A summary of pay system development for the County Engineers Office is presented in Chapters 3, 4, and 5. The pay structure used is shown in Table 6-3; it is a hybrid structure coupling a pay range structure with movement based on merit with a locked step structure based on seniority. This hybrid represents the intersection of the current organizational culture with the future strategic intent of the office. The culture is heavily based on a seniority-driven system, as one would expect in a unionized organization. The future strategic direction of the organization is reflected in the merit pay increases used for each seniority step based on performance ratings of individual contributions.

It should also be noted that the pay range widths are wider for higher-level than for lower-level jobs. This was done to emphasize the core technical capability of the organization, which was viewed as a critical compo-

TABLE 6-3
Engineers office—bargaining unit pay structure.

Pay Range	Base	Step 1 Min	Step 1 Max	Step 2 Min	Step 2 Max	Step 3 Min	Step 3 Max
A	$10.11	$10.41	$12.33	$10.77	$12.74	$11.17	$13.40
B	10.91	11.22	13.20	11.59	13.62		
C	11.07	11.37	13.56	11.74	13.93	12.12	14.42
D	11.29	11.60	13.79	11.95	14.20		
F	11.96	12.27	14.57	12.64	15.00	13.01	15.42
G	12.34	12.65	14.96	13.02	15.38	13.39	15.97
H	12.79	13.10	15.51	13.45	15.93	13.84	16.53
I	13.03	13.33	15.75	13.70	16.18	14.06	16.75
J	13.47	13.78	16.26	14.11	16.64	14.68	17.38
K	13.94	14.25	16.84	14.51	17.11		

Pay Structures

nent of this mission. To emphasize technical expertise, not only were those with technical degrees placed in higher-level jobs through a job evaluation system that put heavy weight on technical knowledge and skills, but they were also eligible for higher wage levels, as reflected in the wage structure. Finally, consistent with the future strategic direction of the office, the number of pay grades was substantially reduced.

CASE 3

County Children Services Agency

The business and compensation strategies of Wright County Children Services are covered in Chapter 5. The pay structure for this agency is shown in Table 6-4. As can be seen from this pay structure, and consistent with the strategy, the pay structure is a very straightforward one. Pay range widths are narrow to reflect the need to be sensitive to costs. Pay grade midpoints are set at the exact market average in order to pay no more than was needed to be competitive. Jobs (e.g., case provider, grant writer) related to the core capabilities of the organization (e.g., care, fund-raising) were placed in higher pay grades, which had wider pay ranges.

TABLE 6-4
Services agency—bargaining unit pay structure.

	Annual Increments								Longevity						
									10 yrs	12 yrs	14 yrs	16 yrs	18 yrs	20 yrs	22 yrs
Pay Ranges	Step 1	Step 2	Step 3	Step 4	Step 5	Step 6	Step 7	Step 8	Step 9	Step 10	Step 11	Step 12	Step 13	Step 14	Step 15
Section I
1	$ 6.73	$ 7.07	$ 7.42	$ 7.79	$ 8.18	$ 8.59	$ 9.02	$ 9.26	$ 9.50	$ 9.74	$10.00	$10.26	$10.52	$10.80	$11.08
2	7.28	7.65	8.03	8.43	8.85	9.29	9.76	10.01	10.27	10.54	10.81	11.09	11.38	11.68	11.98
3	7.57	7.95	8.35	8.77	9.20	9.66	10.15	10.41	10.68	10.96	11.25	11.54	11.84	12.15	12.46
4	7.88	8.27	8.68	9.12	9.57	10.05	10.55	10.83	11.11	11.40	11.69	12.00	12.31	12.63	12.96
5	8.19	8.60	9.03	9.48	9.96	10.45	10.98	11.26	11.55	11.85	12.16	12.48	12.80	13.14	13.48
6	8.52	8.94	9.39	9.86	10.35	10.87	11.41	11.71	12.02	12.33	12.65	12.98	13.32	13.66	14.02
7	8.86	9.30	9.77	10.26	10.77	11.31	11.87	12.18	12.50	12.82	13.16	13.50	13.85	14.21	14.58
8	9.21	9.67	10.16	10.67	11.20	11.76	12.35	12.67	13.00	13.33	13.68	14.04	14.40	14.78	15.16
9	9.58	10.06	10.56	11.09	11.65	12.23	12.84	13.17	13.52	13.87	14.23	14.60	14.98	15.37	15.77
10	9.96	10.46	10.99	11.54	12.11	12.72	13.35	13.70	14.06	14.42	14.80	15.18	15.58	15.98	16.40
11	10.38	10.88	11.43	12.00	12.60	13.23	13.89	14.25	14.62	15.00	15.39	15.79	16.20	16.62	17.00
12	10.78	11.32	11.88	12.48	13.10	13.76	14.44	14.82	15.20	15.60	16.01	16.42	16.85	17.29	17.70
13	11.21	11.77	12.36	12.98	13.62	14.31	15.02	15.41	15.81	16.22	16.65	17.08	17.52	17.98	18.40
Section II
14	11.24	11.81	12.40	13.02	13.67	14.35	15.07	15.46	15.86	16.27	16.70	17.13	17.58	18.03	18.50
15	11.69	12.28	12.89	13.54	14.21	14.92	15.67	16.08	16.50	16.93	17.37	17.82	18.28	18.76	19.24
16	12.16	12.77	13.41	14.08	14.78	15.52	16.30	16.72	17.16	17.60	18.06	18.53	19.01	19.51	20.01
17	13.15	13.81	14.50	15.23	15.99	16.79	17.63	18.09	18.56	19.04	19.53	20.04	20.56	21.10	21.65
18	13.68	14.38	15.08	15.84	16.63	17.46	18.33	18.81	19.30	19.80	20.31	20.84	21.38	21.94	22.51
19	14.23	14.94	15.69	16.47	17.29	18.16	19.07	19.56	20.07	20.59	21.13	21.68	22.24	22.82	23.41
20	14.80	15.54	16.31	17.13	17.98	18.88	19.83	20.34	20.87	21.42	21.97	22.54	23.13	23.73	24.35

TABLE 6.4 (cont.)
Services agency—Nonbargaining unit pay structure.

Pay Ranges	Minimum	Midpoint	Maximum
10	$ 9.92	$12.59	$15.66
11	10.29	13.62	16.94
12	11.14	14.73	18.33
13	11.58	15.32	19.06
14	11.64	15.39	19.15
15	12.10	16.01	19.92
16	13.62	18.01	22.41
17	14.72	19.48	24.23
18	15.31	20.26	25.20
19	17.42	23.04	28.65
20	18.11	23.96	29.81
21	18.83	24.92	31.01
22	20.37	26.95	33.53
23	21.20	28.72	36.25
24	23.83	31.52	39.21

PART 3

PERFORMANCE MEASUREMENT AND REWARDS

Chapter 7: Individual Rewards

Chapter 8: Team Rewards

Chapter 9: Organizational Rewards

A model of corporate business strategy and pay policy integration.

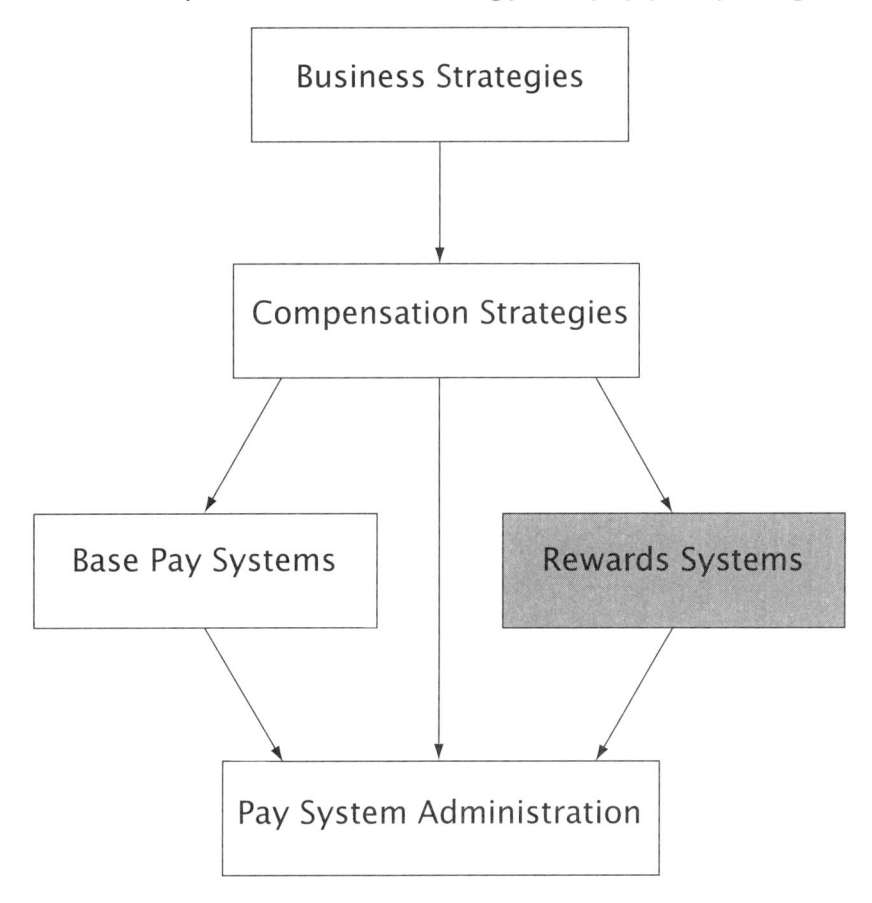

```
        ┌─────────────────────┐
        │ Business Strategies │
        └──────────┬──────────┘
                   │
                   ▼
       ┌─────────────────────────┐
       │ Compensation Strategies │
       └───────┬─────┬─────┬─────┘
            ↙       ↓       ↘
┌──────────────────┐   ┌─────────────────┐
│ Base Pay Systems │   │ Rewards Systems │
└────────┬─────────┘   └────────┬────────┘
          ↘       ↓       ↙
       ┌─────────────────────────┐
       │ Pay System Administration │
       └─────────────────────────┘
```

CHAPTER 7

Individual Rewards

Four major steps are taken to develop individual rewards based on the business strategies and compensation strategies. These steps are summarized in Exhibit 7-1. Each step will be reviewed in turn, followed by case examples of this process.

Performance Standards

Reward systems are based on the concept of pay-for-performance, whereby rewards are linked to past performance in order to motivate future performance.[1] The first step in this process is to clearly define performance of the employee so that the employee is motivated to deliver the level of performance desired by the organization. Performance is usually defined by standards that the employee is expected to meet by the organization. In order for the organization to achieve its goals, the goals of individual employees must be brought into alignment with those of the organization. This step is best accomplished by developing performance standards that are based on the business and compensation strategies of the organization.

Absolute vs. Relative Comparisons

One way to categorize performance standards is by whether absolute or relative comparisons are made. When absolute comparisons are made, employees are compared to a written standard. When relative comparisons are made, employees are compared to one another. Most organizations use absolute rather than relative comparisons for a simple reason,

EXHIBIT 7-1

Establishing individual rewards.

```
          Business and Compensation Strategies
           /            |            \
          /             |             \
  Performance  ←——————————————→  Evaluators
  Standards            |
          \            |            /
           \           ↓           /
            →      Weighting     ←
                       |
                       ↓
                    Rewards
```

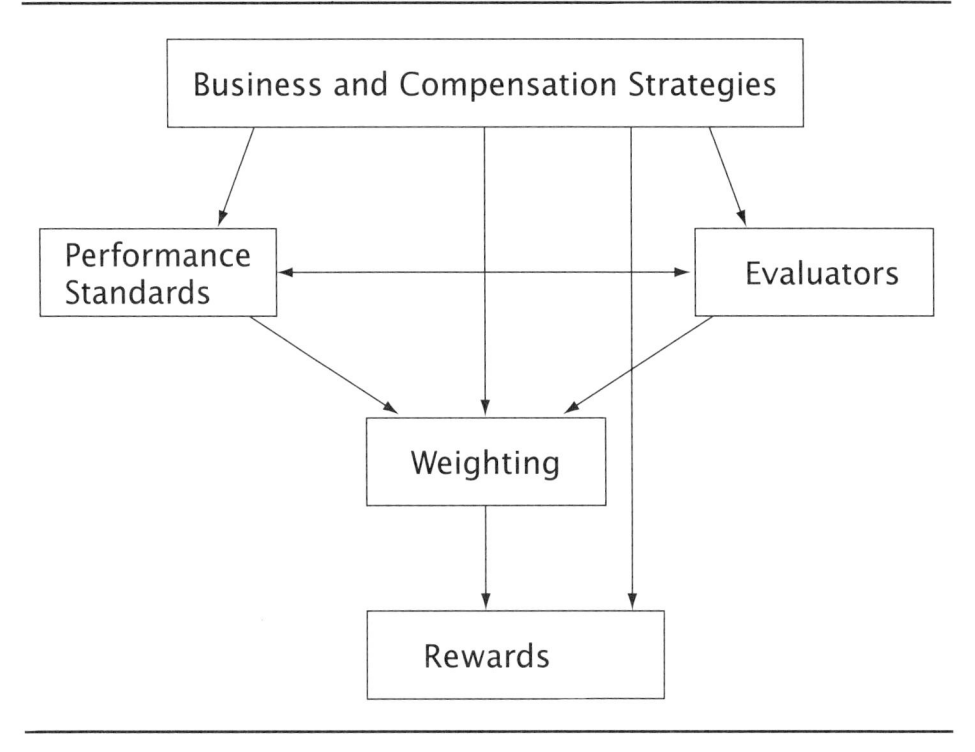

namely, that written standards are needed for employees to learn what it is they must do in order to earn rewards.

A common form of relative comparisons is to rank employees from the highest to the lowest performance in a work group. While this process is very efficient and reliable, it fails to teach employees how to improve. After all, how likely is it for someone to improve in the desired manner when the only feedback given is that he or she was rated number three out of five employees? Moreover, when rankings are made by different departments, the rank orderings are not comparable across departments. Because of these problems, relative comparisons are used only under a limited set of circumstances. These circumstances include a small number of employees, so that all employees can be compared to one another and a cost- or finance-driven business strategy in which an efficient system is demanded.

Types of Absolute Standards

There are several categories of performance standards for absolute comparisons. As will be shown, the appropriateness of each depends upon the business and compensation strategies of the organization.

Traits

Traits refer to performance standards that emphasize the personality of the employee. Typical standards here include "temperament" or "drive"; the evaluator is asked to make a judgment about the degree to which the employee possesses this trait on a 1 to 5 scale. Like relative comparisons, traits are very easy to develop and efficient to use. As such, they are also used by cost- and finance-driven organizations. Traits are sometimes used by organizations with other business and compensation strategies as well, but for a different reason. Organizations that focus on innovation and learning often want to have flexible employees to go along with flexible work practices. Customer service–focused organizations with a great deal of customer interface may desire certain personality characteristics to present a good front to customers and retain customer loyalty.

While traits appear to be related logically to the business strategies just mentioned, they conflict with another business and compensation strategy, namely, legal compliance. Traits as an appraisal method to determine rewards have repeatedly been shown to be illegal under employment discrimination laws.[2] Moreover, they are a poor source of developmental feedback to employees.[3] Fewer employees feel motivated to improve when they are told that they have, for example, a "bad temperament." That is a subjective designation, and employees are likely to resent being labeled in this manner. As a result of these concerns, traits are not to be recommended as an absolute performance standard regardless of business strategy.

Behaviors

You are probably wondering how an organization can provide good customer service if it is not allowed to groom employees with a good temperament. The answer comes in the second category of absolute standards—behaviors. Behaviors refer to observable actions taken by employees to perform their job. Problems with traits can be overcome by using behaviors to define traits. Thus, for example, a customer service representative has as a performance standard "not swearing at customers" and other observable behaviors, rather than temperament. Behaviors are much more likely to be seen as being legal standards by the courts and are more likely to be well received by employees as a source of feedback because they know explicitly what is meant and what needs to be done. As a result, behaviors work well in organizations that put a premium on the flexibility of their workforce. Desired behaviors can be spelled out that are associated with customer service, quality, innovation, organizational learning, and other characteristics needed for organizations to be flexible.

Results

Another type of absolute comparison refers to tangible outcomes produced by employees, such as cost, sales, production, waste, and profit. Results, like behaviors, are far more likely to be viewed as legal and are more likely to be accepted and acted upon by employees than are traits. Companies often couple behaviors and results together because results spell out what is to be accomplished, while behaviors can be used to show how it is to be accomplished. Results lend themselves well to cost-, productivity-, quality-, and finance-oriented business plans because of their bottom-line orientation. Organizations pursuing a business plan on the basis of a balanced scorecard are likely to use both results and behaviors to assess employee performance.

Actual vs. Potential Performance

Behavioral standards come in two forms: actual performance and potential performance. Actual performance refers to performance that has already contributed to the organization, while potential performance refers to behaviors that may contribute to the organization. Behavioral standards with an emphasis on potential are known as competencies and refer to the observable knowledge, skills, and other determinants (e.g., motivation) of effective performance. Knowledge-, skills-, and competency-based pay systems sometimes link rewards to potential rather than actual performance. That is, rewards are allocated for the acquisition of competencies that will eventually be used on the job once they are mastered. Obviously this approach is a desirable one when the organization hopes to develop behaviors in the workforce consistent with quality, productivity, customer service, learning, and innovation. Competency-based pay systems are usually not used by cost-driven and financially-driven organizations because they are very expensive both in terms of direct (increased wage rates) and indirect (training, certification) upfront costs.

Evaluators

It used to be the case that the only evaluator for reward decisions was the immediate supervisor of the employee. The thought was that supervisors had the best opportunity to observe employees and were ultimately held accountable by the organization for their performance. Times have changed, however, and it can no longer be assumed that supervisors have ample opportunity to observe employees or that it is supervisors rather than others to whom the employees are accountable. For example, many supervisors now have a very large number of direct reports due to organizational downsizing or direct reports in remote geographic locations. As a result, they have less opportunity to observe employee performance. Also, in the case of teams, for example, employees may be self-directed and held accountable by their peers rather than by a supervisor. For these reasons and others, raters other than the supervisor are being used to evaluate employee performance, sometimes for purposes of rewards as well as employee development. This process is known as a multi-rater or 360-degree assessment process. Because of the costs of administration, it is usually not used by cost-driven firms.

In selecting evaluators to use, it is usually recommended that evaluators be knowledgeable about the job and have the opportunity to observe performance. While this is certainly good advice, attention should also be paid to the business and compensation strategies in deciding which parties should be part of the evaluation process.

Self

Employee empowerment is often made a part of the compensation strategy in response to business strategies such as customer service, quality, productivity, innovation, learning, and the balanced scorecard. If employees are to be truly involved in decision making in the organization, then they should have the opportunity to assess their own performance.

Peers

Peers can be very useful in the rating process for two reasons. First, they typically have more opportunity to observe employee performance than do supervisors and may also have better knowledge of the job than do supervisors. Second, they may be seen by employees as a more credible source of information than are supervisors.

As a result of these virtues, peers are an excellent source for behavioral ratings of both actual and potential performance. They are less useful for results-oriented standards because they may not always have knowledge of the larger financial context usually held by management. Because of their behavioral knowledge, peers work well as evaluators in organizations that emphasize innovation, quality, productivity, customer service, or organizational learning.

Subordinates

Subordinates can be a good evaluation source for managerial positions, especially in those companies that believe in employee empowerment. If employees are to be truly empowered, then they should be asked about their reactions to the performance of the person they work for. Similarly, managers should be held accountable for employee empowerment if it is a business goal, and employees are likely to know best if they are being empowered by their supervisors to do the job. For example, subordinates can evaluate those they work for by using behavioral scales on dimensions such as delegation of authority, and resources and supervision needed to do the job.

Customers

As a consultant it never ceases to amaze me how many organizations focus completely or in part on customer service as their business plan but fail to gather any form of customer service ratings. If customer service is truly important, then it must be measured and rewarded. Using customers as a source of performance information is to be encouraged not only for those companies following a customer service strategy, but also by organizations following other strategies. Customers can be a tremendous source of ideas for quality, customer service, and innovation enhancements as well as an important part of organizational learning.

Weighting

When providing pay on the basis of performance, an eventual summary judgment must be made to determine the overall level of performance. When multiple standards or multiple evaluators are used, this overall assessment requires weighting. The weighting to arrive at a final assessment should be based on the business and compensation strategy of the organization. Typical weights by business strategy and performance standards are shown in Table 7-1. Typical weights by business strategy and evaluator are shown in Table 7-2.

Rewards

Although one continues to hear the phrases "Cash is king" and "Show me the money," and money is an important reward to most people, organizations often overlook other types of rewards that also have value to employees—namely, time off, recognition, and development. To some employees, these other rewards may have more value than cash. Types of

TABLE 7-1

Typical weights by business strategy and performance standards.

Strategy	Standards	Weighting
Customer Service	Results	50%
	Behaviors	50%
Quality	Results	70%
	Behaviors	30%
Innovation and Time to Market	Results	35%
	Behaviors	65%
Productivity	Results	70%
	Behaviors	30%
Cost	Results	100%
	Behaviors	0%
Human Capital	Results	0%
	Behaviors	100%

TABLE 7-2
Typical weights by business strategy and evaluators.

Business Strategy	Evaluators	Weighting
Customer Service	Customers	45%
	Supervisor	45%
	Self	10%
Quality	Customers	40%
	Peers	30%
	Supervisor	20%
	Self	10%
Innovation and Time to Market	Customers	20%
	Supervisor	35%
	Peers	35%
	Self	10%
Productivity	Supervisor	45%
	Peers	45%
	Self	10%
Cost	Supervisor	100%
Human Capital	Supervisor	40%
	Peers	40%
	Self	20%

rewards also seem to vary by type of business strategy, as will now be described.

Money

Money has a very powerful effect on employee performance and as such is the number one reward used by organizations to motivate employee performance. Although there are claims from time to time that money does not motivate, this argument runs contrary to the evidence.[4] Money can be in the form of a permanent increase to base pay or in the form of a cash bonus. When cost is the business strategy, bonuses are more likely to be used because a permanent increase to base pay compounds itself over time. Increasingly, not only are cost-conscious companies providing cash bonuses rather than pay increases, but so too are organizations with other business strategies. This approach is being taken to make bonuses more salient to employees and less of an entitlement. It is also being used to more closely correlate with business conditions so that employees become more sensitive to the larger business confronting their companies. Although bonuses are increasingly popular, most companies still provide permanent increases to pay in the form of merit pay because of the culture that has arisen around merit pay in American organizations. It is very difficult to break the merit pay expectation of employees.

Time Off

Given the increased number of family members working, time off is an important commodity to many. In order to take care of children or parents while the other spouse is working, or to attend to personal affairs, paid time off may be an option that can be provided to employees. An innovative reward such as this is obviously consistent with a business strategy of innovation. Time off may also allow people to get more rest and, in turn, be more productive and careful at work, thereby being consistent with a business strategy of productivity and quality. Time off may conflict with customer service as a business strategy because there may not be the luxury of deviations from a fixed schedule, which may be required in order to serve the needs of customers.

Recognition

A low-cost alternative to cash is employee recognition for a job well done. This approach is often used by organizations with a low-cost business strategy. Even when cost is not an issue, recognition is important because it confers status upon the recipients. It may also be an important form of social capital to the recipients, because they may become more visible to influential people inside and outside the organization. It is common to offer recognition awards for innovation, quality, and customer service in organizations.

Development

Some reward systems, especially pay for knowledge, skills, and competencies plans, help employees further develop their human capital. That is, the reward system helps them develop knowledge and skills that not only assist them in their current jobs, but also are transportable to future jobs. Rewards such as these are very important to organizations that compete on the basis of human capital. The development of human capital is important as well to be innovative, deliver excellent customer service, and provide quality products and services. Employees, especially at lower levels, sometimes overlook the value of acquiring new skills so the organization needs to carefully communicate the value of this reward.

Case Studies

CASE

1

County Engineers Office

Background information about the County Engineers Office, including the business and compensation strategies, has been detailed in Chapters 3, 4, 5, and 6. The County Engineers Office uses an individual reward system based on critical behaviors required of all employees. Behaviors were developed for all employees, rather than developing specific behaviors for specific groups, such as bargaining unit versus nonbargaining unit employees, in order to promote the strategic goal of labor-management cooperation. To do so, some generic behavioral categories, such as quantity, safety, quality, and timeliness, were used. Categories of behaviors created included leadership, ethics, teamwork (working with others), self-development, adaptability, and initiative; all of these categories are consistent with the strategy of high-performance work systems. The actual form used to make evaluations and the pay matrix are shown in Exhibit 7-2.

EXHIBIT 7-2
County Engineers Organization performance evaluation.

```
TYPE OF APPRAISAL
_____ Mid-Probational
_____ Final Probation
_____ Annual
_____ Special
```

COUNTY ENGINEERS ORGANIZATION

PERFORMANCE EVALUATION

PERMANENT PERSONNEL RECORD

NAME: _____ TITLE: _____

APPRAISAL PERIOD: (FROM) _____ (TO) _____

APPRAISAL PREPARED BY: _____ ISSUED: _____

REMEMBER: SINCE THIS RATING WILL BECOME AN IMPORTANT PART OF THIS INDIVIDUAL'S RECORD, IT IS EXPECTED THAT YOU WILL GIVE AS MUCH CARE AND ATTENTION TO IT AS YOU WOULD LIKE FROM THOSE WHO MIGHT BE RATING YOU.

INSTRUCTIONS

The supervisor should complete items 1 through 53 of this evaluation, including comments for each section, and then meet with higher supervisor to review the evaluation. After the review, the supervisor meets with the employee to discuss the evaluation. Following the rating section, the supervisor is given the opportunity to set performance goals for the next evaluation period and detail any self-improvement efforts that the employee made during the evaluation period; the employee can add to these areas during the meeting and can offer any additional comments regarding the evaluation. The rater then signs and dates the form. The employee also signs indicating that the supervisor has reviewed the form with him or her. The human resources department completes the information in the Data section. The next supervisory level then reviews the completed evaluation form, final remarks are written, and the reviewer(s) and the County Engineers Organization sign and date the form.

In order to complete the rating, indicate the frequency with which the

Performance Measurement and Rewards

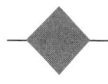

EXHIBIT 7-2 (cont.)

employee exhibits each behavior using the scale provided next to the employee's name and department:

EMPLOYEE'S NAME	N/A = Not Applicable
	1 = Almost Never
DEPARTMENT	2 = Seldom
	3 = Sometimes
	4 = Frequently
	5 = Almost Always

Supervision: the direct responsibility for the work of subordinates, including the planning and scheduling of work, performance appraisal, and policy and safety enforcement.

1. Prioritizes employee tasks to ensure work completion   N/A 1 2 3 4 5
2. Coordinates employee tasks to ensure work completion   N/A 1 2 3 4 5
3. Maintains high ethical standards for staff   N/A 1 2 3 4 5
4. Takes disciplinary steps when necessary   N/A 1 2 3 4 5
5. Promotes fair treatment of employees   N/A 1 2 3 4 5
6. Evaluates employees on a regular basis throughout the evaluation period   N/A 1 2 3 4 5
7. Evaluates employees objectively   N/A 1 2 3 4 5
8. Completes performance evaluations in a timely manner   N/A 1 2 3 4 5
9. Consistently interprets and enforces policies and procedures including work rules   N/A 1 2 3 4 5

Leadership

10. Monitors completion of employee tasks   N/A 1 2 3 4 5
11. Effectively delegates work when appropriate and applicable   N/A 1 2 3 4 5

Individual Rewards

12. Promotes good relationships between all employees and management	N/A	1	2	3	4	5
13. Provides employees with feedback	N/A	1	2	3	4	5
14. Provides guidance to others when appropriate	N/A	1	2	3	4	5
15. Organizes work activities of others to achieve goals	N/A	1	2	3	4	5
16. Provides a positive example for people to follow	N/A	1	2	3	4	5

Ethics

17. Adheres to FCEO Code of Ethics	1	2	3	4	5
18. Promotes agency/department commitment to achieve the highest degree of integrity, honesty, and ethics in the conduct of agency/department business	1	2	3	4	5

Quantity

19. Consistently performs amount of work expected	1	2	3	4	5
20. Minimizes nonproductive activity	1	2	3	4	5
21. Exceeds quantity expectations	1	2	3	4	5
22. Completes assignments on time	1	2	3	4	5

Working with Others

23. Cooperates with others to achieve common goals		1	2	3	4	5
24. Develops a positive, cooperative relationship with other agencies	N/A	1	2	3	4	5

EXHIBIT 7-2 (cont.)

25. Develops a positive, cooperative relationship with other departments — N/A 1 2 3 4 5
26. Develops a positive relationship with the public — N/A 1 2 3 4 5
27. Follows appropriate chain of command — 1 2 3 4 5

Safety

28. Follows safety rules and regulations — 1 2 3 4 5
29. Maintains safe work area — 1 2 3 4 5
30. Maintains well-organized work area — 1 2 3 4 5
31. Reports unsafe working conditions — N/A 1 2 3 4 5
32. Makes useful suggestions for safety improvements — N/A 1 2 3 4 5
33. Uses and maintains equipment in a safe and proper manner — 1 2 3 4 5

Self-Development

34. Takes steps to learn new skills on the job — N/A 1 2 3 4 5
35. Attends work-related conferences, seminars, training sessions, and educational activities — N/A 1 2 3 4 5

Adaptability

36. Learns new duties, approaches, or routines — N/A 1 2 3 4 5
37. Accepts changes in workload priorities and procedures — 1 2 3 4 5

Individual Rewards

38. Accepts changes in policies and procedures   N/A 1 2 3 4 5

___

Planning/Organizing

39. Preplans work   1 2 3 4 5
40. Organizes work   N/A 1 2 3 4 5
41. Sets priorities in completing work   N/A 1 2 3 4 5

___

Quality

42. Work assignments are accurately completed   1 2 3 4 5
43. Work assignments are completed in a neat   1 2 3 4 5
    fashion
44. Work assignments are well-organized   1 2 3 4 5

___

Initiative

45. Suggests reasonable ideas to improve work   N/A 1 2 3 4 5
    methods and procedures
46. Seeks additional knowledge and skills   N/A 1 2 3 4 5
47. Seeks additional work to perform when   N/A 1 2 3 4 5
    assigned work is completed
48. Works with minimum supervision   1 2 3 4 5

___

Accepts Responsibility

49. Accepts responsibility for own work   1 2 3 4 5
    performance

EXHIBIT 7-2 (cont.)

50. Consistently completes work assignments   1   2   3   4   5

Timeliness

51. Arrives at assigned work area by designated time   1   2   3   4   5
52. Does not leave work area before designated time   1   2   3   4   5
53. Adheres to amount of time set for lunches and breaks   1   2   3   4   5

REVIEW OF PREVIOUS GOALS:

RATER'S OVERALL COMMENTS:

PERFORMANCE GOALS FOR NEXT EVALUATION PERIOD:

Individual Rewards

SELF IMPROVEMENT EFFORT MADE THIS YEAR:

_____

_____

_____

EMPLOYEE'S COMMENTS:

_____

_____

_____

RATER'S SIGNATURE	DATE

EMPLOYEE'S SIGNATURE	DATE

My signature indicates that the form has been reviewed with me by my supervisor.

REVIEWED BY:

_____

_____

EMPLOYEE's NAME
_____
DEPARTMENT
_____

EXHIBIT 7-2 (cont.)

—DATA—

TOTAL ABSENCES SICK: _____ TOTAL HOURS SICK: _____

TOTAL ABSENCES UNDOCUMENTED SICK/UNEXCUSED SICK: _____

—SCORING—

Complete the following tally sheet.

Performance

(A) _____ Number of statements answered with a number rather than N/A.

(B) _____ Total of all the scores added together.

(C) _____ B ÷ A = Total Performance Score. Maximum equals 5.

Adjustments

		(0–7.5)	(8–11.5)	(12 +)
(D)	TOTAL SICK LEAVE OCCURRENCES _____	0	-0.25	-0.5

			(0–6.5)	(7 +)
(E)	UNDOCUMENTED SICK/ UNEXCUSED SICK _____		-0	-0.25

		(0)	(2 or more verbal or 1 or more written/suspensions)
(F)	NUMBER OF DISCIPLINES	0	-0.25

TOTAL _____
   C + D + E + F

Individual Rewards

Please place a checkmark in the box below the total score after adjustments:

0.0–0.49	0.5–0.99	1.0–1.49	1.5–1.99	2.0–2.49	2.5–2.99	3.0–3.49	3.5–3.99	4.0–4.49	4.5–5.0

For DAS purposes only:

Total, after adjustments: ☐ multiplied by 20 = ☐ GRAND TOTAL

Total Performance Evaluation Score after Adjustments

Distance from the top of your current pay range step		2.5–2.99	3.0–3.49	3.5–3.99	4.0–4.49	4.5–5.0
	3.50% or less					
	3.51%–4.00%					
	4.01%–4.50%					
	4.51%–5.00%					
	5.01%–5.50%					
	5.51%–6.00%					
	6.01%–6.50%					
	6.51% or greater					

—RATE—

PAY RANGE (CURRENT): _____   LONGEVITY: _____

CURRENT RATE: $_____

INCREASE AMOUNT: $_____

INCREASE PERCENTAGE   _____%

NEW RATE: $_____

EFFECTIVE DATE OF INCREASE   _____

EXHIBIT 7-2 (cont.)

REMARKS:

_____

_____

_____

Reviewer's Signature	Date
County Engineer	Date

CASE 2

Education Agency

The business and compensation strategies of StarNet are described in Chapter 4. A concentrated effort was made in this case to clearly show employees the line of sight from their job to the overall goals of StarNet using an individual reward system. Results were used in the performance evaluation to show what needs to be accomplished, while behaviors were used in the performance evaluation to show how to best accomplish the results. The critical behaviors shown were generated by senior management to be consistent with strategy as well as the values deemed important by senior management to the successful accomplishment of goals across business units in the agency.

Excerpts of the actual performance management manual can be seen in Exhibit 7-3. Actual strategies followed by the agency were omitted to maintain the anonymity of StarNet.

EXHIBIT 7-3

The performance management process at StarNet.

Performance Management Process at StarNet

HR Task Force

Introduction

The purpose of this manual is to provide guidance on how to link organizational goals with individual employee goals at StarNet. The manual is organized as follows:

Overview of the Performance Management Process

Organizational Strategy

Department, Infrastructure, and Program Roles, Goals, and Project Management

Individual Objectives

Calendar of Events

Overview of the Performance Management Process

Explanation

Goals at StarNet cascade from the highest level of the organization to the lowest levels of the organization. Goals must be in alignment with one another at all levels of the organization in order to ensure that organizational effectiveness is achieved.

At the highest level of the organization, goals are spelled out in general terms. These general goals include the vision for StarNet, its mission and strategic directions.

In order for the highest-level goals to be accomplished, department, infrastructure, and program goals must be carefully aligned with vision, mission, and strategic directions. This is accomplished by setting forth department and program goals, roles, and projects.

At the lowest level of the organization, goals are very specific and pertain to individual employees. They are carefully aligned with organizational, departmental, and program goals. The specific goals for each employee are set forth in the performance evaluation.

◆ EXHIBIT 7-3 (cont.)

```
           Organizational Strategy
                     │
                     ▼
     Department, Infrastructure, and Program
      Roles, Goals, and Project Management
                     │
                     ▼
            Individual Objectives
                     │
                     ▼
          Organizational Effectiveness
```

Organizational Strategy

Explanation

The StarNet strategy is defined in three documents: vision statement, mission statement, and strategic directions. Vision refers to the ultimate end state or what the organization hopes to accomplish. Mission refers to the core capabilities of the organization that enable it to move toward accomplishment of the vision. Strategic directions refer to the actual sets of activities that need to be undertaken at StarNet to meet the vision and to support it.

The vision, mission, and strategic directions are set forth by StarNet and StarNet executives for the organization. They are periodically updated to reflect changes in the environment, which must be accommodated by StarNet.

```
   Vision
     ↓
   Mission
     ↓
Strategic Diretctions
```

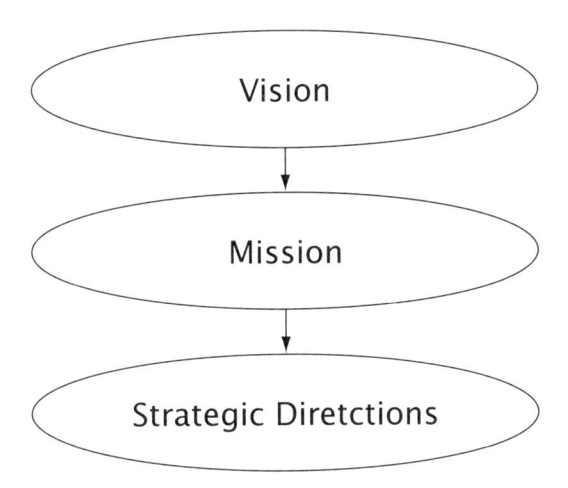

Department, Infrastructure, and Program Roles, Goals, and Project Management

Explanation

In order for the vision, mission, and strategic directions of StarNet to be enacted, departments, infrastructure, and programs must be fully integrated into the strategy of StarNet. Goals, roles, and projects are initiated by senior staff to be consistent with the strategy of StarNet. Roles refer to the expectations that departments, infrastructure, and programs have for one another. These expectations are defined in terms of both results and behaviors. Goals refer to the outputs that are needed from the department, infrastructure, and programs in order to accomplish the strategy. Project management refers to the organization of activities in an efficient and effective manner, so that the department, infrastructure, and program goals are met.

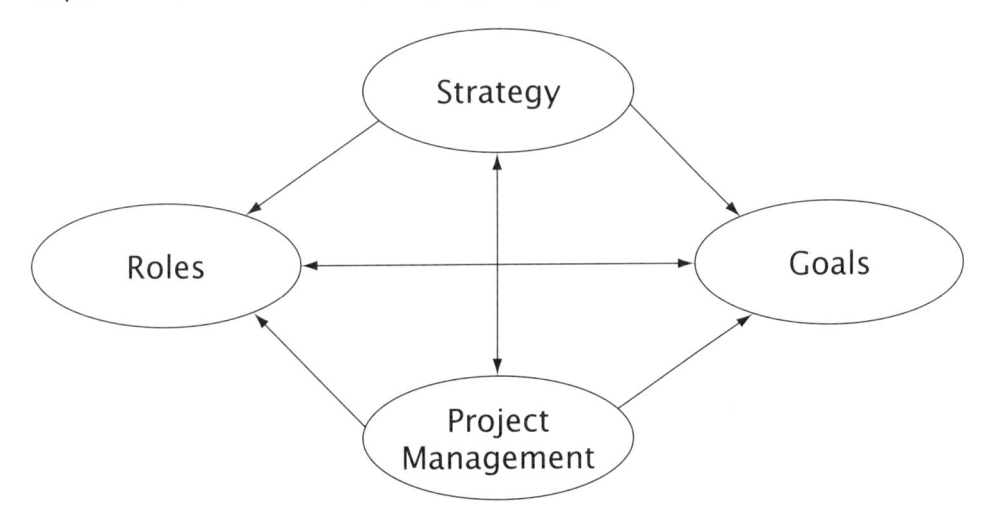

```
         Strategy
        ↙   ↕   ↘
    Roles ←→ Goals
        ↖   ↕   ↗
      Project
     Management
```

EXHIBIT 7-3 (cont.)

Goals

Goals are spelled out in the StarNet document "Programs-at-a-Glance."

Roles

Business unit expectations held by other StarNet business units.

Operations

1. Results: Project Management Methodology
2. Behaviors: StarNet Values

Results Expected

The expected results for each business unit are spelled out in the StarNet Project Methodology worksheets.

Project Management is defined by the following steps in the Project Management Manual.

- Objectives
- Standards
- Governance
- Action Plan
- Budget

Individual Objectives

Explanation

The performance planning process at the organizational, department, program, and project levels culminates in individual performance objectives for each StarNet employee. Individual performance objectives come directly from organizational strategy; from department, infrastructure, and program goals, roles, and project management; and from the job description.

Performance objectives for the individual employee are set forth in the annual performance review by the supervisors in conjunction with the employee. Some standards, expected organizational behaviors, are the same for all StarNet employees. Others, results, may vary from position to position. By having these performance standards for each position, employees should be able to see how they directly contribute to the overall strategy of StarNet and to departmental, program, and infrastructure goals.

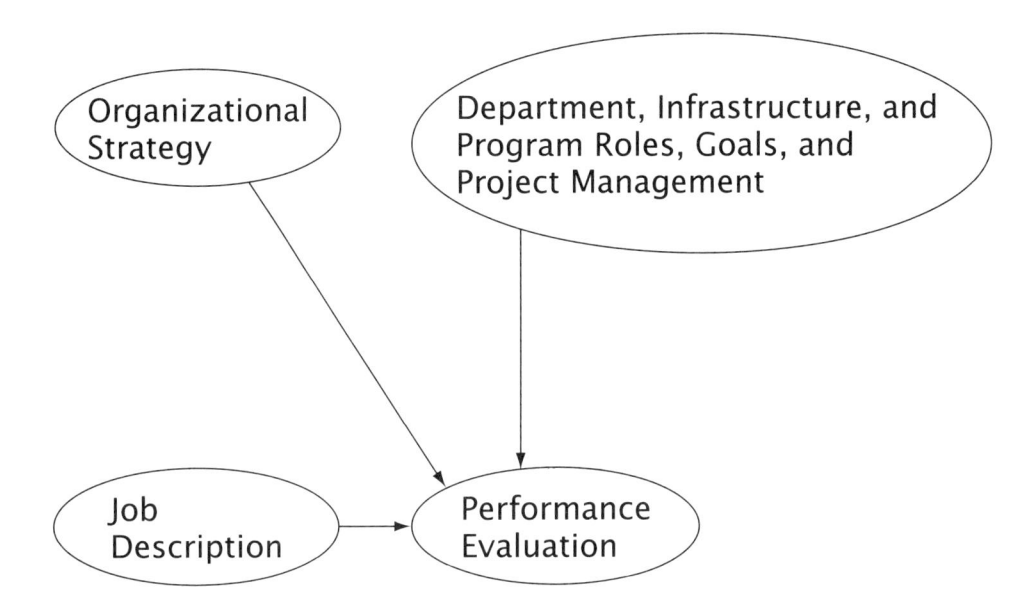

Individual Rewards

```
                                   ┌─────────────────────────┐
┌──────────────┐                   │ Department, Infrastructure, and │
│ Organizational│                  │ Program Roles, Goals, and │
│   Strategy   │                   │   Project Management    │
└──────┬───────┘                   └────────────┬────────────┘
       │                                        │
       │          ┌──────────────┐              │
       │          │     Job      │              │
       │          │ Description  │              │
       │          └──────┬───────┘              │
       │                 │                      │
       ▼                 ▼                      ▼
              ┌──────────────────┐
              │   Performance    │
              │   Evaluation     │
              └──────────────────┘
```

Performance Evaluation

A performance evaluation form has been created to evaluate each StarNet employee.

StarNet Performance Evaluation
August 4, 1998

Background Information:

Employee _____

Position _____

Immediate Supervisor _____

Date of Last Review _____

Current Review Date _____

Instructions:

Performance standards should be set jointly with the employee in June of each year. Performance objectives should be in alignment with the goals for the department and the entire organization. Objectives spell out what is to be accomplished. Well-developed objectives have the following characteristics:

183

EXHIBIT 7-3 (cont.)

- **S**pecific
- **Me**asurable
- **A**ttainable
- **R**esults-oriented
- **T**ime-dated

Performance objectives should be spelled out for each major area of responsibility of the position. A major area of responsibility is a category or segment of work defined in the job description. Most duties in the job description can be categorized into one to nine major areas of responsibility. There may be multiple objectives for each major area of responsibility.

Coaching should be provided on a quarterly review basis with each employee. Objectives should be reviewed to ensure that they are still relevant. Progress relative to the objectives should be reviewed, as should action plans needed for objectives to be met.

At the end of the year, a formal performance evaluation should be conducted. The following rating scale should be used to assess the degree to which each objective was met:

> 5 = Greatly exceeds objective
> 4 = Somewhat exceeds objective
> 3 = Meets objective
> 2 = Partially meets objective
> 1 = Below expectations

An average rating should be calculated as shown on the last page of this form. Please fill in the ratings and weights from the previous pages. It is not necessary to have nine major areas of responsibility to calculate this average.

The following scale should be used to evaluate each of the behaviors:

> NA = Not Applicable
> 1 = Almost never
> 2 = Seldom
> 3 = Sometimes
> 4 = Frequently
> 5 = Almost always

Each rating indicates the degree to which you have observed this behavior exhibited by the employee. Behaviors reflect how the results were accomplished. For each category of behaviors, the behaviors listed reflect what the employee does, how the employee acts in relation to the team,

Individual Rewards

and how the employee acts in relation to the client. If the employee's job does not require the exhibition of a behavior, mark it "NA." An average of the statements rated should be reached as shown at the end of this form.

The completed form must be reviewed with each employee. Be sure to have the employee sign the completed form to indicate that the completed form has been reviewed with him or her. The signature does not necessarily mean that the employee agrees with the review.

Results:

Major Area of Responsibility: _____ Weight: _____

Performance Objectives:

_____
_____
_____
_____
_____
_____
_____
_____

Results:

_____
_____
_____
_____
_____
_____
_____
_____

EXHIBIT 7-3 (cont.)

Rating: _____

5 = Greatly exceeds objective
4 = Somewhat exceeds objective
3 = Meets objective
2 = Partially meets objective
1 = Below expectations

Supporting Documentation (Document examples for why high (5) and low (1 or 2) scores granted):

_____

_____

_____

_____

_____

(Attach a copy of this page for each major area of responsibility.)

Results Score:

Major Area of Responsibility   Weight × Rating

1. _____ ____ × ____ = ____
2. _____ ____ × ____ = ____
3. _____ ____ × ____ = ____
4. _____ ____ × ____ = ____
5. _____ ____ × ____ = ____
6. _____ ____ × ____ = ____
7. _____ ____ × ____ = ____
8. _____ ____ × ____ = ____
9. _____ ____ × ____ = ____

Total = ____

Individual Rewards

Development Plans:

EXHIBIT 7-3 (cont.)

Behaviors:

	Not Applicable	Almost Never	Seldom	Sometimes	Frequently	Almost Always
	NA	1	2	3	4	5

Leadership:

1. Conducts staff meetings as needed to discuss issues and concerns and provide client feedback.   NA 1 2 3 4 5
2. Listens and responds effectively to staff.   NA 1 2 3 4 5
3. Leads by example, with a "do whatever it takes" attitude; willingly performs a variety of tasks, whether or not they are defined within the job description.   NA 1 2 3 4 5
4. Views all staff as team members and develops a team environment that allows all individuals to be successful by establishing policies, procedures, and goals with team member input.   NA 1 2 3 4 5
5. Communicates openly and honestly the needs and requirements of agency/section/program with subordinates and peers, keeping them up-to-date on pertinent information and events and resolving problems in a timely manner.   NA 1 2 3 4 5

Supporting Documentation (Document examples for why high (5) and low (1 or 2) scores granted):

Individual Rewards

_____
_____
_____
_____
_____
_____
_____

Total score on this dimension: _____ Total statements circled with a number rather than NA _____

	Not Applicable	Almost Never	Seldom	Sometimes	Frequently	Almost Always
	NA	1	2	3	4	5

Quality of Service:

1. Recognizes the authority, legislature, executive branch, school districts, the public, and other employees as clients.

   NA 1 2 3 4 5

2. Seeks client feedback about quality, appropriateness, and timeliness of services provided.

   NA 1 2 3 4 5

3. Maintains knowledge of clients, their environment, organization, and staff to revise the organization's delivery product and services.

   NA 1 2 3 4 5

4. Responsive to client needs through listening to comments and questions and responding in an appropriate time frame.

   NA 1 2 3 4 5

5. Incorporates the results of client feedback into individual, team, and organizational goals.

   NA 1 2 3 4 5

6. Accepts responsibilities for failed commitments.

   NA 1 2 3 4 5

7. Processes payments to vendors upon receipt of invoice in an acceptable period of time.

   NA 1 2 3 4 5

EXHIBIT 7-3 (cont.)

	Not Applicable	Almost Never	Seldom	Sometimes	Frequently	Almost Always
	NA	1	2	3	4	5
8. Informs clients of new programs, changes, and opportunities via all effective means of communication and provides them with the procedures/information they need to participate.	NA	1	2	3	4	5
9. Prioritizes tasks/jobs *efficiently* and *effectively* each time a new task/job is assigned or created.	NA	1	2	3	4	5
10. Takes criticism/critiques from clients, considers possibilities of revision, and makes decision to change.	NA	1	2	3	4	5

Supporting Documentation (Document examples for why high (5) and low (1 or 2) scores granted):

_____

_____

_____

_____

_____

Total score on this dimension: _____ Total statements circled with a number rather than NA _____

	Not Applicable	Almost Never	Seldom	Sometimes	Frequently	Almost Always
	NA	1	2	3	4	5

Professionalism:

1. Demonstrates honesty and integrity in all aspects of performance.	NA	1	2	3	4	5

Individual Rewards

	Not Applicable	Almost Never	Seldom	Sometimes	Frequently	Almost Always
	NA	1	2	3	4	5

2. Understands and can articulate the mission and goals for the organization, including work team and personal goals.	NA	1	2	3	4	5
3. Communicates to assigned supervisor, team members, and other staff the status and progress of his/her work and the impact on individual, team, and organizational goals.	NA	1	2	3	4	5
4. Accepts responsibility for achievement of individual, team, and organizational goals.	NA	1	2	3	4	5
5. Willingly seeks and accepts critical feedback regarding performance from others, including his/her direct supervisor.	NA	1	2	3	4	5
6. Understands, articulates, and willingly complies with organizational procedures, practices, and rules.	NA	1	2	3	4	5
7. Establishes friendly atmosphere for co-workers and is respectful and responsive to peers, management, and employees.	NA	1	2	3	4	5
8. Maintains composure and uses appropriate language conducive to office environment.	NA	1	2	3	4	5
9. Doesn't get defensive and maintains diplomacy.	NA	1	2	3	4	5
10. Makes good judgments about what should be documented for others and what does not need to be documented.	NA	1	2	3	4	5
11. Leaves personal problems at home and doesn't let them interfere with mission/work.	NA	1	2	3	4	5
12. Keeps his/her word on verbal and written agreements.	NA	1	2	3	4	5
13. Cancels appointments/deadlines only when circumstances are not controllable by employee.	NA	1	2	3	4	5

EXHIBIT 7-3 (cont.)

	Not Applicable	Almost Never	Seldom	Some- times	Fre- quently	Almost Always
	NA	1	2	3	4	5
14. Reschedules appointments/ cancellations within an appropriate time period.	NA	1	2	3	4	5
15. Always willing to complete project or task workload even if involves work on weekend or extra hours.	NA	1	2	3	4	5

Supporting Documentation (Document examples for why high (5) and low (1 or 2) scores granted):

_____
_____
_____
_____
_____
_____
_____
_____

Total score on this dimension: _____ Total statements circled with a number rather than NA _____

	Not Applicable	Almost Never	Seldom	Some- times	Fre- quently	Almost Always
	NA	1	2	3	4	5
Learning and Knowledge:						
1. Finds answers to questions/ problems where correct response is not readily available.	NA	1	2	3	4	5
2. Integrates established knowledge and skills into present position, utilizing information to effectively make decisions and perform work.	NA	1	2	3	4	5

Individual Rewards

	Not Applicable	Almost Never	Seldom	Sometimes	Frequently	Almost Always
	NA	1	2	3	4	5
3. Attends in-services that increase job skill level and performance.	NA	1	2	3	4	5
4. Establishes attainable goals and objectives for self.	NA	1	2	3	4	5
5. Seeks to provide unique skills and talents to the team while recognizing that other facts and skills may need to be acquired to accomplish task/job.	NA	1	2	3	4	5
6. Lifelong learning demonstrated by awareness of new thoughts and concepts to improve team and mission of agency and to effectively perform assigned job by reading current theory/books/articles.	NA	1	2	3	4	5
7. Maintains knowledge and understanding of programs provided by agency to enable appropriate feedback/responses to clients.	NA	1	2	3	4	5
8. Seeks to improve overall services/operations of agency.	NA	1	2	3	4	5

Supporting Documentation (Document examples for why high (5) and low (1 or 2) scores granted):

_____

_____

_____

_____

_____

_____

_____

_____

Total score on this dimension: _____ Total statements circled with a number rather than NA _____

EXHIBIT 7-3 (cont.)

	Not Applicable	Almost Never	Seldom	Sometimes	Frequently	Almost Always
	NA	1	2	3	4	5

Change Management:

1. Seeks information about changes in the work environment. NA 1 2 3 4 5
2. Able to synthesize the parts of others or his/her own work into a "whole" for the mission of the office. NA 1 2 3 4 5
3. Employee is proactive, not reactive to possible roadblocks. NA 1 2 3 4 5
4. Employee is flexible, modifies work/plan due to external or internal "forces" with little downtime. NA 1 2 3 4 5
5. Identifies others who have knowledge and abilities and brings them to the table when an issue is raised or strategic planning is necessary. NA 1 2 3 4 5

Supporting Documentation (Document examples for why high (5) and low (1 or 2) scores granted):

_____

_____

_____

_____

_____

_____

_____

Total score on this dimension: _____ Total statements circled with a number rather than NA _____

Individual Rewards

	Not Applicable	Almost Never	Seldom	Sometimes	Frequently	Almost Always
	NA	1	2	3	4	5

Interpersonal:

1. Recognizes when to cordially end a conversation that has potential negative consequences and/or context.   NA 1 2 3 4 5
2. Listens carefully to concerns and suggestions and responds appropriately.   NA 1 2 3 4 5
3. Seeks consensus. Uses alternative decision-making styles when consensus is not found.   NA 1 2 3 4 5
4. Values others' opinions regardless of their position or rank.   NA 1 2 3 4 5
5. Shares new information and resources gathered with appropriate coworkers.   NA 1 2 3 4 5
6. Utilizes effective communication skills, both verbal and nonverbal, that result in an ongoing, productive dialogue with staff, constituents, and clients.   NA 1 2 3 4 5
7. Attends fully to coworker's, client's, subordinate's, and supervisor's needs (no distractions).   NA 1 2 3 4 5
8. Assists others with/without being asked regardless of tasks being requested to perform.   NA 1 2 3 4 5
9. Able to assume new roles and adapt appropriately to changing circumstances/responsibilities.   NA 1 2 3 4 5
10. Respects others and can work despite differences with others to accomplish the work.   NA 1 2 3 4 5
11. Fair in processes and can articulate sound reasoning and justification for decisions.   NA 1 2 3 4 5

Supporting Documentation (Document examples for why high (5) and low (1 or 2) scores granted):

_____

_____

EXHIBIT 7-3 (cont.)

_____
_____
_____
_____

Total score on this dimension: _____ Total statements circled with a number rather than NA _____

Organization Behaviors Score:

Dimension:	(a) # items rated	(b) Total Dimension score	b ÷ a	× weight =	total
Leadership	_____	_____	_____	× .175 =	_____
Quality of Service	_____	_____	_____	× .2 =	_____
Professionalism	_____	_____	_____	× .175 =	_____
Learning and Knowledge	_____	_____	_____	× .175 =	_____
Change Management	_____	_____	_____	× .125 =	_____
Interpersonal	_____	_____	_____	× .15 =	_____
				Total =	_____

Developmental Plans:

_____
_____
_____
_____
_____
_____
_____
_____

Individual Rewards

_____
_____
_____
_____
_____
_____

Summary Evaluation:

Job behaviors score   _____ × .60 = _____

Organization behaviors score   _____ × .40 = _____

                                                                                                            Total = _____

Employee Comments:

_____
_____
_____
_____
_____
_____
_____
_____
_____
_____
_____
_____

Signatures:

_____   _____

Employee   Date

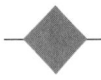

EXHIBIT 7-3 (cont.)

My signature indicates that the completed form has been reviewed with me. My signature does not necessarily indicate my agreement with the review.

_____   _____
Supervisor   Date

_____   _____
Appointing Authority   Date

Calendar of Events

Evaluation

The performance management process at StarNet takes place on a yearly basis. Goals are established at the higher levels of the organization at the start of the calendar year and cascade down to individual objectives by the start of the fiscal year. A calendar of scheduled events follows.

Calendar

January	Executive committee meeting to review vision, mission, and strategic direction
February	Departmental, infrastructure, and program meetings to review business unit role expectations
April	Departmental, infrastructure, and program goals due to fiscal
July	Individual objectives established by supervisor with employee for each position
October	Update with employees on progress toward first-quarter goals and objectives
January	Update on progress toward second-quarter goals
April	Update on progress toward third-quarter goals
July	Update on progress toward fourth-quarter goals and annual performance review

Notes

1. R. L. Heneman, *Merit Pay: Linking Pay Increases to Performance Ratings* (Reading, MA: Addison-Wesley, 1992).
2. H. S. Field and W. H. Holley, "The Relationship of Performance Appraisal System Characteristics to Selected Employment Discrimination Cases," *Academy of Management Journal* (1982): 25, pp. 392–406.
3. G. P. Latham and K. N. Wexley, *Increasing Productivity through Performance Appraisal* (Reading, MA: Addison-Wesley, 1994).
4. G. D. Jenkins, Jr., A. Mitra, N. Gupta, and J. D. Shaw, "Are Financial Incentives Related to Performance? A Meta-analytic Review of Empirical Research," *Journal of Applied Psychology* (1998): 83, pp. 777–787.

CHAPTER 8

Team Rewards

Although most reward systems are still oriented toward the individual, team-based reward systems are increasing in popularity as a result of the increased use of teams to perform work in organizations. To reinforce the importance of teamwork, or to reward employees to function in teams as well as perform their usual assignments, additional pay on the basis of team performance is often needed.

Team pay is usually provided to small groups of employees performing as intact work groups (e.g., self-directed work cell in manufacturing) or as a critical task force (e.g., new product development team). The critical point here is that the team must demonstrably add value to the organization in ways not compensated for by base pay, individual rewards, or organizational rewards.

Just as with individual rewards, team rewards need to be clearly linked to the business strategy of the organization. By doing so, the incremental value of the team can be clearly established. In particular, the standards of performance, the evaluators, and weighting steps must all be linked to the business and compensation strategies.

Standards

For team performance, the contributions of the team can be defined in terms of *what* they accomplish (results) and *how* they accomplish results (process).

Results

In the team context, *results* refers to tangible outcomes achieved by the group in such areas as sales, profit, waste, cost, and production. Results are often emphasized by organizations with cost, quality, innovation, customer service, or productivity as the major strategic goal(s).

Process

Organizations with a focus on human capital, innovation, and organizational learning as objectives are likely to emphasize the process used to achieve results. Process is emphasized in order to build human capital in the organization and to ensure that lessons learned about the most effective ways for groups to operate in the organization are deciphered, stored, and disseminated throughout the organization.

Evaluators

The team as a whole is usually evaluated under a team reward system. Thus, some evaluators different from those used for individual rewards are used to assess the team.

Team Leader

In many teams there is an elected or appointed team leader to coordinate the process and to hold team members accountable for the results. Team leaders are often asked to evaluate their teams in terms of both results and process. Organizations with a cost strategy usually stop here with evaluations because of the increased resources needed to use multiple raters. When self-directed teams are used, there may not be a permanent team leader. Instead, leadership responsibilities may be divided up among team members or team members may rotate into the leadership position for a limited duration. Under these circumstances, team leadership may not be used to make evaluations.

Team Members

Each member of the team may be asked to make an assessment of the results of the team and the processes used. Organizations with an emphasis on human capital are likely to take this approach because it helps the team members develop evaluation skills needed to be a team leader. The different perspectives are also helpful from an organizational learning perspective. Lastly, team member participation is consistent with an employee empowerment strategy likely to be found with organizations attempting to be productive, innovative, and quality- and customer service–conscious.

Senior Management

In order to ensure that the benefits of teamwork outweigh the costs of teamwork, a member of senior management may be asked to assess the performance of the team. The use of a senior manager is likely when cost minimization is the preferred business strategy. It is also likely to take place when human capital is the business strategy because the senior management can mentor the team. A senior manager can also be used for purposes of organizational learning because the senior manager can broadly disseminate helpful team processes to other teams.

Weighting

Emphasis placed on both the standards and evaluators used seems to vary as a function of business strategy. Table 8-1 shows the typical weighting of standards by business strategy. Table 8-2 shows the typical weights used by companies to weight evaluator input by business strategy.

Rewards

In a team environment, rewards are usually allocated to the team rather than to the individual. Once received, distribution of the funds can occur in one of three ways. One approach is to let the team decide how best to allocate the funds. This approach is consistent with an employee empowerment philosophy often found in organizations with quality, innovation, or human capital business strategies. A second approach is to distribute an equal share to each team member. This approach is consistent with an egalitarian compensation philosophy sometimes found in innovation- and quality-driven firms. The third approach is to provide an equal percentage of the pool based on the base pay level of each employee. This is a more

TABLE 8-1

Typical weights for performance standards by business strategy.

Strategy	Standards	Weights
Customer Service	Results	80%
	Process	20%
Quality	Results	70%
	Process	30%
Innovation and Time to Market	Results	35%
	Process	65%
Productivity	Results	80%
	Process	20%
Cost	Results	100%
	Process	0%
Human Capital	Results	0%
	Process	100%

traditional approach that is likely to be found with all business strategies and is based upon the merit pay culture in many organizations.

Money

The more value that teams add to the organization, the more likely that cash will be used as the reward. Teams are often essential in business environments with a human capital, innovation, quality, and customer service focus.

Time Off

Some teams require a large amount of work outside the normal forty-hour week put in by most employees. In recognition of this factor, some organizations grant compensatory time off for team members. Obviously, cost-conscious employers are unlikely to follow this approach.

Recognition

The more difficult it is to demonstrate the ongoing value of teams to the organization, the more likely it is that recognition programs will be used.

TABLE 8-2

Typical weights for evaluators by business strategy.

Strategy	Evaluators	Weights
Customer Service	Team Leader	40%
	Team Members	10%
	Senior Management	50%
Quality	Team Leader	0%
	Team Members	40%
	Senior Management	60%
Innovation and Time to Market	Team Leader	50%
	Team Members	10%
	Senior Management	40%
Productivity	Team Leader	40%
	Team Members	20%
	Senior Management	40%
Cost	Team Leader	0%
	Team Members	0%
	Senior Management	100%
Human capital	Team Leader	40%
	Team Members	40%
	Senior Management	20%

Also, the smaller the budget available for pay increases, the more likely it is that recognition programs will be used.

Stock

Stock options are infrequently used to reward team performance because they dilute the stock base available for shareholders. However, in some innovative, organizational learning, and human capital environments, it makes good sense to issue stock. By doing so, former team members have a vested interest to help current team members. In the absence of stock, previous team members may be less willing to help current team members perform because they no longer receive the rewards. As a result, the organization may lose the benefit of their knowledge. In a balanced scorecard environment, with an emphasis on cost as well as on the business strategies previously mentioned, a vested interest in current team member performance can be created by delaying a portion of the former team members' reward until after the current team's performance is up to the desired standard.

Case Study

CASE

1

Computer Storage Products Company

Background. Techstore is a $6 billion manufacturer of computer storage products. The company has been in business for twenty years. New product development teams are a critical factor in the company's success. A constant flow of new products must be created because once they are on the market, profit margins erode quickly as competitors "reverse engineer" the product and are also able to sell the product. Product development teams are cross-functional in nature and consist of midlevel employees from engineering, marketing, finance, and operations.

Business Strategy. The business strategy of Techstore is firmly grounded in the values of the founding partners of the company. These same values have remained at the heart of the business strategy for twenty years. One of these values is teamwork. Teamwork, along with other values and financial and customer service goals, forms the balanced scorecard that drives the company's business plans.

Compensation Strategies. The company has a strong commitment to employee involvement as part of its value system. Because of the difficult labor market in which Techstore competes, emphasis is placed primarily on external equity. There is also a strong belief that rewards should be on the basis of performance rather than on tenure with the organization.

Base Pay. Because of the emphasis on external equity in order to attract and retain talented personnel, Techstore uses a market-based pay system for base salaries. The plan works well because Techstore is in a labor market in which accurate salary data are readily available through industry, professional, and civic associations. Base pay is set at the seventieth percentile of the labor market.

Rewards. Along with many other high technology companies, Techstore uses a wide variety of reward programs to attract and retain people. There is a merit pay system to reward individual contributions along with a profit-sharing plan to reward organizational success. Spot bonuses and generous benefits are provided as well. Stock is shared with higher-level personnel.

Team Pay. The business case can be clearly made that teams add value to the business. They are the key drivers of financial success, as spelled out in the background section. Hence, even though team members already receive above-market base pay through membership in the organization and are eligible for additional individual and organizational rewards, they can also earn a team bonus because of the value the team adds to the business above and beyond the individual contributions of team members performing their functional roles in the organization.

Team performance is assessed using a balance scorecard of very specific measures. These measures include financials, customer product ratings, and team competencies based on the values of the company. Prior to completion of the product, the team meets with senior management and customers to develop performance levels for each of the balanced scorecard categories based on market projections. Evaluations are then conducted by the team, customers, and, ultimately, senior management. Because of the value-added nature of these teams, a bonus pool is budgeted in advance of actual sales for each product development team. Bonuses are distributed to the product development teams as a percentage of their salary level. Both individual and team contributions are evaluated.

CHAPTER 9

Organizational Rewards

Organizational rewards refer to those rewards provided to business units in the organization other than teams. Organizational rewards usually go to those business units with profit and loss responsibilities and sometimes to cost centers. The philosophy used with organizational rewards is that monetary reinforcement should be provided to employees when the organization is successful in meeting its business goals. Although this notion is very straightforward and consistent with the business strategies of most organizations, three potential pitfalls must be kept in mind when integrating organizational-level compensation policies with business strategy. These warnings are shown in Table 9-1. Methods to minimize these potential trouble spots will be discussed throughout the chapter.

Performance Standards

Business unit performance can be most broadly categorized into two categories: operational and financial measures.[1] Many organizations use a combination of these two sets of standards in creating organizational reward policies.

Operational

Operational standards reflect how the business unit goes about generating economic profit. It includes those internal capabilities of the organization that generate revenues and minimize costs. Typical operational standards include productivity, customer service, and cycle time.

TABLE 9-1

Potential trouble spots with organizational rewards.

Issue	Description
Line of sight	Employees may be frustrated that they cannot influence the performance standards because they are measured at the organizational level and may be outside their control. The higher the business unit level for performance standards, the more likely this problem is.
Open book	Organizational-level reward systems require executives to share operational and financial details of the company. Some owners and executives are unwilling to do so.
Economic downturn	During economic booms, organizational-level rewards can come to be viewed as an entitlement by employees and foster resentment toward the organization when rewards decline or cease upon a downturn in the business cycle.
Free riding	Usually everyone in the business unit shares in the economic gains associated with business unit performance. However, not every person may have contributed equally to the economic gains, and some employees may feel that they did not receive a reward commensurate with their contributions relative to other employees' contributions. Those who contributed less are seen as free riders.

Financial

Financial standards are usually measures of revenue, costs, profits, and shareholder value. They reflect the ultimate goals of the organization that are achieved through meeting operational goals.

Combined

Economic value-added formulas are often used to link operational standards to financial standards.[2] By doing so, line of sight issues can be minimized because operational measures are more under the control of employees than are financial measures in many organizations. Balanced scorecard approaches also help link operational measures to financial measures.[3] Exhibit 9-1 shows an example of an economic value-added tree. A balanced scorecard is shown in Exhibit 9.2.

On the face of things, many of the business strategies covered in this book fall into the financial or operational performance standards categories. For example, cost is financial, while customer service, quality, and productivity are operational. Upon closer examination, this is an oversimplification. If organizations are to overcome the problems associated with organizational reward plans, combined measures must be used. When complete information is available to employees on both sets of measures, when all employees are trained to understand and use these measures in their jobs, then the concept of open-book management has been realized.[4] Line-of-sight issues are kept to a minimum if care is taken to make operational measures under the control of employees salient to them. Resentment due to economic downturns can be decreased because employees have knowledge about how financial markets operate. Free riding can be addressed because employees have the knowledge of who does what and can police themselves. Owner concern about sharing information can be overcome because the owner can see how employees can use this information to help the owner build more wealth. Don't be misled—all of this may sound like nirvana, but it is not. It is very difficult to *eliminate* the problems with organizational-level rewards. It has been clearly shown in the research literature that the productivity gains associated with some individual rewards are far greater than those associated with some organizational

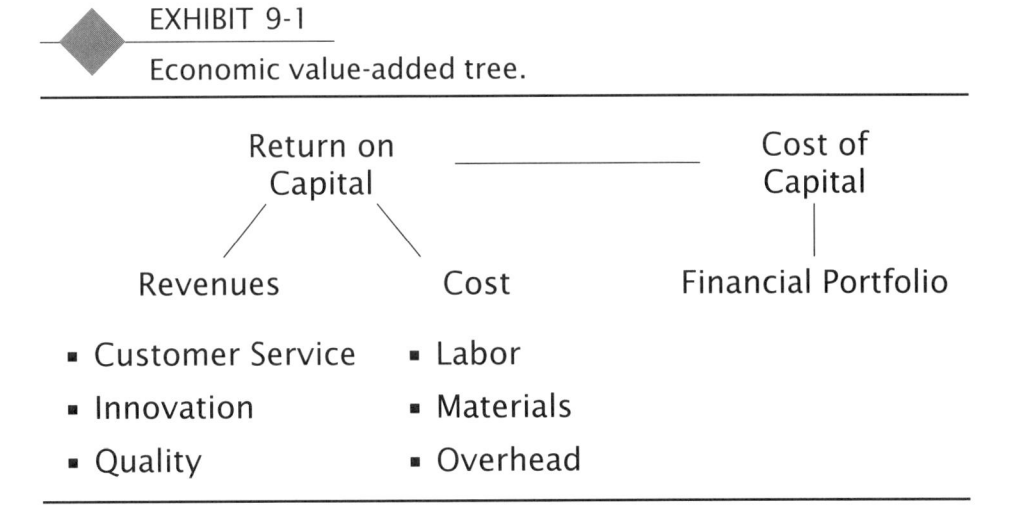

EXHIBIT 9-1
Economic value-added tree.

Return on Capital		Cost of Capital
Revenues	Cost	Financial Portfolio
• Customer Service	• Labor	
• Innovation	• Materials	
• Quality	• Overhead	

EXHIBIT 9-2
Balanced scorecard.

Performance Standard	Weight (W)	Below (1)	Results (R) Meets (2)	Exceeds (3)	Total (W×L)
Financial Goals	0.50		X		2.00
Operational Goals	0.50		X		2.00
				Total	4.00
				Average	2.00

rewards. For example, the productivity associated with formula-driven individual incentives exceeds that associated with profit sharing by a magnitude of about two to one.[5] Smart organizations use both individual and organizational rewards to capitalize on the gains associated with each rather than treating them as alternatives to one another.

Evaluators

Often overlooked in the discussion of organizational rewards is the issue of who calls the shots. There are four possible answers to this question.

Executives

An obvious choice to make decisions about organizational rewards are the senior executives of the company. Unfortunately, when they are the only source of evaluation, using them can lead to the use of discretionary organizational rewards where it is up to the executives to decide when and if to offer rewards. This approach runs contrary to the participation in decision-making philosophy often embodied in the compensation strategy of organizations pursuing a strategy of learning, quality, and innovation. To the extent that the decision-making process of senior executives is made public in advance, this is less of an issue. However, it may not create the organizational knowledge desired in some business strategies.

Controller

The controller possesses a wealth of detailed information with which to make organizational reward decisions. His or her counsel is important regardless of business strategy. If cost minimization is the strategic business objective, then the controller may have major or total say in organizational reward decision making.

Employees

Don't laugh at the thought of employees making financial judgments regarding organizational rewards. It does occasionally happen in organizations with heavy employee empowerment, such as workers co-ops. Employees can be very cautious with organizational reward decisions when their job security is on the line if faulty decisions are made. Employees are also resident experts when it comes to operational measures like customer service and quality.

Team

All of the parties just mentioned, and potentially others, can be on a team to oversee the organizational reward plan(s). Each brings distinct knowledge about various aspects of the plan, an approach that can be very helpful in terms of creating organizational knowledge and ownership around this process.

Weights

Typical weights used for various performance standards and evaluators are shown in Table 9-2 and 9-3, respectively.

Case Studies

CASE 1

Human Resources Services Providers

Background. Personnel Resources is a high-growth human resources services firm in a large metropolitan area. Human resources services provided

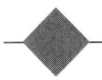

TABLE 9-2
Typical weights for performance standards by business strategy

Strategy	Performance Standards	Weights
Customer service	Operational	50%
	Financial	50%
Quality	Operational	50%
	Financial	50%
Innovation and Time to Market	Operational	60%
	Financial	40%
Productivity	Operational	70%
	Financial	30%
Cost	Operational	40%
	Financial	60%
Human Capital	Operational	70%
	Financial	30%

to small and medium-sized companies include staffing, payroll, and consulting. The company has been in existence for ten years. The corporate offices consist of the following functional areas: secretarial, computer systems, and finance/accounting. It also maintains one satellite office in a large suburban business park.

Business Strategy. The company is pursuing a delicate process of balancing growth, customer service, and innovation in order to be as profitable as possible. Recently, it has become clear that the major product lines (staffing, payroll, and consulting) have been operating very autonomously of one another to the detriment of the company. That is, the potential synergy among these units is not being capitalized upon. In conducting business with its clients, each business unit should also be attempting to bring business from the same client to other business units.

Compensation Strategy. External equity is a primary concern for the company because high turnover is detrimental to customer satisfaction. Performance is to be assessed on the basis of corporate, team, and individual performance. To do so, a balanced scorecard should be formed. All employees are thought to contribute to the success of the company, so all

TABLE 9-3
Typical weights for evaluators by business strategy.

Strategy	Evaluators	Weights
Customer Service	Executive	35%
	Controller	35%
	Employee	30%
Quality	Executive	35%
	Controller	35%
	Employee	30%
Innovation and Time to Market	Executive	30%
	Controller	20%
	Employee	50%
Productivity	Executive	40%
	Controller	40%
	Employee	20%
Cost	Executive	60%
	Controller	40%
	Employee	0%
Human Capital	Executive	30%
	Controller	30%
	Employee	40%

employees, including corporate staff, should be provided with incentives. Benefits are kept to a minimum to keep costs low. Bonuses are meant to be large enough to compensate for the lower level of benefit coverage and to serve as an incentive to remain with this smaller company rather than leave for a larger company with better benefits.

Base Pay. The base pay system is market driven, and the company pays at the market rate for corporate staff positions and above the market rate for business unit positions.

Rewards. A profit-sharing plan was created to reward corporate, team, and individual performance. This approach was taken to ensure that the business units recognized the interdependencies among the units while at the same time being aware of their own functional and individual goals. All employees were eligible for the plan. Weights given to the various areas of the business by performance goal are shown in Table 9-4.

TABLE 9-4
Typical weights for business area by performance goal.

Area of Business	Corporate-Level Performance (Operating gross margin amount)	Team-Level Performance (Operating gross margin amount)	Individual Plan Execution (Critical events and competencies)
Staffing	30%	50%	20%
Payroll	30%	50%	20%
Consulting	30%	50%	20%
Systems	80%	0%	20%
Finance and Accounting	80%	0%	20%
Reception	80%	0%	20%
Remote Site	30%	0%	70%

There are zeros in the matrix because of the lack of sound financial or operational measures of performance for staffing jobs. Also, corporate level performance is weighted more heavily for staff jobs than for line jobs (80 percent versus 30 percent, respectively) to recognize that staff jobs provide assistance to all business units, not just one. Individual performance for all employees is measured using the form shown in Exhibit 9-3.

CASE 2

Gourmet Products

Background. Gourmet Foods is a manufacturer of gourmet food products such as jams, olive oil, and sauces. It is a small, privately owned company in the Midwest. It has been in operation for thirteen years. The company consists of a kitchen, assembly line, and warehouse for distribution. A small corporate support staff and internal and external sales staff complete the labor force. The business is very seasonal in nature, with the bulk of its sales in September through January.

Business Strategy. The company prides itself on quality and the financial success of the business. Only premium ingredients are used (purchased, not raised) along with high-quality containers (glass imported from Italy). With prices at the high end of the market, financial success is driven

Organizational Rewards

Plan Execution Review Form

Name:

Position:

Immediate Supervisor:

Date:

Instructions

The immediate supervisor of the job incumbent is expected to complete a review of the job incumbent's individual contribution to the team plan using the attached form. It is to be completed on a quarterly basis. In order to complete the review form, the following steps should be taken:

1. Meet with the job incumbent at the start of the quarter to establish critical events that must be performed by the job incumbent in order for the plan to be executed.
2. At the end of the quarter, *both* the job incumbent and immediate supervisor should complete a review form for the job incumbent. A discussion should then take place to reach agreement on the level of performance attained by the job incumbent. For legal purposes, the completed form should be signed by both the job incumbent and immediate supervisor.

Critical Events

List the three most important or critical events that must be accomplished by the job incumbent this quarter in order for the team plan to be successfully executed. Evaluate how successful the job incumbent was in accomplishing each critical event.

Critical Event	Evaluation (accomplished or not accomplished)
1. _____	_____
2. _____	_____
3. _____	_____

Competencies

Evaluate the competencies displayed by the job incumbent in executing the team plan. Behavioral descriptions of each competency are attached.

Competency	Evaluation (needs development or meets description)
1. Teamwork	_____
2. Commitment	_____
3. Quality	_____
4. Business Skills	_____

Development

Indicate any areas in which the job incumbent needs further development in order to successfully execute his or her portion of the team plan.

Area	Development Plan
1. _____	_____
	_____
	_____
2. _____	_____
	_____
	_____

Overall Assessment

Indicate whether the overall assessment of individual contribution to team plan execution is satisfactory or unsatisfactory.

☐ Satisfactory   ☐ Unsatisfactory

Signatures

Signatures indicate that the form was reviewed by the job incumbent with the supervisor.

Organizational Rewards

_____   _____
Job incumbent's signature   Date

_____   _____
Immediate supervisor's signature   Date

Attachment: Behavioral Description for Each Competency

Teamwork

- Respects others' needs and negotiates when necessary
- Presumes competence of the other members
- Respects team actions and decisions over own opinion and individual agenda
- Works together to create the best group output possible
- Assists others outside the area of responsibility
- Keeps time commitments to other team members
- Gives constructive feedback
- Is willing to present opposing ideas
- Shares information/knowledge for the benefit of the team
- Supports team decisions even if not in full agreement

Commitment

- Puts in the time necessary to perform 100 percent for the client
- Chooses to live within consensus decisions even when he/she disagrees
- Keeps promises and/or commitments to others
- Meets deadlines and helps others do the same
- Follows projects through to their completion
- Strives to exceed client expectations, both internally and externally
- Believes in value and importance of what is being done, as an individual and as a team

Quality

- Delivers services that meet or exceed expectations
- Has foresight to anticipate future problems and addresses them right away
- Strives for higher levels for personal performance
- Takes the time to do a task correctly the first time; eliminates duplication of work
- Evaluates actions based on goals
- Focuses on tasks as they relate to objectives

- Ensures that the client is more than satisfied through follow-up communication
- Solicits feedback from customers regarding quality of services provided
- Shows caring attitude in every step of every interaction with the client
- Follows through and follows up on projects
- Is able to evaluate and communicate how the company's services are value-added to the client
- Proofreads and researches information to ensure information that has been passed on is accurate
- When a problem occurs, takes the time to discover what happened in order to ensure that it will not happen again
- Seeks out different ways to meet the client's needs
- Focuses on desired end result and is not restricted by systems or processes
- Evaluates actions against known best practices and responds
- Ensures consistent quality and continuous improvement

Business Skills

- Possesses phone skills for appropriate interaction with clients
- Produces documents and materials in a professional manner
- Asks for help to learn how to do something new
- Has working knowledge in utilizing and troubleshooting office equipment
- Meets with IS to discuss possibilities for improvements or enhancements to systems
- Strives to educate others about equipment capabilities
- Uses available resources
- Is competent with computer, various software applications, and all office equipment
- Understands business management and HR theories and best practices
- Understands financial concepts such as profit

---

by profit margins rather than volume. In this family business, employees, suppliers, and customers are viewed as family members. Innovation is also an important part of the business strategy because custom orders form an important part of the business.

Compensation Strategy. This small company is in a rural labor market with several large manufacturing companies. As a result, considerable emphasis is placed on variable pay to make up for the base pay differential between Gourmet Products and the manufacturing firms. Also, total rewards such as a friendly workforce, flexible schedule, and the like can be used to make up for the base wage differential. Employees are viewed as an important asset because they are a vital source of markets and new product ideas for the company. In addition, a skilled workforce is needed to maintain high quality.

Base Pay. A market-based pay system is used. Pay is set at the fiftieth percentile for small employers, and a generous benefit package is offered.

Rewards. In addition to the nonmonetary rewards mentioned, an organization-wide incentive plan was developed. Goals of the project, consistent with the business and compensation strategies, follow:

- Tied to the goals of the business
- Understandable to employees
- Employee contribution explicitly tied to reward
- Many opportunities for feedback
- Employees motivated to achieve a common goal (i.e., teamwork)
- Employees can clearly see how their performance impacts the rewards they receive
- Affordable (possibly self-funding)
- Employee commitment to plan
- Must further company vision/mission
- Improved productivity
- Stability (maintain head count)
- Increase understanding of the business to facilitate and encourage employee participation
- Employee empowerment (participation and involvement)
- Consistent administration of plan and follow-through
- Plan goals and objectives clearly communicated to employees

In order to meet these objectives, an organization-wide incentive plan was developed. Funding for the plan was based on corporate performance as measured by change in return on assets. The amount made available for cash bonuses from the funding pool was determined by business performance by the whole company relative to standards in the following categories: quality, "controllable" cost savings, and sales. Actual payouts from each of these three sources was determined by individual performance, as assessed by a performance appraisal system, and tenure with the organization. Although this is an elaborate formula, it meets the understandability objectives by employees because employees helped develop the formula and because extensive training was provided to the employees.

Line-of-sight issues with companywide performance measures were dealt with in three ways. First, only those measures were selected that employees on the design team thought were under the control of employees. For example, large capital expenditures (e.g., new equipment) under the control of senior managers rather than employees were not counted as "controllable" costs. Second, a participating governance system was established whereby employees came up with and implemented innovations to influence the organizational measures. Third, employees were trained on what these measures meant and how they would be influenced. It should also be noted that the line-of-sight issue is not as large an issue in a small company like Gourmet Products as it is in a large company.

Notes

1. J. L. McAdams and E. J. Hawk, *Organizational Performance and Rewards* (Scottsdale, AZ: American Compensation Association, 1995).
2. A. Ehrbar, *Eva: The Real Key to Creating Wealth* (New York: John Wiley, 1999).
3. R. S. Kaplan and D. P. Norton, *The Balanced Scorecard* (Boston: Harvard Business School Press, 1996).
4. J. Stack, *The Great Game of Business* (New York: Currency Doubleday, 1992).
5. G. D. Jenkins, Jr., A. Mitra, N. Gupta, and J. D. Shaw, "Are Financial Incentives Related to Performance? A Meta-analytic Review of Empirical Research," *Journal of Applied Psychology* (1998): 83, pp. 777–787; M. L. Weitzman, and D. L. Kruse, (1990). "Profit Sharing and Productivity," In *Pay for Productivity,* edited by A. S. Blinder (Washington, D.C.: The Brookings Institution, 1990), pp. 95–142.

PART 4

PAY SYSTEM ADMINISTRATION

Chapter 10: Strategic Pay Design

Chapter 11: Strategic Pay Implementation

Chapter 12: Strategic Pay Evaluation

Pay System Administration

A model of corporate business strategy and pay policy integration.

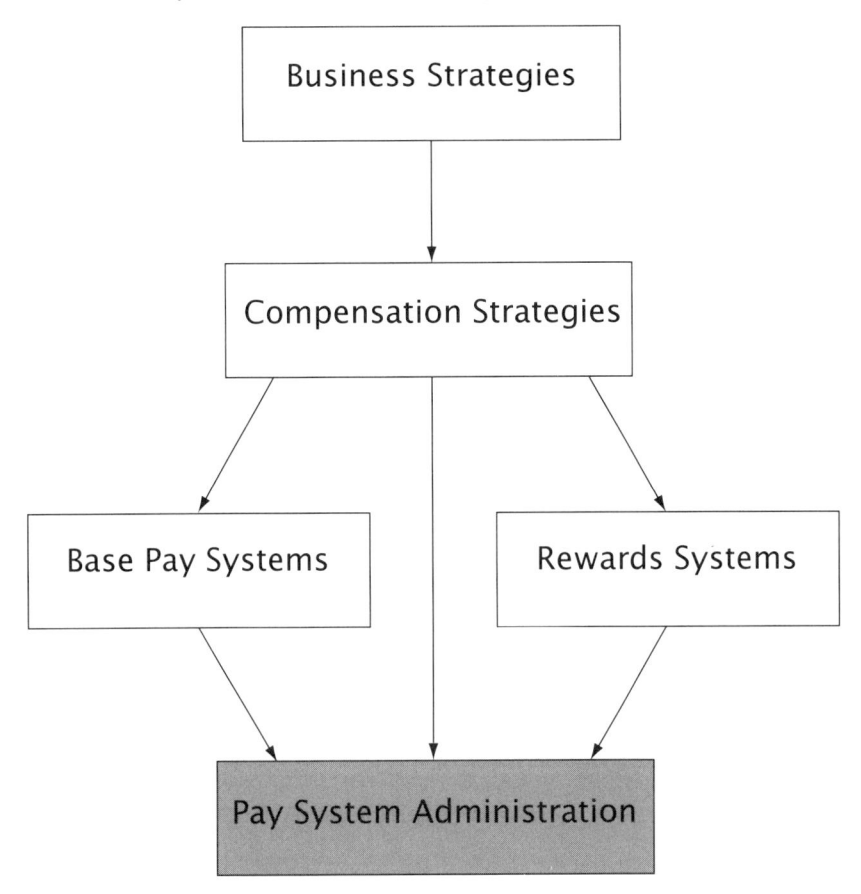

```
           ┌──────────────────────┐
           │  Business Strategies │
           └──────────┬───────────┘
                      │
                      ▼
         ┌────────────────────────┐
         │ Compensation Strategies│
         └────┬──────────────┬────┘
              │              │
              ▼              ▼
    ┌──────────────────┐  ┌──────────────────┐
    │ Base Pay Systems │  │  Rewards Systems │
    └────────┬─────────┘  └─────────┬────────┘
             │      │               │
             ▼      ▼               ▼
         ┌─────────────────────────────┐
         │   Pay System Administration │
         └─────────────────────────────┘
```

CHAPTER 10

Strategic Pay Design

Business and compensation strategies not only need to guide the determination of base pay and rewards, but also to guide the design process in establishing base pay and reward systems. As shown in Exhibit 10-1, the foundation of the design phase is the strategy.

Managers, employees, and human resources professionals draw upon these strategies to guide their actions. A design team working with each of these groups and outside consultants establishes objectives for the design. Each of these facets of pay plan design will be considered relative to business and corporate strategies. Several case studies showing how the design process is linked to business and compensation strategies will be presented as well.

Pay Plan Objectives

Pay plan objectives are essential because, when driven by corporate business strategy and compensation strategy considerations, the objectives determine the type of pay plan to be designed or the changes that need to be made to existing plans. In order for pay plan objectives to reflect the actual strategies of the organization, pay plans cannot simply be designed by the human resources group alone using documented strategic plans. In order for there to be a set of pay plan objectives that are truly consistent with the direction of the organization, the strategies must be interpreted by those who develop the strategies and who are affected by the strategy, as shown in Exhibit 10-1. Managers and employees translate written strategies into actual direction.

EXHIBIT 10-1
The design process.

```
                    Design
                   Objectives
                Outside Consultant
                   Design Team
        Senior                          HR
      Management    Employees       Department
         Business and Compensation Strategies
```

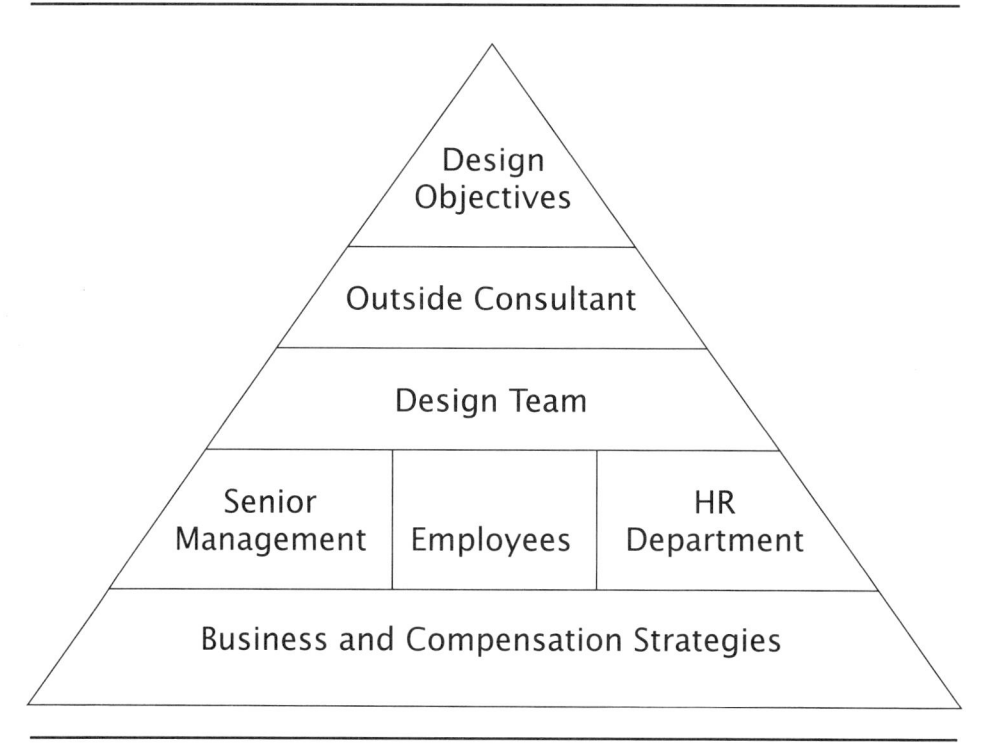

The objectives of the pay plan spell out in detail the desired end state and the scope of the project.

The desired end state indicates what is to be designed and specifies not only whether a base pay and/or reward system is to be created, but also what type of base pay and/or reward system is to be created. Each of the components selected should be consistent with the corporate business and compensation strategies as per the guidelines offered in Chapters 3–9 of this book.

The scope of the project provides guidance on who is to be covered by the pay plan to be designed. Eligibility for participation in the pay plan comes directly from the corporate business strategy and compensation strategy as well. Typical groups of employees who cause deliberation as to their eligibility include sales and support staff. Cost-driven organizations usually exclude sales and support personnel from teamwide and organization-wide reward systems. In the case of sales, this is done because sales personnel usually have commissions, and additional rewards would be an unnecessary cost. Support staff personnel are excluded because they do not directly deal with the product or service being provided. Hence, their value added to the organization is very difficult to assess, and in order to err on the side of caution, they are excluded from team and organization reward plans.

Other corporate business strategies and compensation strategies may argue for inclusion of sales and/or support personnel. Quality-driven and innovative organizations often put a great emphasis on teamwork, and if any personnel are excluded from the pay plan, then teamwork is threatened. Similarly, in productivity-driven organizations, the productivity of support staff may be just as likely to be assessed as that of line personnel.

In short, objectives need to spell out what types of pay are to be used and who is eligible for each type of pay plan used.

Standards must accompany the desired end states and scope of the pay plans to be designed. Standards allow us to gauge when the desired end states have been reached. Categories of standards for pay plan design are as follows:

- Laws and regulations to be followed
- Values to be adhered to
- Corporate business objectives to be adhered to
- Compensation objectives to be adhered to
- Products and services to be provided
- Reliability and validity of measures
- Acceptability to affected parties
- Deadlines to be adhered to
- Evaluation criteria
- Cost parameters
- Level of employee involvement
- Link to existing decision-making bodies in organization

The types of standards required by various organizations may vary by corporate business strategy and compensation strategy. Obviously, this is true for the business and compensation strategy objectives, but it may also be the case for other standards in this list. For example, in organizations that use human capital as a source of competitive advantage, there may need to be an evaluation of attendance and turnover to gauge plan effectiveness. Organizations that focus on customer service, quality, or productivity should use measures in each of these categories to evaluate pay plan effectiveness.

The Design Team

The design team plays a critical role in translating corporate business and compensation strategy into compensation policies fully integrated with the corporate business strategy. To do so, it must clearly sort out the true strategic direction of the organization from the background "noise." Because of the economic impact of the design team on the welfare of employees in the organization, there are many "noisy" factors for the design team to contend with, including employee needs, office politics, and uncertainty. As a result, it is absolutely crucial for the design team to have very talented members who are well connected in the organization and have the respect of various constituents.

There is usually a core set of design team members regardless of business and compensation strategies. This cadre includes a financial expert, a human resources expert, and a representative from senior management. Additional representation varies by corporate business and compensation strategy. When customer service, productivity, and quality are heavily weighted business objectives, measurement experts are needed in these areas. In organizations that focus on human capital and innovation, organizational development specialists are needed to ensure the full integration of the compensation system with the organic nature of business processes found in these types of organizations.

The Role of Management

Obviously, senior management is a key player in the design of compensation systems when the goal is to fully integrate compensation policies with the corporate business and compensation strategies. This need exists regardless of strategies. The senior management representative plays a critical role both in terms of content of the pay plan and process. In terms of process, the senior management representative serves as a figurehead to employees and places an air of legitimacy around the plan design. Also, the senior management representative serves as a communication vehicle between the design committee and the executives in the organization.

In order for the senior manager to be a champion for the plan, and to legitimize the importance of the plan to the organization, the senior manager should represent the core strategic capability of the organization. When cost minimization is the goal of the business, a senior manager with a financial background is needed. When customer service, quality, or productivity are being pursued as corporate business strategies by the organization, then a senior manager with an operations background is needed. In balanced scorecard environments, both financial and operational representation may be needed in order to ensure that the proper balance is struck between finance and operations. When innovation and human capital are the critical strategic capabilities of the organization, the senior human resources executive is a logical choice for the design team.

Representation from the supervisory ranks is needed as well. They are often overlooked in the design process but should not be as they play a vital role in linking the pay plan to corporate business strategies and compensation strategies. On a day-by-day basis, it is the first-line supervisor that needs to make the link for employees. Research clearly shows that compensation plans are much less likely to be effective when first-line supervisors are left out of the process.[1] As with senior managers, supervisors on the design committee should represent the strategic core of the organization.

The Role of the Consultant

It is very difficult for the design team to develop a pay plan without the use of an outside consultant. In the absence of an outside consultant, the design team is more likely to be seen as having a hidden agenda. An outside consultant can bring more of a detached perspective to bear on the design of the pay plan. The consultant should have experience designing pay plans in organizations with a similar strategic focus. This need is especially important in organizations that are using innovation or human capital as their core capability. There are many consultants who have designed compensation plans in organizations that focus on cost, quality, productivity, and customer service. There are far fewer consultants who possess the skills and experiences needed to design a compensation plan in a freewheeling environment that focuses on highly specialized personnel (e.g., scientists and engineers) in very loosely defined organizational structures needed to foster innovation and creativity.

The Role of Employees

Employee representation on the design team is a very difficult issue because there are so many employees and only a few slots on the design team for their participation. Design teams should have no more than eight to ten members in order for it to be a workable size. Usually, employee representatives should be well respected by their peers and represent the major business areas in the organization.

Representation can take forms other than design team membership. Subcommittees of employees can be formed on an as-needed basis by the design team to help carry out various parts of the design process. For example, subject matter experts may need to be brought in to evaluate jobs using a new job evaluation system. Also, groups of employees can be used as sounding boards to get employee reactions to various components of the compensation system prior to their implementation. Another form of participation is company surveys or focus groups in which employee input is sought prior to the development of components of the pay plan. While employee opinion across all employee locations is usually desirable, it is not always possible to do so due to time or money constraints. When this is the case, it is best to over sample employees from those parts of the organization most closely aligned with the corporate business and compensation strategies.

The Role of the Union

A fatal flaw in the design of pay plans in unionized organizations is to fail to include the union in the design stage. Eventually, the plan will be part of the collective bargaining process as required by labor relation laws in the United States. Union receptivity to ratifying such a plan in the union contract or as a letter agreement is much more likely when the union has played a role in developing the plan rather than being handed the plan for approval at the last minute. By participating in the process, the union has a much greater understanding of why it is designed in a certain way and has had the opportunity to solicit rank and file opinion throughout the process. Issues of concern can be worked out by the parties doing the design process prior to pressure-packed negotiations. Although union involvement in the design process does not guarantee passage of the plan at the bargaining table, the lack of union involvement at the design stage almost always results in failure at the bargaining table.

The Role of the Human Resources Department

If human resources professionals are to be true strategic partners with management, then the linking of compensation policies to corporate business strategies is a crucial task confronting the HR department. HR people are urgently needed to make this link because they possess full knowledge of the components of pay, such as job evaluation, that must be linked with strategy for a complete integration to occur. Note, however, that a traditional HR person will not be able to successfully fulfill this role. Traditional HR is reactive and focuses on administration rather than on the strategy of the organization. Contemporary HR is proactive and focuses on the aims of the business.[2] Therefore, the HR representative must be well versed in business as well as in human resources methods. In addition, the skilled HR professional on the design team needs to have the analytical skills required to show the validity of the designed compensation system. The competence just described is seldom gained through experience alone. A master's degree in human resources is needed from a top-notch program.

The HR representative on the team must be well networked in the organization's HR staff as well. As will be seen in the next chapter, the compensation system needs to be fully integrated with the performance management system, career development system, payroll system, human resources information system, staffing system, and training system.

Case Studies

Design teams used in some of the previous cases in the book will now be described.

CASE 1

Educational Distributor

The details of this case are presented in Chapters 3, 4, 5, and 6. The design team consisted of the CFO, operations manager, human resources manager, and the consultant. In order to ensure representation by lower-level employees, subcommittees were created and led by design team members. Usually, the human resources manager served as head of the subcommittees because of the time pressures on the CFO and operations manager.

Pay System Administration

Subcommittees were formed around major project segments (e.g., job analysis, job evaluation, market surveys, performance appraisal). Employees from all levels and functions served on these subcommittees and developed recommendations such as job evaluation factors for the design team.

CASE 2

County Engineers Office

The details of this case are presented in Chapters 3, 4, 5, 6, and 7. The design team consisted of the chief of engineering, the chief of operations, the manager of human resources, a human resources generalist, an engineer, and an operations manager.

Because the operations workforce was represented by a union, the local union president served on the committee, as did a staff person from the national union. Both the national union and the local union needed to be represented because the staff representative of the union coordinated bargaining of similar employees in the geographic region. The two union members played a vital role on the committee vehicle with rank and file members to assess the receptivity of the proposed changes throughout the process. They also were at the table for collective bargaining, so they had a thorough understanding of the issues to be bargained over regarding wages. Bargaining went very smoothly because many of the potential sticking points had already been resolved during design team meetings. Lastly, the union members brought some very helpful wage survey data collected by the union to the design team.

In order to ensure employee participation in the process, additional employees were used in the job analysis and job evaluation stages. They were needed not only for employee participation reasons, but also as "subject matter experts" to ensure that accurate descriptions of the job were generated and that accurate evaluations were made as well.

Another subcommittee was created with senior management of the organization to ensure that the strategic objectives of the county were being met. It would meet periodically before design team meetings to go over issues so that management could present a unified front during discussions with the design team.

Strategic Pay Design

CASE 3

Computer Storage Products Company

The background of the Techstore case appears in Chapter 8. The design team for this project consisted of two consultants and an internal organizational development consultant. A very small design team was consistent with the lean organizational structure at Techstore as well as the need for a short cycle time in its business process. Greater representation would have meant slower development of the team pay plan.

Although very small, the design team interacted with a variety of constituents. There was frequent interaction with the chief financial officer to ensure that the financial requirements of the plan were realistic. A subcommittee of seasoned team members was convened to conduct a needs analysis. Performance measures were developed with a subcommittee of operations managers. The evaluation process was constructed with a subcommittee of executives. The entire design team usually met with each one of these constituent groups.

Notes

1. J. L. McAdams and E. J. Hawk, *Organizational Performance and Rewards* (Scottsdale, AZ: American Compensation Association, 1995).
2. D. Ulrich, *Human Resource Champions* (Boston: Harvard Business School Press, 1997).

CHAPTER 11

Strategic Pay Implementation

A properly implemented compensation plan must "fit," or be consistent with, the corporate business strategies, compensation strategies, and other human resources policies, as shown in Exhibit 11-1. In order for these strategies and policies to fit with one another, sound design alone will not do. Additional action steps need to be taken. Alignment, as shown in Exhibit 11-2, is achieved by providing training for the pay plan, communicating the pay plan, and rewarding employees. Integration is achieved by linking the compensation plan to staffing, development, human resources information systems, and payroll policies, as shown in Exhibit 11-3. Both sets of activities will be reviewed and several cases will be presented to illustrate these points.

Alignment

The translation of the newly designed compensation plan to employee behaviors consistent with the corporate business strategies and compensation strategies is not automatic. Training, communication, and reward activities must be carefully implemented.

Training

Extensive training needs to take place in order for business plans and compensation policies to be firmly connected in the minds of employees. It is extensive training because both employees and managers need to be trained. It is also extensive because not only must the training program

EXHIBIT 11-1

The concept of strategic fit.

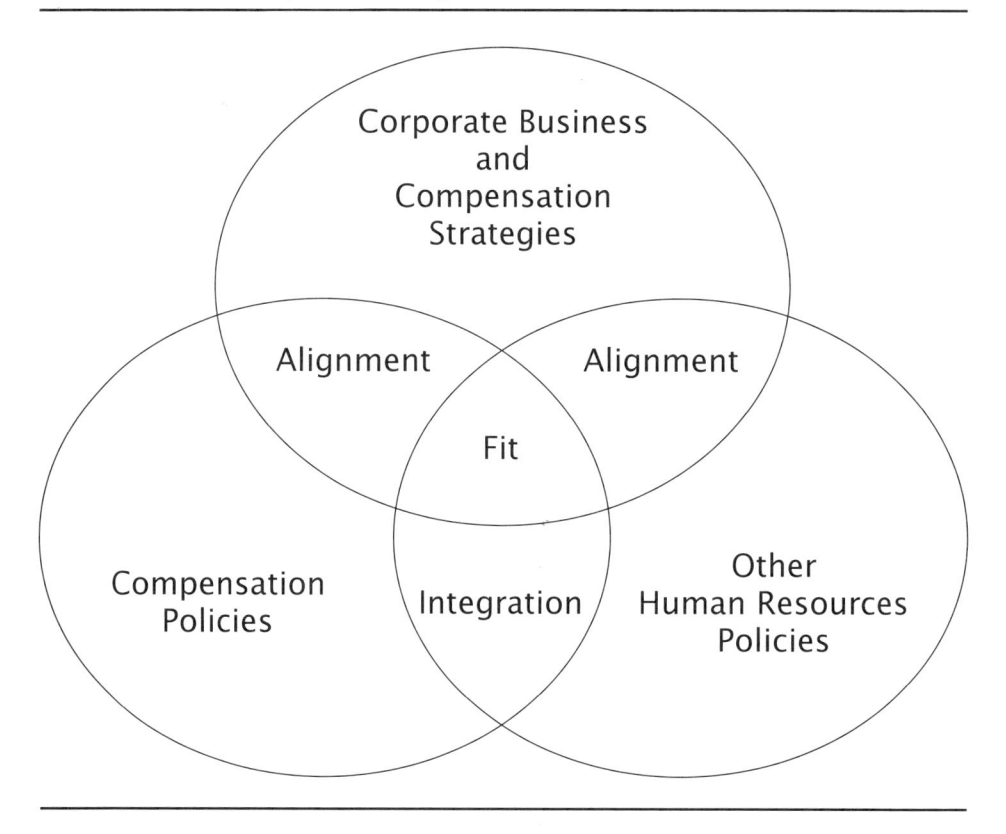

```
           Corporate Business
                  and
            Compensation
              Strategies

         Alignment    Alignment
                  Fit

   Compensation            Other
     Policies    Integration  Human Resources
                              Policies
```

show how the pay system is intended to work, but it must also show how to make the pay system work best.

Management Training

Managers need to learn how each component of the compensation plan is consistent with the corporate business and compensation strategies. Hence, more than the mechanics of each pay plan component must be discussed. For example, managers need to be shown how each factor in the job evaluation system relates back to corporate business objectives. By doing so, three advantages are likely to be attained. First, managers are likely to view the compensation plan as a device that facilitates accomplishment of their business objectives, rather than as a paperwork exercise from the human resources department that is an obstacle to the accomplishment of their business objectives. Second, this type of training is likely

Strategic Pay Implementation

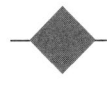

EXHIBIT 11-2
The concept of alignment.

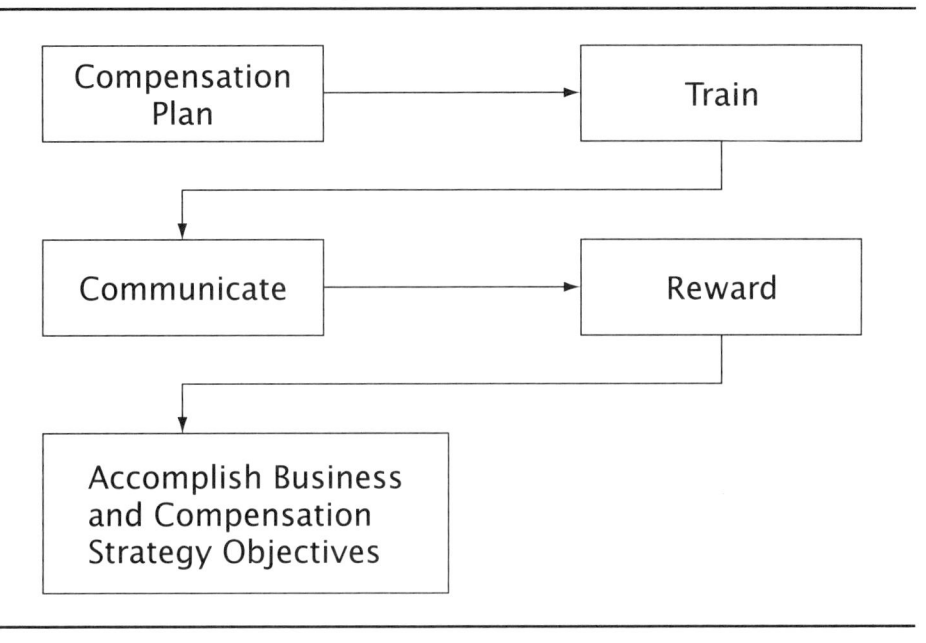

```
┌──────────────┐         ┌──────────────┐
│ Compensation │────────▶│    Train     │
│     Plan     │         │              │
└──────────────┘         └──────────────┘
       │                        │
       ▼                        │
┌──────────────┐         ┌──────────────┐
│ Communicate  │────────▶│    Reward    │
└──────────────┘         └──────────────┘
       │
       ▼
┌──────────────────────┐
│ Accomplish Business  │
│ and Compensation     │
│ Strategy Objectives  │
└──────────────────────┘
```

EXHIBIT 11-3
The concept of integration.

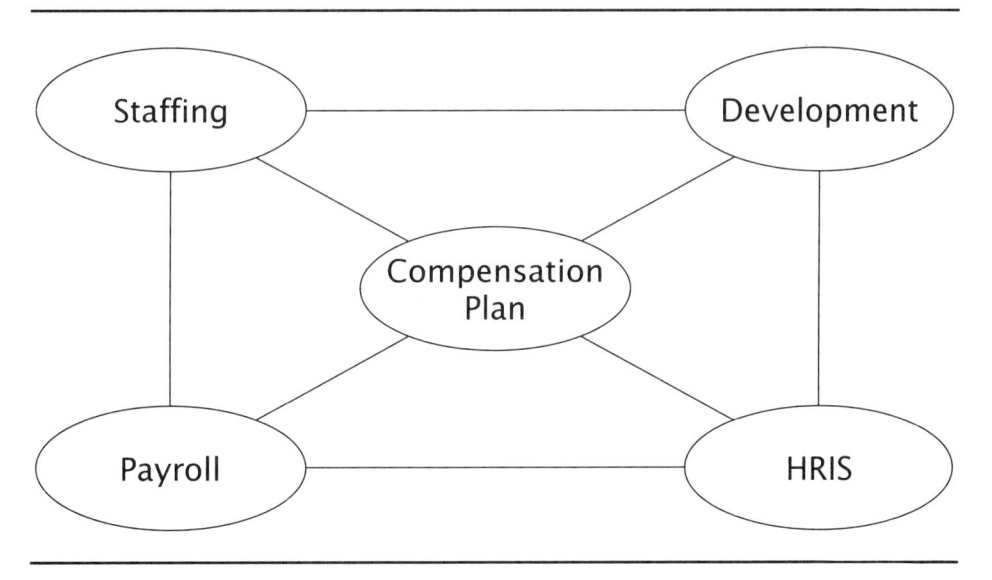

```
    Staffing ────────────── Development
       │  \              /      │
       │    \          /        │
       │    Compensation        │
       │       Plan             │
       │    /          \        │
       │  /              \      │
    Payroll ──────────────── HRIS
```

to eliminate common evaluation errors made by managers in compensation decision making, such as:

>Halo Error: Rating all aspects of performance above average when not deserved
>
>Horns Error: Rating all aspects of performance below average when not deserved
>
>Central Tendency Error: Rating all aspects of performance average when not deserved

Third, there is a much better chance that managers will spend time explaining the compensation system to employees because the managers both understand and appreciate each component of the compensation plan.

Employee Training

As with managers, employees also need to be trained on each of the components of a new compensation plan. The training they receive, however, needs to emphasize how they can best impact the measures that will help them maintain or improve upon their pay status. One way to do so is to work in small groups with employees to brainstorm ways that they can best go about influencing their pay in a manner consistent with the business and compensation objectives of the organization.

Communications

As previously pointed out, individual and small-group discussions with the immediate supervisor are more likely to produce the desired results than are mass training sessions by the HR department or written communications about the plan alone. Of course, larger meetings with the HR department can be used to set the stage for follow-up discussions with the supervisor. Also, written communications can be distributed to employees after these conversations in order to reinforce the principles. An example of a written communication of this nature is shown in the Appendix (see pages 293–316).

Timing

Most often, pay is distributed to satisfy the goal of administrative ease rather than that of having maximum impact on employee behavior to be consistent with corporate business goals. Probably the best example here is the use of employee anniversary dates to make merit increase decisions. If employee actions are to be aligned with the goals of the organization, then the payouts of compensation plans should mirror the business cycle of the organization as closely as possible. Thus, for example, common review dates for merit pay reviews can be made consistent with yearly financial results of the organization.

Integration

Pay systems are not likely to be viewed as credible by employees unless they are fully integrated with one another. For example, a competency-based pay system is not likely to work unless there are training opportunities for employees to develop specific competencies required by the organization.

Staffing

Pay goals are unlikely to be reached if the wrong people are selected. That is, the applicants chosen must have the requisite knowledge, skills, and abilities to master the job at a level such that they have the capacity to influence the outcomes needed to maintain or improve upon their pay status. In addition, the pay system can be self-defeating if it leads to the decline of job offers by qualified job applicants because the compensation plan components don't match up with employee preferences. This is a very important issue, as evidenced by recent research showing that employees do not favor the latest forms of rewards offered by employers: variable pay and team pay. Instead, they prefer permanent additions to base pay based on individual performance, as in merit pay systems.[1]

Development

As organizations shift to person-based pay systems such as skill-based pay and competency-based pay, the stakes for developmental opportunities for employees increase. While general training and development activities are common in organizations, the development of firm-specific competencies is a source of competitive advantage for companies.[2] A real synergy is likely to occur between staffing and compensation systems when person-based pay is used. Even when traditional merit pay plans are used, a developmental portion can be attached to the performance standards. Employees are far more likely to act on these development plans when they lead to the development of competencies consistent with the goals of the organization, which in turn may produce a performance increase associated with a pay increase.

HRIS

An HRIS can be very helpful in lessening the burden of pay reviews by supervisors. As a result, they can focus more on the substance of pay systems (i.e., linking individual to organizational goals) rather than worry about filling out the proper form at the proper time. A sound HRIS when networked with the compensation plan can automatically bring the review to the supervisor's attention, provide real-time training online, and automatically make changes to pay and distribute them to employees. In addition, real-time spreadsheets can be made available to supervisors to financially model alternate compensation decisions that they make.

Payroll

It is crucial that a compensation plan interface with the payroll system. Otherwise, many of the other elements of total compensation (e.g., workers compensation) may not be made part of compensation decision making. As a result, overestimates or underestimates may be made as to the real cost of new pay programs to organizations. For example, increases to base salary often lead to increases in pensions that must be included to determine the real costs of pay plans. Also, real-cost figures have a bearing on the communication of pay to employees. Employers need to get as much credit as possible with employees for their total contributions to employee income.

Case Studies

Because training is such an important component of successful implementation, several examples of training used by companies will now be presented.

Strategic Pay Implementation

CASE 1

Gourmet Products

Background information on Gourmet Products appears in Chapter 9. The design team conducted a daylong training program with all Gourmet Products employees to introduce the organization-wide incentive plan. All of the design team members, not just the consultant, led the training in order to give credibility to the incentive plan. People were trained in the mechanics of the plan and in the financial and operational measures used in the payout formula. Because the employees were more knowledgeable about the operational measures used in the formula as a result of their day-to-day activities, more time was spent on return on assets (ROA). ROA was used to fund the plan. In essence, the pay plan served as a lead system (described in Chapter 2) to present a model of the business to all the employees for the first time. The goal here was, of course, to bring the interests of the owners and employees in alignment with one another for mutual gain.

An important feature of the training was to divide the employees into breakout groups to discuss the business model and to develop activities that they could undertake in their positions to influence the success of the business. Breakout groups were formed around each of the operational measures: quality, sales, controllable costs, and individual performance. The groups then shared the results of their discussions with the other groups. A copy of the actual training outline is shown in Exhibit 11-4.

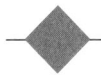

EXHIBIT 11-4
Training outline.

Training Objectives:
1. To create enthusiasm for the new gain-sharing plan
2. To communicate company commitment to the success of the new plan
3. To create employee commitment to the plan
4. To communicate the parameters of the new plan in a way that is easily understandable to employees
5. To teach employees how they can influence the variables within the plan to maximize their own gain and enhance the success of the company

Pay System Administration

I. Overview of agenda (including all of the elements to follow)
II. Welcome and introduction
   A. Goal; communicate company commitment to and enthusiasm for the plan
   B. Include company mission
III. Introduction of the committee members and the process
   A. Explanation of the process
   B. Overview and explanation of plan objectives (see attached sheet)
IV. What is gain-sharing?
   A. What do employees think gain-sharing is?
   B. Definition
      1. Based on individual, group, and company performance
      2. Tie back to mission statement
V. The plan
   A. Brief overview of entire plan
   B. Main goals of plan (explain slight difference between these and committee goals)
      1. Something that reflects the goals of the company
      2. Something that employees could influence
      3. Something that allows employees to share in the gains generated by their efforts
   C. Participation—all current employees are eligible to participate with the exception of the owners
      1. Fair
      2. Larger "pot to share"
   D. Review of specific measures of the three-step plan
      1. Financial measures
         a. Financial model of company
         b. Terms and definitions
         c. Overview of ROA and how employees can influence it
      2. Employee performance measures
         —Purpose—important to company and capable of being influenced by employees
         —Review of the four "buckets" and percentages attributable to each
         a. Quality (group measure)
            1. Measures of quality to be used—amount of scrap minus that attributable to shipping company error
            2. Amounts of payout
            3. Review the basis for historical and projected standards
            4. Review feedback methods—how will employees know their progress
         b. Sales (group measure)
            1. Measure of sales to be used—growth in quarterly sales
            2. Amounts of payout
            3. Reiterate historical versus projected standards

Strategic Pay Implementation

           4. Review feedback methods—how will employees know their progress
        c. Costs (group measure)
           1. Measures of costs to be used
           2. Amounts of payout
           3. Reiterate historical versus projected standards
           4. Review feedback methods—how will employees know where they stand
        d. Performance (individual measure)
           1. Review performance appraisal form and proper techniques for using the form
           2. Amounts of payouts—review percentages
           3. Review feedback methods—how will employees know where they stand
      3. Seniority and individual pay level—review percentages and methods of calculation
    E. Sample plan calculation
VII. Administration of the plan
    A. Administered by controller
    B. Review committee
      1. Composed of three senior-level managers and one elected member from each of the four METLs teams
      2. Quarterly meetings
      3. Purpose—to help develop suggestions as to how employees can maximize their rewards by impacting the above criteria
    C. Special issues—may contribute gain-sharing funds to 401(k) without company matching
VIII. Goal setting
    A. Explanation of goal-setting theory—why it is important
    B. Breakouts—divide into approximately eight groups of six. The groups will be assigned the task of determining how they can impact the plan criteria individually and as members of the group. Two groups will be assigned to each of the following:
      1. Sales
      2. Quality
      3. Costs
      4. Individual performance
IX. Questions and answers

Pay System Administration

CASE 2

Computer Storage Products Company

Background information on Techstore is presented in Chapter 8. A three-phased training program was needed at the company to mirror the three sets of evaluators used in the team pay system: senior management, team members, and customers. Although the performance criteria used by all three groups differed to reflect the different opportunities that they had to observe team performance, the same heuristic was used. Cases were created based on actual team performance data available in the archives. The evaluators then made evaluations using these cases in small groups. They then received feedback from other evaluators in their groups as well as design team members as to the accuracy of their ratings and the subsequent impact on bonuses. This exercise was prefaced with instruction on how the system works and how to make accurate assessments.

CASE 3

Lawn Care Products

Background. Lawn Food is a large manufacturer of lawn-care products. It is located in a rural area and has been in business for over twenty years.

Business Strategy. A balanced scorecard approach is used by the company. Emphasis is placed upon developing high-quality and innovative lawn-care products at a reasonable price. Employee teamwork is believed to be the key to being highly productive and in turn keeping costs down.

Compensation Strategy In order to foster innovation, teamwork, quality, and productivity, the compensation system needs to be flexible, responsive to business needs, and heavily influenced by employee contributions to Lawn Food.

Base Pay. Flexibility is established by using broad-banded job classifications linked closely to market pay. Pay is set at the fiftieth percentile of the market.

Strategic Pay Implementation

Rewards. Team-based and organizational incentive plans are used throughout the organization at both the plant and corporate levels to emphasize performance. The plans must pay for themselves in order to minimize costs. Individual productivity is stressed as well and is reinforced by setting individual objectives for each position.

Training. The human resources group is charged with helping each Lawn Food employee develop a performance plan that is tied to merit pay increases. Training provided to the human resources department by a consultant and the vice president of human resources is shown in Exhibit 11-5.

◆ **EXHIBIT 11-5**
Topical outline.

Day One

- I. Introduction
- II. Performance management process
- III. Developing a performance plan
- IV. The scanning process
- V. Developing performance standards

Out-of-class assignment

Day Two

- VI. Critique of performance standards
- VII. Developing action plans
- VIII. Teaching the process to others
- IX. Application goals back at work
- X. Conclusion and next steps

- I. Introduction
  - A. Objectives
    1. To develop performance goals that are measurable, valid, and fair
    2. To develop and be conversant about performance planning at Lawn Food
  - B. Process
- II. Performance management process
  - A. Why it is important
  - B. Objectives
  - C. Steps

Performance Management Process

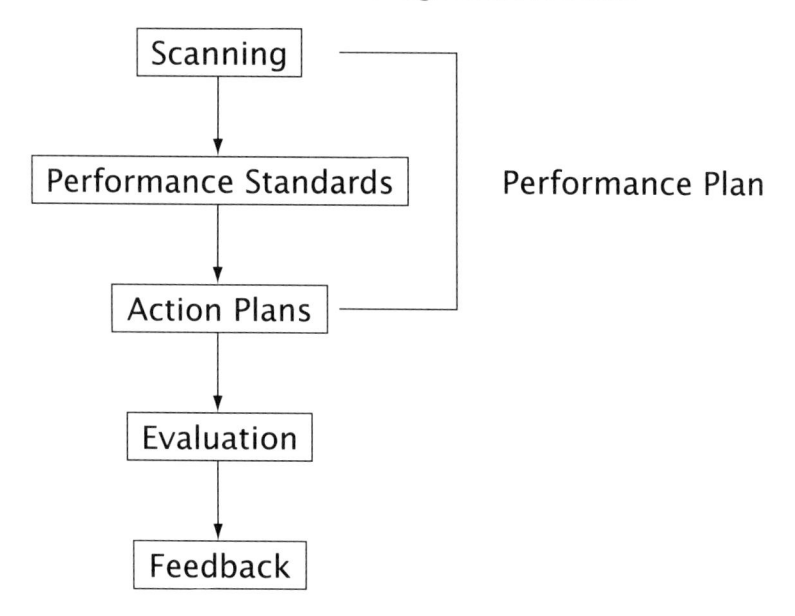

```
        Scanning ─────────┐
            │              │
            ▼              │
    Performance Standards  │   Performance Plan
            │              │
            ▼              │
       Action Plans ───────┘
            │
            ▼
        Evaluation
            │
            ▼
         Feedback
```

III. Developing a performance plan
  A. Steps
  B. Documentation

Strategic Pay Implementation

Developing a Performance Plan: Steps

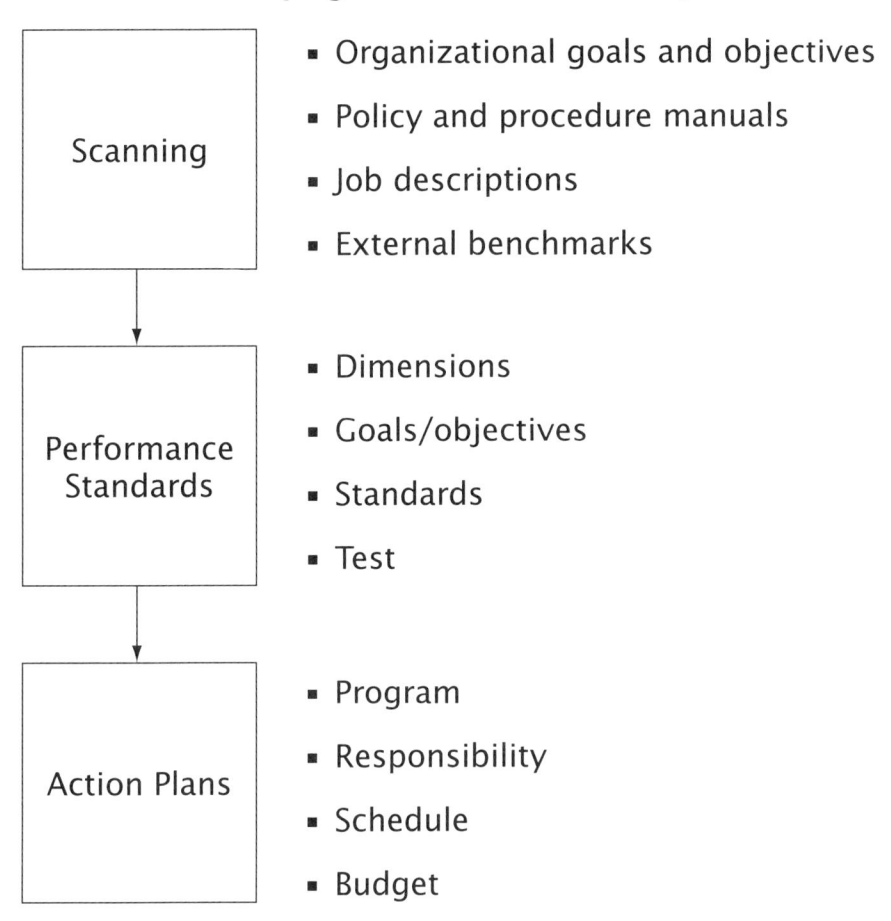

Scanning
- Organizational goals and objectives
- Policy and procedure manuals
- Job descriptions
- External benchmarks

Performance Standards
- Dimensions
- Goals/objectives
- Standards
- Test

Action Plans
- Program
- Responsibility
- Schedule
- Budget

Developing a Performance Plan: Documentation

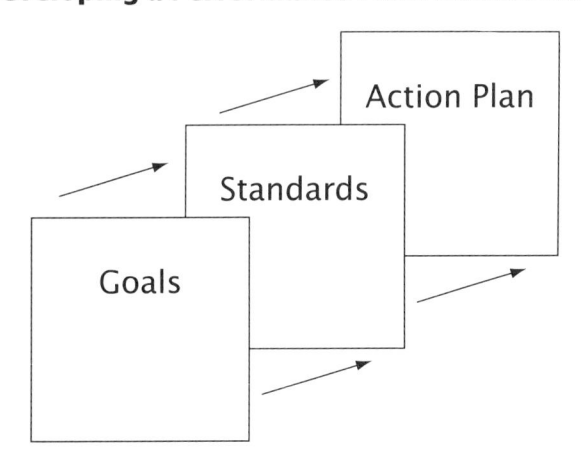

Goals → Standards → Action Plan

IV. The Scanning Process
   A. Organizational goals and objectives
   B. Policy and procedure manuals
   C. Job descriptions
   D. External benchmarks

Planning Process

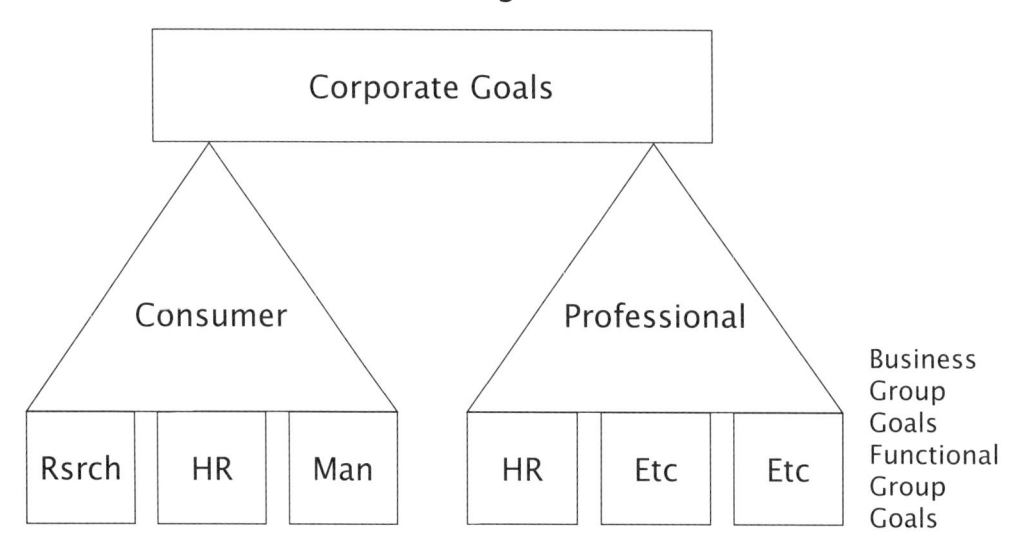

```
                    ┌─────────────────────────┐
                    │     Corporate Goals     │
                    └─────────────────────────┘
                       /                    \
                  Consumer              Professional       Business
                                                           Group
                                                           Goals
         ┌──────┬──────┬──────┐     ┌──────┬──────┬──────┐ Functional
         │Rsrch │  HR  │ Man  │     │  HR  │ Etc  │ Etc  │ Group
         └──────┴──────┴──────┘     └──────┴──────┴──────┘ Goals
```

V. Developing performance standards
   A. Dimensions
   B. Goals/objectives
   C. Standards
   D. Test
   E. Assignment for next time

Strategic Pay Implementation

Performance Dimensions

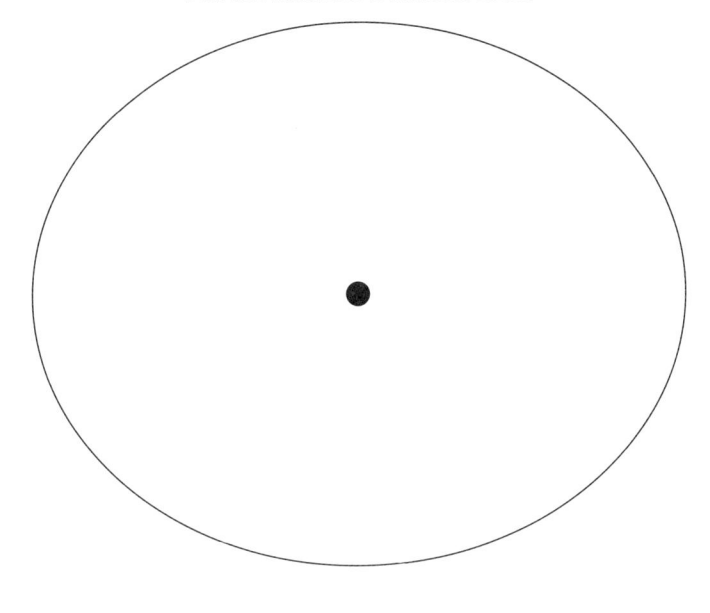

Goals
_____
_____
_____
_____
_____
_____
_____

Standards
_____
_____
_____
_____
_____
_____
_____

Checklist to Test Standards

Effective standards should be:
1. Complete
2. Free from bias
3. Consistent with the business plan
4. Measurable
5. Specific
6. Challenging
7. Realistic
8. Critical to the success of the position
9. Under the control of the employee

   VI.   Critique of performance standards
        A. Content
           1. Process followed
           2. Actual standards
        B. Process
           1. Teams
           2. Entire class
   VII. Developing action plans
        A. Purpose
        B. Components
           1. Program
           2. Responsibility
           3. Budget
           4. Schedule

Strategic Pay Implementation

Action Plan

Program (list steps)	Responsibility (list people)	Schedule (completion dates)	Budget (time and money)

VIII. Teaching the process to others
   A. Motivation to learn
   B. Skills to impart
   C. Resources to use

IX. Exercise: Application goals back at work

Goals

_____

_____

Obstacles

_____

_____

Solutions

_____

_____

X. Conclusion and next steps

Notes

1. P. LeBlanc and P. Mulvey, "How American Workers See the Rewards of Work," *Compensation and Benefits Review* (1998): 30, pp. 24–28; D. M. Cable and T. A. Judge, "Pay Preference and Job Search Decisions: A Person-Organization Fit Perspective," *Personnel Psychology* (1994): 47, pp. 317–348.
2. J. B. Barney, "Firm Resources and Sustained Competitive Advantage." *Journal of Management* (1991): 17, pp. 99–120.

CHAPTER 12

Strategic Pay Evaluation

Executives expect to see a return on the investment (ROI) that they make in compensation systems. Compensation systems can be huge investments. In service organizations, for example, the direct cost of total compensation is 70 percent or more. In very large organizations, the direct cost can be in the billions of dollars. These large figures do not even include the indirect costs of designing and administering compensation systems. Given these large costs, it can certainly be argued that the evaluation of compensation systems is the most critical step in pay system administration. The goal with evaluation is to assess, if, indeed, compensation is linked to the corporate business goals, and to see if this link generates a return on the investment. The purpose of this chapter is to examine how to tell if the pay plan is actually working.

Measures

The measures that we use to assess pay plan effectiveness come in various forms:

Level 1: Attitudes
Level 2: Behaviors
Level 3: Operational Results
Level 4: Financial Results

The closer the categories of measures are to level one, the more they are under the control of employees and are likely to show a positive gain as a result of the pay plan. The closer the categories of measures are to level four, the more difficult it is to show a positive gain for the pay plan because these results are less under the control of employees and subject to other forces (e.g., technology, business cycle). The different types of measures for each category are:

Attitudes

- Pay satisfaction
- Job satisfaction
- Pay-for-performance perceptions

Behaviors

- Absenteeism
- Turnover
- Job performance

Operational Results

- Quality
- Productivity
- Waste

Financial Results

- Costs
- Sales
- Profits

In addition to being influenced by the amount of control employees have over outcomes, the level of gain that we can expect varies by business strategy:

Objective	*Measure Category*
Customer service	- Operational Results
Quality	- Operational Results
Innovation	- Attitudes
	- Behavior
Productivity	- Operational Results

Objective	Measure Category
Cost	• Financial Results
Human Capital	• Attitudes
	• Behavior

The closer our evaluation measure is to the purpose of the pay plan, the more likely we are to be able to demonstrate a gain in effectiveness.

The amount of gain that we can demonstrate also varies by the reliability of our measures. Low reliability limits the gains that we can show with our effectiveness criteria. The use of multiple evaluators and multiple measures in each category helps improve reliability. The end result of this discussion is that we must choose our criteria carefully to show the effectiveness of our compensation plans:

- Lower-level measures are more likely to show success than higher-level measures.
- The level of measuring effectiveness should be closely matched to the level of the objectives of our compensation plan in order to demonstrate success.
- Care must be taken to measure variables in a reliable manner.
- Reliability can be increased with the use of multiple measures and multiple evaluators.

Design Factors

Our ability to show success with our pay plans also varies by the research design that we use. Our arguments can be much more convincing if we can show that there was a change in our effectiveness measures from "before" the pay intervention to "after" it. That is, we can show that a change in effectiveness took place rather than the status quo being maintained. Another way to bolster our pay plan effectiveness arguments is to show the gain associated with the new pay plan relative to a comparable group of employees who did not participate in the new pay plan. By comparing a group with and without the pay plan, we can make more firm statements that it was the pay plan rather than influences extraneous to our pay plan (e.g., technology) that impacted the change in effectiveness outcomes. Alternatively, we could gather data using the same effectiveness criteria at multiple time periods before the implementation of the pay plan. Then, to rule out extraneous influences, an assessment could be made to see if any events took place other than pay that would logically have influenced the level of the measures from time period to time period prior to the implementation of the pay plan. Lastly, higher-level outcomes may take longer to develop. Hence, whenever possible, data should be collected not only immediately after the implementation of the new pay plan, but several time periods later as well.

Benchmark Comparison

Many evaluation studies of pay have already been conducted and can be used in two fashions. First, positive results in similar organizations facing similar situations may argue for the need for a less rigorous evaluation because it has been established elsewhere. Conditions necessary to have confidence in benchmark comparisons are as follows:

- Findings revealed in organizations similar to own organization
- People in study similar to people in own organization
- Same results found in multiple studies
- Study has a large number of observations
- Reliable measures were used
- Results reported in peer-reviewed journal

Second, previous studies provide information with which to expect and/or interpret the magnitude of the results found in our study. Remember that differences between studies may reflect differences in the factors shown above, rather than actual differences between pay plan results in each study.

Economic Modeling

A very sophisticated methodology to show the impact of a pay plan is to create an economic model of the likely impact of a pay plan between the variable categories shown in the list on page 254. That is, an expected sequence of events is detailed using the list of criteria on page 254–255. Then, statistical techniques are used to show the actual sequence of events. For example, in one study, it was shown that new human resources systems, including pay, resulted in increased employee job satisfaction. In turn, increased job satisfaction was related to improved customer service ratings. Lastly, improved customer service ratings were shown to be related to increased revenue generation.[1] An economic model such as this one makes an excellent argument to management that it is getting a return on human resources investments.

Case Study

CASE

1

Flight Simulation Company[2]

It is becoming increasingly common for senior managers to ask compensation professionals to provide economic data to justify the need for new pay systems. Such requests are certainly not unexpected, given the large direct and indirect costs of compensation to organizations. Ideally, management would like to see how the investment in pay systems directly translates to the bottom line in terms of productivity and economic value added.

Making this link, however, can be very difficult—for several reasons. First, some jobs (e.g., support staff) lack objective measures of profitability because they do not directly touch the final service or product. Second, profitability is often subject to external forces, such as the state of the economy, that are outside the control of individual employees. Third, most organizations are undergoing massive change and restructuring, and it is very difficult to disentangle the impact of a new pay system on organizational performance from the impact of other changes taking place simultaneously.

The need for economic justification for pay plans and the difficulties of measuring economic impact pose a dilemma for compensation professionals. How can one overcome the measurement difficulties inherent in this process and thus provide an accurate assessment of a pay program's economic impact? One solution, described here, is to assess the direct impact of pay systems on employee attitudes toward the pay system.

At first blush, the use of employee attitude surveys to measure this impact appears to be unacceptably "soft"—not the kind of data that will impress senior management. After all, people can feel good, but business performance can be lousy.

In response to this criticism, one can argue that "hard" data may also be misleading. For example, profitability may be more a function of cutting costs than a new pay plan. More important, however, various studies have shown a direct relationship between soft and hard data. In particular, studies on pay satisfaction clearly show that positive attitudes toward pay are associated with better attendance, less turnover, and a lower profitability of employees voting for a union.[3]

The point here is that neither soft nor hard data are perfectly objective. Obviously, hard data are preferable, but for some occupations it is difficult if not impossible to obtain. Because research has established a link between soft data and behaviors, there is some basis to use soft data as a measure of effectiveness. Moreover, when multiple changes are taking place in an organization, pay satisfaction data may arguably be preferable because attitudes toward pay can be directly linked to the pay system rather than to other interventions going on simultaneously.

Fortunately for compensation professionals, the measurement of employee attitudes toward pay is a straightforward process. The remainder of this article presents a case study from a high technology firm on how pay satisfaction can be measured and used to guide strategic pay decisions. The objective is to show a rigorous approach to the assessment of attitudes toward pay.

Although straightforward, such a process is not easy. Hastily constructed measures of attitudes toward pay will likely lack reliability and validity. As such, they can be more problematic than no assessment of the effectiveness of pay plans because they may send a false signal to senior management. On the other hand, the vigorous assessment of employee attitudes toward pay can provide a very useful barometer on pay plan effectiveness.

Need for a New Pay System. Simcom is a small, privately held, ten-year-old company with locations in Orlando and Phoenix. It is in the business of building flight simulators and training pilots on twin propeller planes as well as small jets. The company's approximately eighty employees are organized into teams based on functional units: production, marketing, sales, training, computer services, and clerical.

Growth has been rapid. In 1990, Simcom trained only 54 pilots; in 1997, approximately 2,650 pilots received Simcom training. The company is recognized as a leader in its industry, as evidenced by a "Best of the Best" award from *Flying* magazine.

In 1992, Simcom's senior management asked the lead author of this article to assess the need for an incentive pay plan. At the time, the organization was in a start-up/growth phase with a large investment in technology. The pay system then in place was based on market pricing with seniority-based increases.

The company's new president expected associates to act like owners and placed heavy emphasis on customer service as a business strategy. The president and the company's owner wanted to examine the possibility of incentive pay as a method to emphasize performance within that framework.

Phases of The Project. In response to this situation, Simcom implemented a three-phase project. In Phase One, the company developed a survey to assess the need for incentive pay. In Phase Two, it developed and implemented an incentive pay system. In Phase Three, management assessed the effectiveness of the incentive pay system by comparing the survey results prior to pay system implementation with survey results after implementation.

The Survey. The initial survey aimed at assessing the readiness of employees for an incentive pay plan. An internal survey of all associates was chosen over an external survey of similar-company incentive practices because senior management valued employee input and wanted to develop an incentive system unique to its business and culture. Rather than viewing incentive pay as a separate system, management took a more holistic approach in which it viewed incentive pay as part of the larger system of compensation and rewards (both monetary and nonmonetary). The results of the survey were validated in both Phase One and Phase Three by conducting focus groups with a sample of employees and by statistically calculating the reliability of the survey measures each time.

The survey measured attitudes in four areas:

- Job satisfaction
- Pay satisfaction
- Performance ratings
- Pay for performance

Exhibits 12-1 through 12-4 show the dimensions covered in each area. For job satisfaction and pay satisfaction (Exhibits 12-1 and 12-2), the instrument used multiple statements to define each dimension. Survey participants responded using the 5-to-1 scale shown. The pay and pay-for-performance measures (Exhibits 12-3 and 12-4) were shorter and consisted of the statements and rating scale shown in the exhibits. All of these measures had been used in previous research and their statistical reliability had been documented (see notations for each exhibit).

Initial Survey Results. The first column in Exhibit 12-5 shows the survey results for Phase One of the project. As the data show, associates had favorable job satisfaction scores, especially with regard to the work itself (intrinsic satisfaction). Satisfaction with pay, however, was somewhat

EXHIBIT 12-1
Job satisfaction measure.

Dimensions

- Intrinsic Satisfaction
  Satisfaction with work itself
- Extrinsic Satisfaction
  Satisfaction with conditions surrounding work

Rating Scale

5 = Very Satisfied
4 = Satisfied
3 = Neutral
2 = Dissatisfied
1 = Very Dissatisfied

Source: Weiss, D. J., Davis, R. V., England, G. W., and Lofquist, R. H., *Manual for the Minnesota Satisfaction Questionnaire (Minnesota Studies in Vocational Rehabilitation: XXII)* Minneapolis, MN: University of Minnesota Industrial Relations Center, Work Adjustment Project, 1985.

EXHIBIT 12-2
Pay satisfaction measure.

Dimensions

- Pay Level
- Pay Raise
- Structure/Administration
- Benefits

Scale

5 = Very Satisfied
4 = Satisfied
3 = Neither Satisfied nor Dissatisfied
2 = Dissatisfied
1 = Very Dissatisfied

Source: Heneman, H. G. III and Schwab, D. P., "Pay Satisfaction: Its Multidimensional Nature and Measurement," *International Journal of Psychology*, Vol. 20 (1985), pp. 129–141.

EXHIBIT 12-3
Performance ratings measure.

Statements

- Quality
- Quantity
- Following of procedures
- Ability to help others
- Productivity under pressure
- Acceptance of responsibility
- Adaptation to different situations
- Overall performance

Scale

5 = Excellent
4 = Above Average
3 = Average
2 = Below Average
1 = Poor

Source: Heneman, R. L., Greenberger, D., and Ananyou, C., "Attributions and Exchanges: The Effects of Interpersonal Factors on the Diagnosis of Employee Performance," *Academy of Management Journal*, Vol. 32 (1989), pp. 466–476.

EXHIBIT 12-4
Pay for performance measure.

Statements

"If I perform especially well on my job it is likely that I will get a pay raise."
"The best workers in the company get the highest pay raises."
"The pay raises that I receive on my job make me work harder."
"High performers and low performers get the same pay raises."

Scale

5 = Strongly Agree
4 = Agree
3 = Neither Agree nor Disagree
2 = Disagree
1 = Strongly Disagree

Source: Heneman, R. L., Greenberger, D. B., and Strasser, G. "The Relationship between Pay for Performance Perceptions and Pay Satisfaction," *Personal Psychology*, Vol. 41 (1988), pp. 745–759.

low, especially for benefits. In addition, the link between pay and performance was not clear to employees nor was administration of the pay system.

The focus groups confirmed these results. For example, researchers heard a consistent theme related to the need to tie pay to performance. One employee, for example, indicated that associates should have the opportunity to "earn what they deserve." A manager indicated that employees at the company were very "dedicated and committed and should be rewarded accordingly."

The Reward Plan. Based on the results in Phase One, senior management decided that a new reward plan would, indeed, be appropriate. Phase Two consisted of the development of the plan. Goals for the reward system included providing a share in company success, rewarding customer service, establishing above-market salaries, and providing job security. The reward plan consisted of three components: clarification of role expectations, a new performance management system, and profit sharing.

Role expectations were clearly communicated through a written, personalized document for each employee. The document lists required tasks, core competencies needed to perform each task, and employee and team leader expectations. The performance management system spells out the performance competencies on which employees will be assessed. The system measures a number of dimensions believed to be critical to customer service. These include:

- Understanding and support of company goals
- Relationships with supervisors and coworkers
- Doing "whatever it takes"
- Creativity
- Self-improvement
- Communications

Ten percent of operating profit is set aside for the profit sharing plan. The plan pays out twice a year and is administered by a management-associate committee. The amount an individual receives depends on his or her performance rating, pay level, and seniority. All employees and managers are eligible. Due to a downturn in business conditions at the start of the plan, the first payout came in 1996 with another payout anticipated for 1997.

Effectiveness of the Reward Plan. Prior to the 1997 payouts, Simcom readministered the survey conducted in Phase One (in 1992) to assess the effectiveness of the plan to date. The second column of Exhibit 12-5 shows the results. As with Phase One, the lead author conducted a series of focus groups to confirm the numerical results from the survey.

As the data show, scores increased in all categories except perform-

EXHIBIT 12-5
Employee attitude survey results.

Measure	Pre-Plan 1992	Post-Plan 1997
Job Satisfaction	3.55	3.99
Extrinsic Satisfaction	3.64	4.36
Intrinsic Satisfaction	3.80	4.05
Pay Satisfaction	2.80	3.27
Benefits	2.58	3.19
Level	2.87	3.35
Raise	2.90	3.22
Structure/Administration	2.73	3.21
Pay for Performance	2.69	3.02
Performance	4.07	3.84

Scale: 1 = Low, 5 = High

ance. Although the increases are not large, they are statistically significant—and take on additional meaning when we consider that the plan had only paid out once. At the same time, however, score increases cannot be totally attributed to the pay plan because there was also turnover among employees during the five-year period. Although the performance scores dropped somewhat, this may actually be a positive event if we interpret it as meaning that supervisors now take the evaluation process more seriously because pay is involved and are thus less lenient in their ratings.

The pattern of scores also underscores the effectiveness of the plan. For example, in 1992 intrinsic satisfaction was greater than extrinsic satisfaction. In 1997, extrinsic satisfaction was greater than intrinsic satisfaction. Moreover, the increase in pay satisfaction was greater than the increase in job satisfaction. These sets of data show that pay as a source of satisfaction at work had grown relative to satisfaction with other aspects of work.

Based on the results of the survey and focus groups, senior management plans to continue to use the reward plan. In the future, the plan will be further refined by several ideas currently under consideration. Multiple raters may be used to gather a more complete picture of employee performance. Training may be provided to raters to ensure that accurate ratings are being made. In order for the process to lead to the development of new skills, learning contracts may be established with employees through the performance management process. To make the performance management process a "living, working" document for employees, personal mission statements may be used to supplement the company mission statement.

Care must be exercised in refining the system because associates expressed concern during the focus groups about changes taking place too frequently with the plan.

Discussion and Conclusions. The results of this case study suggest that "soft" data in the form of employee attitudes toward pay can be successfully used to assess the effectiveness of a pay system. In this instance, senior management accepted soft data as a basis for deciding whether to use a new pay plan, how to design and refine the plan, and whether to continue the plan.

As shown in this case, well-developed measures of employee attitudes toward work already exist and can be readily used. To develop a comprehensive understanding of these surveys, the numerical results should be supplemented with focus group data, as in the present case. As new forms of reward plans are developed, additional measures will be needed and are being worked on at universities like Ohio State University. However, in the meantime, the currently available surveys provide a good starting point.

Taking this approach to assessing the economic impact of pay in the organization is critical because of the established link between pay satisfaction and absenteeism, turnover, and union vote. Senior management cannot ignore the potential costs associated with these three indicators of organizational effectiveness.

Notes

1. J. A. Rucci, S. P. Kirn, and R. T. Quinn, "The Employee-Customer-Profit Chain at Sears," *Harvard Business Review* (1998): January–February.
2. Robert L. Heneman, Don E. Eskew, and Julie A. Fox, "Using Employee Attitudes to Evaluate a New Incentive Program," *Compensation and Benefits Review*, Vol. 28(1), pp. 40–44.
3. Robert L. Heneman, *Merit Pay: Linking Pay Increases to Performance Ratings* (Reading, MA: Addison-Wesley, 1992); Herbert G. Heneman III, "Pay Satisfaction," in K. N. Rowland and G. R. Ferris (eds.), *Research in Personnel and Human Resources Management*, Vol. 3 (Greenwich, CT: JAI Press).

PART 5

CHECKLIST SUMMARIES

Chapter 13: General Do's and Don'ts

Chapter 14: Business Strategy Checklist

A word of caution needs to be placed in this final part of the book. The do's and don'ts list presented here should *not* be viewed as a substitute for reading the rest of the book. It is provided as a summary only. Developing business-driven compensation plans is a very complex process and cannot be narrowed down to a simple laundry list of do's and don'ts. The complexity of the process can begin to be appreciated only by reading the text and cases in each chapter.

A model of corporate business strategy and pay policy integration.

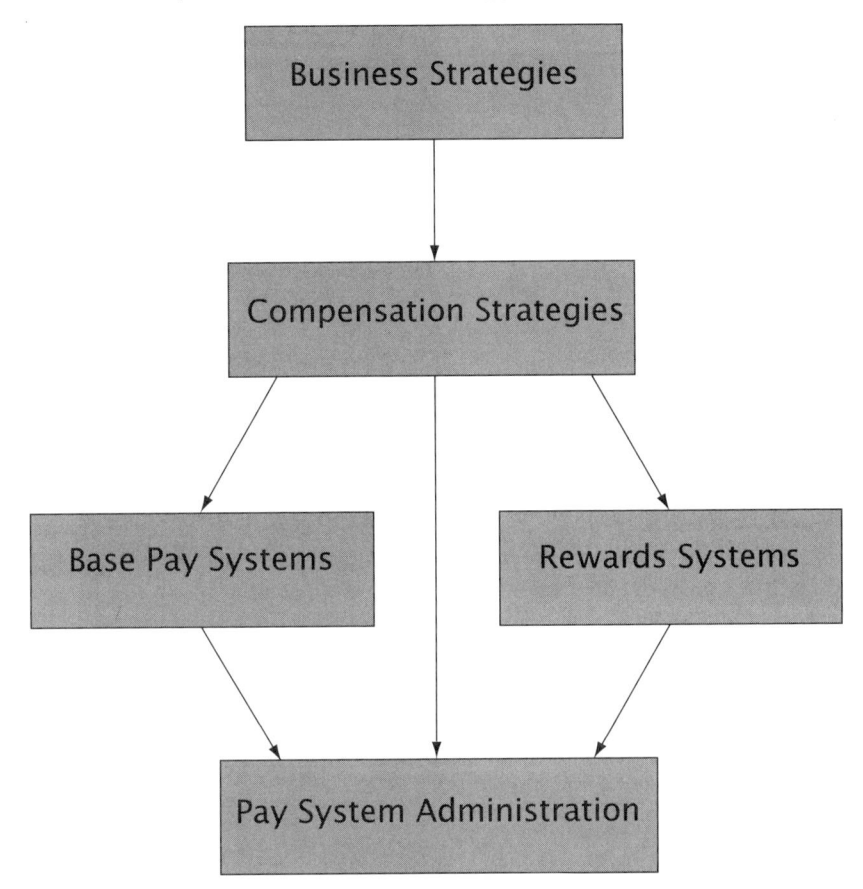

```
            ┌─────────────────────┐
            │ Business Strategies │
            └──────────┬──────────┘
                       ▼
          ┌────────────────────────┐
          │ Compensation Strategies│
          └───┬──────────┬─────────┘
              │          │         
     ┌────────▼──┐       │    ┌────▼──────────┐
     │ Base Pay  │       │    │ Rewards       │
     │ Systems   │       │    │ Systems       │
     └────────┬──┘       │    └────┬──────────┘
              │          ▼         │
           ┌──▼──────────────────▼──┐
           │ Pay System Administration│
           └──────────────────────────┘
```

CHAPTER 13

General Do's and Don'ts

Chapter 1: Overview and Model

DO:
- ☐ Educate employees on goals of company and reward them on accomplishment of those goals.
- ☐ Integrate corporate business strategy and compensation policies to create a compensation system.
- ☐ Allow corporate business strategy to be the force that guides pay policy formation and administration.
- ☐ Permit new compensation strategy to set the stage for deciding which pay system to be included or excluded.

DON'T:
- ☐ Ignore integrating other business systems such as laws and regulations, structure, business process, and culture of organization when creating a compensation system.
- ☐ Create a stand-alone pay system without a concrete foundation in the business plan.

Chapter 2: Corporate Business Strategies and Compensation Strategies

DO:
- ☐ Tailor-make compensation systems to the needs of the business.
- ☐ Develop a unique approach to the organization's product or service that competitors have a difficult time imitating.
- ☐ Align strategic plans at the business unit with strategic plans at the corporate level prior to the development of a new compensation plan.

- [ ] Consider pay philosophy, pay assessment, pay form, pay delivery, and pay plan design when developing compensation strategy.
- [ ] Consider both internal and external pay equity in developing pay philosophy.
- [ ] Evaluate both human capital and job characteristics to determine value that a person makes to the organization.
- [ ] Clearly articulate and address importance of seniority versus performance trade-off in the compensation strategy.
- [ ] Emphasis significance of education so that employees have the breadth of knowledge needed to add value to the firm.
- [ ] Move toward variable pay system so that cost incurs only if the business prospers.

DON'T:
- [ ] Assume that organizations have perfect market information when following an external equity pay strategy.
- [ ] Ignore importance of employee performance as part of company's compensation strategy.
- [ ] Change compensation system unless significant business changes have occurred.
- [ ] Use business strategy independent of other contingency factors when developing a compensation strategy formulation.

Chapter 3: Work Analysis

DO:
- [ ] Make competencies specific to the business strategy of the organization.
- [ ] Consider all three layers of job analysis: person, job, and context.
- [ ] Assure that qualifications and competencies that define the person for the job be both very precise and related to the business strategy of the organization.
- [ ] Account for context in which work takes place when making compensation decisions by looking at environment, work flow process, and network analysis.
- [ ] Consider both top-down and bottom-up perspectives to gain an accurate portrayal of a job.
- [ ] Use multiple data collection methods to reduce sampling and measurement error.

DON'T:
- Depend on job titles alone to make sound compensation decisions.
- Eliminate job descriptions in human resources decisions especially when it comes to compensation decisions.

Chapter 4: Work Evaluation

DO:
- Base job evaluation method upon compensation and business strategy.
- Select enough compensation factors to encompass all-important aspects of the business and compensation strategies.
- Always weight compensation factors depending upon most important portion of business strategy.
- Custom develop competencies specific to the specific strategy of the organization.
- Measure competencies at different levels of the organization and consider the level of the competency needed.

DON'T:
- Assume that job evaluations are anachronistic and unnecessary.
- Reject job evaluation systems due to legal and employee relations reasons related to organizational effectiveness.

Chapter 5: Market Surveys

DO:
- Take great care in the external market survey process to minimize sampling error and measurement error.
- Consider business and compensation strategies and the job analysis the guiding lights in the market survey process.
- Conduct organizational surveys in the same industry for higher-level jobs and in multiple industries for lower-level jobs.
- Consider benchmark jobs that are well known, employee large numbers of people, and have stable job contents.

DON'T:
- Assume that market survey data is free of bias when relying on an external equity pay philosophy.
- Treat the salary midpoint and averages in a synonymous fashion when analyzing compensation data.

Chapter 6: Pay Structures

DO:
- [ ] Adhere to the pay structure in the organization because it supports the aims of the business and compensation strategies of the organization.
- [ ] Utilize pay ranges in all compensation systems other than cost business strategies to increase flexibility.

Chapter 7: Individual Rewards

DO:
- [ ] Clearly define performance of the employee so that the employee is motivated to deliver the level of performance desired by the organization.
- [ ] Align goals of individual employees to goals of the organization.
- [ ] Develop performance standards that are based on the business and compensation strategies of the organization.
- [ ] Pay attention to business and compensation strategies when deciding which parties should be part of the performance evaluation process.
- [ ] Utilize both the business and compensation strategies of the organization in weighting the final assessment of the performance standards.
- [ ] Align types of awards given to the type of business strategy of the organization.

DON'T:
- [ ] Use traits as an absolute performance standard regardless of business strategy.
- [ ] Fail to gather feedback from customers as part of the performance evaluation process if customer service is truly important.
- [ ] Underestimate the value of money to motivate employee performance.

Chapter 8: Team Rewards

DO:
- [ ] Consider team pay if teams demonstrably add value to the organization in ways not compensated for by base pay, individual rewards, or organizational awards.
- [ ] Link the standard of performance, the evaluators, and weighting steps to the business and compensation strategies.
- [ ] Define contributions in terms of what they accomplish and how they accomplish results.

Chapter 9: Organizational Rewards

DO:
- ☐ Utilize economic value-added formulas to link operational standards to financial standards.
- ☐ Combine performance standard measures to overcome the problems associated with organizational reward plans.
- ☐ Include the controller as an evaluator in making organizational reward decisions regardless of business strategy.

Chapter 10: Strategic Pay Design

DO:
- ☐ Utilize business and compensation strategies to guide the design process in establishing base pay and reward systems.
- ☐ Allow strategies to be interpreted by those who develop the strategy and by those who are affected by the strategy in order for pay plan objectives to be consistent with business direction.
- ☐ Utilize corporate business and compensation strategies to determine eligibility for participation in the pay plan.
- ☐ Assure that pay plan objectives spell out what types of pay are to be used and who is eligible for each type of pay plan.

DON'T:
- ☐ Exclude first-line supervisors from the compensation plan process.
- ☐ Fail to include the union in the design stage of pay plans in a unionized organization.

Chapter 11: Strategic Pay Implementation

DO:
- ☐ Assure that compensation plan "fits" and is consistent with the corporate business strategies, compensation strategies, and other human resources policies.
- ☐ Achieve alignment in compensation plans by providing training and communication regarding the pay plan and by rewarding employees.
- ☐ Achieve integration in compensation plans by linking the plan to staffing, development, human resources information systems, and payroll policies.
- ☐ Show managers how each factor in the job evaluation system relates back to corporate business objectives.

☐ Train employees on how they can best impact the measures that will help them maintain or improve upon their pay status.
☐ Align the payouts of compensation plans with the business cycle of the organization.

Chapter 12: Strategic Pay Evaluation

DO:
☐ Realize the critical step of the evaluation of compensation systems in pay system administration.
☐ Carefully chose evaluation criteria to show the effectiveness of the compensation plan.

CHAPTER 14

Business Strategy Checklist

Customer Service Business Strategy

Pay Philosophy	☐ External Equity—consistent with setting product/service prices at market value ☐ Match Market—not competing on labor costs ☐ Retention—focus on meeting demands of customer now; no time to attract better customer service–oriented employees
Pay Assessment	☐ Behavior Based—behavior crucial to delivery of services ☐ Performance Based—performance essential to business strategy above seniority ☐ Education and Skills—equally important
Pay Form	☐ Nonmonetary Rewards—to reward excellence in customer service ☐ Fixed Pay System—used to buy loyalty of employees to the organization ☐ Individual Compensation—to consider only in team-based work system
Pay Delivery	☐ Broad Bands—reward people for performing outside their normally defined job duties ☐ Midrange Communication System—individuals' pay levels not made available; pay ranges and averages made public

Checklist Summaries

Pay Plan Design	☐ Participative Pay Plan Design—empowered workforce essential to business strategy ☐ Centralized and Decentralized Pay Plan—standardization among plans while allowing modifications for local circumstances ☐ Static and Dynamic Pay Plan—significant business changes must occur to change compensation plan ☐ Lag System—designed to reinforce the change in business strategy
Work Evaluation	☐ Factor Evaluation System: Customer Service Problem Solving Contacts ☐ Competency Evaluation System: Communication Skills Interpersonal Skills Product Knowledge
Work Analysis	☐ Emphasis on the job
Pay Structure	☐ Utilize Pay Ranges ☐ Utilize Broadbanding ☐ Broad Bands ☐ Small Band Overlap
Individual Rewards	☐ Performance Standards: Results—50% Behaviors—50% ☐ Absolute Comparisons: Traits Behaviors Potential Performance ☐ Evaluator: Supervisor Rating—45% Self-Rating—10% Customer Rating—45% ☐ Rewards: Money Recognition

Team Rewards	☐ Standards: Results—80% Process—20% ☐ Evaluator: Team Leader—40% Team Members—10% Senior Management—50% ☐ Rewards: Cash Time Off
Organizational Rewards	☐ Performance Standards: Operational—50% Financial—50% ☐ Evaluator: Executive—35% Controller—35% Employee—30%
Pay Design	☐ Customer Service Standards ☐ Customer Service Expert on Design Team ☐ Senior Management with Operations Background
Pay Evaluation	☐ Evaluation Measures: Operational Results

Quality Business Strategy

Pay Philosophy	☐ External Equity—administrative steps and cost associated with internal equity inconsistent with TQM philosophy ☐ Lead Market—attract people who don't need monitoring ☐ Retention Focus—focus on meeting demands of customers now; no time to attract better employees
Pay Assessment	☐ Person Emphasis—flexibility in roles is essential to delivery of services

	☐ Results Based—consistent with team philosophy of valuing overall system rather than individual ☐ Performance Based—performance essential to business strategy above seniority ☐ Skills—put emphasis on skills that are specific to the business strategy
Pay Form	☐ Nonmonetary Rewards—to celebrate new process innovation that produces higher-quality product ☐ Variable Pay System—performance measures used are often based on metrics employed by the business to gauge business strategy success ☐ Team Compensation—likely have team-based work systems
Pay Delivery	☐ Large Band Overlap—allows employees to be rewarded for multiskilled efforts ☐ Midrange Communication Systems—individuals' pay levels not made available; pay ranges and averages made public
Pay Plan Design	☐ Participative Pay Plan Design—empowered workforce essential to business strategy ☐ Decentralized Pay Plan—strategy localized so it is logical to link pay system to decentralized strategy formulation ☐ Static and Dynamic Pay Plan—significant business changes must occur to change compensation plan ☐ Lag System—designed to reinforce the changes in business strategy
Job Evaluation	☐ Factor Evaluation System: Know-How Leadership Problem Solving ☐ Competency Evaluation System: Teamwork

Business Strategy Checklist

	Quality Training
	Leadership
Work Analysis	☐ Emphasis on the context
Pay Structure	☐ Utilize Pay Ranges
	☐ Broad Bands
	☐ Small Band Overlap
Individual Rewards	☐ Performance Standards:
	Results—70%
	Behavior—30%
	☐ Absolute Comparisons:
	Behaviors
	Results
	Potential Performance
	☐ Evaluator:
	Supervisor Rating—20%
	Self-Rating—10%
	Peer Rating—30%
	Customer Rating—40%
	☐ Rewards:
	Money
	Time Off
	Recognition
Team Rewards	☐ Standards:
	Results—70%
	Process—30%
	☐ Evaluator:
	Team Leaders—0%
	Team Members—40%
	Senior Management—60%
	☐ Team Members Allocate Funds
	☐ Rewards:
	Cash
	Time Off
Organizational Rewards	☐ Performance Standards:
	Operational—50%
	Financial—50%
	☐ Evaluator:
	Executive—35%

Checklist Summaries

	Controller—35% Employees/Teams—30%
Pay Design	☐ Include Sales and Support Staff ☐ Quality Standards ☐ Quality Expert on Design Team ☐ Senior Management with Operations Background
Pay Evaluation	☐ Evaluation Measures: Operational Results

Innovation and Time to Market Business Strategies

Pay Philosophy	☐ External Equity—consistent with setting product/prices at market value ☐ Match Market—not competing on labor costs ☐ Attraction—necessary to go outside market for employees with desired skill sets not available in-house
Pay Assessment	☐ Person Emphasis—flexibility in roles essential to business strategy ☐ Performance Based—performance essential to business strategy above seniority ☐ Education and Skills—equally important
Pay Form	☐ Monetary and Nonmonetary Rewards—equal emphasis placed to provide creative rewards for creative people ☐ Variable Pay System—motivational properties ☐ Team Compensation—likely to have team-based work system
Pay Delivery	☐ Broad Bands—reward people for performing outside their normally defined job duties ☐ Large Band Overlap—allows employees to be rewarded for multiskilled efforts

	☐ Midrange Communication System—individuals' pay levels not made available; pay ranges and averages made public
Pay Plan Design	☐ Participative Pay Plan Design—empowered workforce essential to business strategy ☐ Decentralized Pay Plan—strategy localized so it is logical to link pay system to decentralized strategy formulation ☐ Static and Dynamic Pay Plan—significant business changes must occur to change compensation system ☐ Lead System—used to make change more salient to employees
Job Evaluation	☐ Factor Evaluation System: Knowledge Autonomy Research ☐ Competency Evaluation System: Analytical Skills Motivation Judgment
Work Analysis	☐ Emphasis on the person
Pay Structure	☐ Utilize Pay Ranges ☐ Utilize Broadbanding ☐ Utilize Market Pricing ☐ Broad Bands ☐ Small Band Overlap
Individual Rewards	☐ Performance Standards: Results—35% Behaviors—65% ☐ Absolute Comparisons: Traits Behaviors Potential Performance ☐ Evaluator: Customer Rating—20% Supervisor Rating—35%

	Peer Rating—35% Self-Rating—10% ☐ Rewards: Money Time Off Recognition
Team Rewards	☐ Standards: Results—35% Process—65% ☐ Evaluator: Team Leader—50% Team Members—10% Senior Management—40% ☐ Team Members Allocate Funds ☐ Rewards: Cash Time Off
Organizational Rewards	☐ Performance Standards: Operational—60% Financial—40% ☐ Evaluator: Executive—30% Controller—20% Employee/Teams—50%
Pay Design	☐ Include Sales and Support Staff ☐ Organizational Development Specialist on Design Team ☐ Senior Management with HR Background ☐ Strategic Consultant Suggested
Pay Evaluation	☐ Evaluation Measures: Attitudes Behaviors

Productivity Business Strategy

Pay Philosophy	☐ Match Market—not competing on labor cost

	☐ Attraction and Retention Focus—balance between two
Pay Assessment	☐ Job Emphasis—easier and more relevant to build a job- rather than person-based accounting system
	☐ Results and Behavior Based—results focus on output side of productivity ratio; behavior focuses on input side of productivity ratio
	☐ Performance Based—performance essential to business strategy above seniority
	☐ Education and Skills—equally important
Pay Form	☐ Monetary Rewards—form of pay is consistent with accounting and measurement system
	☐ Variable Pay System—performance measures used are often based on metrics employed by the business to gauge business strategy success
	☐ Individual Compensation—to consider only in team-based work system
Pay Delivery	☐ Broad Bands—reward people for performing outside their normally defined job duties
	☐ Large Band Overlap—allows employees to be rewarded for multiskilled efforts
	☐ Midrange Communication System—individuals' pay levels not made available; pay ranges and averages made public
Pay Plan Design	☐ Participative Pay Plan Design—empowered workforce essential to business strategy
	☐ Centralized and Decentralized Pay Plan—standardization among plans while allowing modifications for local circumstances
	☐ Static and Dynamic Pay Plan—significant business changes must occur to change compensation plan
	☐ Lag System—designed to reinforce the change in business strategy

Job Evaluation	☐ Factor Evaluation System: Effort Responsibility Economic Impact ☐ Competency Evaluation System: Management Skills Finance Knowledge Accounting Skills
Work Analysis	☐ Emphasis on the job
Pay Structure	☐ Utilizes Pay Ranges ☐ Utilizes Broadbanding ☐ Narrow Bands ☐ Small Band Overlap
Individual Rewards	☐ Performance Standards: Results—70% Behavior—30% ☐ Absolute Comparisons: Potential Performance ☐ Evaluator: Supervisor Rating—45% Peer Rating—45% Self-Rating—10% ☐ Rewards: Money Time Off
Team Rewards	☐ Standards: Results—80% Process—20% ☐ Evaluator: Team Leader—40% Team Members—20% Senior Management—40% ☐ Rewards: Time Off
Organizational Rewards	☐ Performance Standards: Operational—70% Financial—30%

	☐ Evaluator: Executive—40% Controller—40% Employee/Teams—20%
Pay Design	☐ Includes Sales and Support Staff ☐ Productivity Standards ☐ Senior Management with Operations Background
Pay Evaluation	☐ Evaluation Measures: Operational Results

Cost Business Strategy

Pay Philosophy	☐ External Equity—consistent with setting products/services at market value ☐ Lag Market—competing on cost ☐ Attraction—fewer new entrants to be paid to the organization than there are current employees to be paid
Pay Assessment	☐ Job Emphasis—due to cost of person-based approach ☐ Results Based—allows people to pay for themselves ☐ Performance Based—performance essential to business strategy above seniority ☐ Education—to minimize cost; education to be obtained off the job and paid for by incumbent
Pay Form	☐ Nonmonetary Rewards—due to cost savings ☐ Variable Pay System—increased costs to be incurred only if business prospers ☐ Individual Compensation—to consider only in team-based work system
Pay Delivery	☐ Narrow Bands—help organization minimize labor cost

	☐ Large Band Overlap—allows employees to be rewarded for multiskilled efforts ☐ Closed Communication System—minimizes turnover by keeping employees ignorant about pay levels
Pay Plan Design	☐ Nonparticipative Pay Plan Design—more emphasis placed on capital than on people; financial matters more essential to business strategy ☐ Centralized Pay Plan—most finances including compensation controlled at corporate level ☐ Static and Dynamic Pay Plan—significant business changes must occur to change compensation plan ☐ Lag System—designed to reinforce the change in business strategy
Job Evaluation	☐ Factor Evaluation System: Working Conditions Experience Responsibility ☐ Competency Evaluation System: Financial Knowledge Accounting Skills Product Knowledge
Work Analysis	☐ Emphasis on the job
Pay Structure	☐ Utilize Single-Rate Structure ☐ Utilize Locked Step Structure ☐ Utilize Broadbanding ☐ Utilize Market Pricing ☐ Narrow Bands ☐ Large Band Overlap
Individual Rewards	☐ Performance Standards: Results—100% Behaviors—0% ☐ Evaluator: Supervisor—100%

Business Strategy Checklist

	☐ Rewards: Money Recognition
Team Rewards	☐ Standards: Results—100% Process—0% ☐ Evaluator: Senior Management—100%
Organizational Rewards	☐ Performance Standards: Operational—40% Financial—60% ☐ Evaluator: Executive—60% Controller—40%
Pay Design	☐ Excludes Sales and Support Staff ☐ Senior Management with Financial Background
Pay Evaluation	☐ Evaluation Measures: Financial Results

Financial Business Strategy

Pay Philosophy	☐ External Equity—consistent with setting products/services at market value ☐ Match Market—not competing on labor cost ☐ Attraction and Retention—balance between two
Pay Assessment	☐ Job Emphasis—due to cost of person-based approach ☐ Results Based—allows people to pay for themselves ☐ Performance Based—performance essential to business strategy above seniority ☐ Education—to minimize cost; education to be obtained off the job and paid for by incumbent

Checklist Summaries

Pay Form	☐ Monetary Rewards—importance of capital to business strategy ☐ Variable Pay System—increased costs to be incurred only if business prospers ☐ Individual Compensation—to consider only in team-based work system
Pay Delivery	☐ Narrow Bands—help organization minimize labor cost ☐ Large Band Overlap—allows employees to be rewarded for multiskilled efforts ☐ Midrange Communication System—individuals' pay levels not made available; pay ranges and averages made public
Pay Plan Design	☐ Nonparticipative Pay Plan Design—more emphasis placed on capital than on people; financial matters more essential to business strategy ☐ Centralized Pay Plan—most finances including compensation controlled at corporate level ☐ Static and Dynamic Pay Plan—significant business changes must occur to change compensation plan ☐ Lag System—designed to reinforce the change in business strategy
Job Evaluation	☐ Factor Evaluation System: Working Conditions Experience Responsibility ☐ Competency Evaluation System: Financial Knowledge Accounting Skills Product Knowledge
Work Analysis	☐ Emphasis on the job
Pay Structure	☐ Utilize Pay Ranges ☐ Narrow Bands ☐ Large Band Overlap

Individual Rewards	☐ Performance Standards: Results—100% Behaviors—0% ☐ Evaluator: Supervisor—100% ☐ Rewards: Money Recognition
Team Rewards	☐ Standards: Results—100% Process—0% ☐ Evaluator: Senior Management—100%
Organizational Rewards	☐ Performance Standards: Operational—40% Financial—60% ☐ Evaluator: Executive—60% Controller—40%
Pay Design	☐ Excludes Sales and Support Staff ☐ Senior Management with Financial Background
Pay Evaluation	☐ Evaluation Measures: Financial Results

Human Capital Business Strategy

Pay Philosophy	☐ Internal Equity—due to intrinsic value of human capital to company and business strategies ☐ Lead Market—differentiate from competitors on basis of labor quality ☐ Attraction and Retention—balance between two
Pay Assessment	☐ Person Emphasis—flexibility in roles essential to business strategy

Checklist Summaries

	☐ Behavior Based—crucial to the delivery of exemplary service ☐ Performance—performance essential to business strategy above seniority ☐ Education and Skills—equally important
Pay Form	☐ Monetary and Nonmonetary—focus on both forms of compensation emphasizes the importance of human capital to business strategy ☐ Variable Pay System—motivational properties ☐ Individual Compensation—to consider only in team-based work system
Pay Delivery	☐ Broad Bands—reward people for performing outside their normally defined job duties ☐ Small Band Overlap—motivates employees to acquire more skills ☐ Open Communication System—no secrets kept in order to retain highly talented employees
Pay Plan Design	☐ Participative Pay Plan Design—empowered workforce essential to business strategy ☐ Centralized and Decentralized Pay Plan—standardization among plans while allowing modifications for local circumstances ☐ Static and Dynamic Pay Plan—significant business changes must occur to change compensation plan ☐ Lag System—designed to reinforce the change in business strategy
Job Evaluation	☐ Factor Evaluation System: Knowledge Skills Ability ☐ Competency Evaluation System: Skills

Business Strategy Checklist

	Personality
	Leadership
Work Analysis	☐ Emphasis on the person
Pay Structure	☐ Utilize Pay Ranges
	☐ Broad Bands
	☐ Small Band Overlap
Individual Rewards	☐ Performance Standards:
	Results—0%
	Behaviors—100%
	☐ Absolute Comparisons
	☐ Evaluator:
	Supervisor Rating—40%
	Peer Rating—40%
	Self-Rating—20%
	☐ Rewards:
	Money
Team Rewards	☐ Standards:
	Results—0%
	Process—100%
	☐ Evaluator:
	Team Leaders—40%
	Team Members—40%
	Senior Management—20%
	☐ Team Members Allocate Funds
	☐ Rewards:
	Cash
	Time Off
	Stock
Organizational Rewards	☐ Performance Standards:
	Operational—70%
	Financial—30%
	☐ Evaluator:
	Executive—30%
	Controller—30%
	Employee/Teams—40%
Pay Design	☐ Organizational Development Specialist on Design Team

Checklist Summaries

	☐ Senior Management with HR Background
	☐ Strategic Consultant Suggested
Pay Evaluation	☐ Evaluation Measures:
	Attitudes
	Behaviors

APPENDIX

Example Pay Communication*

Introduction

One of the best-kept secrets in American business is how organizations make decisions about the amount of pay employees receive. Regretfully, this secrecy leads to a number of unfortunate consequences for employees and organizations. Employees want to do their best at work but don't know the rules of the game. If employees don't know the rules of the game, their efforts may not be directed toward those goals valued by the employer. As a result, employees don't receive the pay they really deserve, become frustrated, and may withdraw their best efforts. The organization suffers because well-intentioned employees' best efforts are thwarted rather than captured by the organization.

The purpose of this section is to show readers the rules of the game regarding compensation decisions in organizations and how to use these rules to their advantage to get the pay raise they deserve. By knowing the rules of the game, readers learn what is expected at work and how to direct their best efforts toward getting the best rewards. Based on my twenty years of compensation consulting with a variety of organizations across the country, this book recognizes that knowledge is an important source of power in organizations and shows readers how to attain this power over their pay by sharing some of the best-kept secrets on how organizations compensate employees.

This appendix is arranged in a user-friendly format, complete with charts and check-off lists, to best guide the reader through the process. First, a model of the pay raise process will be presented to show four key influencers held by employers in making pay raise decisions and how to impact them. Next, each one of these influencers will be covered in detail so that readers have an understanding of where the leverage points are

---

* The Appendix was written by Rob Heneman and Chris Naylor.

with the organization in getting a pay raise. Finally, powerful techniques that can be used with employers show how to make the pay raise model work in the readers' best interests.

Understanding How Employers Make Pay Raise Decisions

Today's employers provide pay increases based on measures that ensure that the organization is getting a good return on its investment. In many organizations, pay can account for 50 percent or more of total costs to the employer. In return for this investment of money, employers expect employees to work hard, perform work of importance to the employer, remain with the organization, and upgrade their capabilities.

What many employees do not know is that employers use the following four factors to determine who is eligible for pay raises, the amount of the pay raise, and how often to give raises:

1. *Performance.* Pay raises are given to those employees who are the most productive. Other typical indicators of performance are new skills learned, quality of job done, and service orientation.
2. *Job Value.* Pay raises are given to employees based on the value their jobs have to the organization. Job value is typically determined by a variety of things, including number of people managed by the employee and the job's potential to impact company strategy and the bottom line.
3. *Market Value.* Pay raises are given to employees based on value of their job in the labor market outside the organization.
4. *Potential.* Pay raises are given to those employees with the potential to perform in jobs of higher value to the organization than their current jobs.

The method used by employers to make pay raise decisions shows that in order to get a pay raise, a larger pay raise, or a more frequent pay raise, you must show the employer that you add value to the organization and that the employer is wisely investing in a pay increase for you. How you go about showing that you add value and, in turn, deserve a pay raise, is shown in Exhibit A-1.

Example Pay Communication

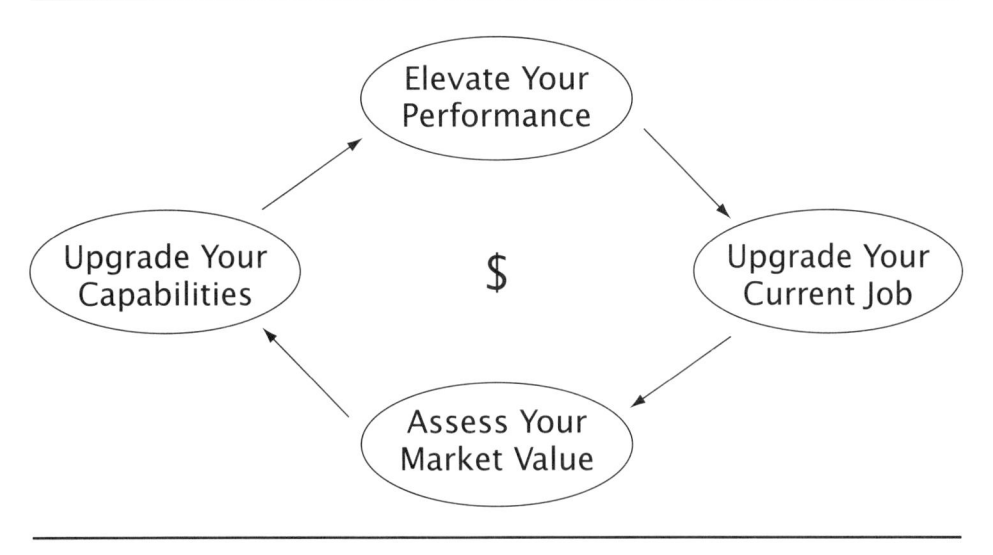

EXHIBIT A-1

Pay raise model.

```
         Elevate Your
          Performance
         ↗           ↘
Upgrade Your    $    Upgrade Your
Capabilities         Current Job
         ↖           ↙
         Assess Your
         Market Value
```

Evaluate Your Performance

By elevating or improving your performance on your current job, you become eligible for a merit increase or a bonus because you have exceeded the performance expectations for your position. You are creating value for the employer by exceeding the expectations of the job. In turn, the employer is likely to reward you with a pay increase. Methods to evaluate your performance are discussed in the section on raises based on performance.

Upgrade Your Current Job

Upgrading your current job refers to expanding the scope of your current job so that it is of greater value to your employer. Expanding the scope of your job, as will be described in the section on job value, usually entails increasing the number of duties performed, increasing your accountability, and increasing the complexity of your job. Because these new assignments are of greater importance to the employer and because it is more difficult to find people to perform these expanded duties, employers are more likely to provide a pay raise when there is a significant change in the scope of the job.

Assess Your Market Value

Assessing your market value involves finding out how much your job is worth to other employers. You may be asking yourself, how in the world can I establish my market value? Do I need to apply to jobs outside my company to see how much I would get paid elsewhere? Fortunately, as will be shown in the section on market adjustments, market data are available to you as a result of organizations that periodically conduct surveys on the market value of jobs. Surveys are conducted by the U.S. Government, trade and professional associations, and consulting firms. Survey data can be used to verify the importance of your job to the organization because they show the importance of your job to the rest of the industry that you are in. The market validates your employer's internal assessment of the value of your job. Employers are typically very interested in the market value of your job, in order to attract top job candidates and avoid losing qualified employees to the competition.

Upgrade Your Capabilities

A final way to receive a pay raise is to upgrade your capabilities. In order to do so, you may need to increase your skills and knowledge by taking such steps as attending company-specific training courses, going back to school, or obtaining a certificate or degree. By taking these steps, you are showing your employer that you have the potential to be promoted into jobs of greater scope and responsibility than that of your current job. Potential adds value to the organization because you can "fit" in more places in the organization, especially in jobs of greater value than the one you currently hold. Potential is often associated with promotions in organizations, a topic that will be covered later in this appendix.

Raises Based on Performance

High performers are more productive than low performers; hence, high performers add more value to the organization and receive larger raises. Increasingly, organizations are placing a premium on granting pay raises on the basis of performance. Indeed, in some organizations the *only* way to get a pay raise is by your performance. As a result, it is imperative that you understand what employers are looking for in employee performance, how to bring your performance to the attention of the organization, and what boundaries are placed on what employers can pay for performance.

What Employers Look for in Employee Performance

Historically, performance was assessed by how much time you put in on the job. The more seniority you had, the larger the raise you received. It was just assumed that more senior employees were more productive employees. Times have changed, and today many organizations have moved away from basing pay on seniority or assuming that more seniority is associated with more productivity. For example, the skills of more senior employees may be more obsolete than those of junior employees, and thus the productivity of senior employees may be lower, not higher.

Time spent at work as a standard of performance has been replaced in some organizations by *quantity* of products produced or services provided. In such an environment, in contrast to those in which seniority is counted, simply putting in your time is not enough. Instead, you must show that you are adding value by producing or providing service at a level beyond normal expectations in order to get a pay raise. And, while quantity counts in today's organization, it is not enough to lead to a large pay raise. Why? Because simply producing a large number of products or services does not guarantee that they will be used by consumers of the products or services. Consumers expect to receive high-quality products or services and to be treated well. Consequently, pay raises are allocated on the basis of the *quality* of your work and of the *customer service* that you provide, as well as the quantity of work. This means that your work must be accurate, error free, responsive to the needs of customers, and provided in a timely manner. By emphasizing the quality of your work and customer service, you add value to the organization because the customer is more likely to purchase your product or service, rather than that of a competitor.

New technology and the design of work have brought about additional performance standards monitored by employers. Advances in technology have made it possible for employers to be more responsive to customer needs than ever before. For example, the Internet makes it possible to provide consumers with an almost infinite number of services. In order to do so, however, the computer must be guided by employees to provide meaningful services. As a result, employees increasingly are being held accountable for being *innovative*. Innovative employees add value to the production or service chain and are rewarded accordingly. But innovation alone is not always practical from a business perspective. There are lots of good ideas, but they must be produced or provided at low cost to be profitable. Hence, *efficiency*, or "doing more with less," is another aspect of performance examined by employers in making pay raise decisions.

In terms of changes in work design, employees are expected not only to perform their own individual work, but also to perform in work teams. Many times these teams are charged with providing new and better products or services. Being an effective team member requires employees to exhibit new critical behaviors to earn a pay raise. One such behavior is *leadership*. Employees who can significantly influence the direction of the group in a fashion such that new and innovative products or services are added to the organization are leaders and receive larger increases. Even if one is not a leader in a group, one can also add value by being a good team player. In order to be a *good team player*, it is important to be supportive of team members and pitch in where needed. Both leaders and team members need to be good *organizational citizens* and contribute to the larger mission of the employer. This could include arriving early and staying late, volunteering to work on companywide projects, and helping newcomers learn about the organization.

In summary, simply putting in time is not enough to earn the pay raise that you deserve. Value must be added by your activities at work. Exhibit A-2 offers a checklist for you to see to what extent you are adding value to the organization in the form of your work activities.

How to Bring Your Performance to the Attention of the Organization

As important as performance is to organizations, not all organizations do a good job at measuring and keeping track of employee performance. Many employees have failed to receive the pay raise they really deserve not because a lack of performance, but because the organization did not have a system to record their accomplishments. Thus, if you want a raise, you need to develop a system to gather performance data that will convince your boss of your value to the organization and your need for a corresponding pay raise.

In order for your performance to be noticed in the organization, it must be periodically assessed. If performance is to be assessed, then there must be a standard to compare your performance against. Thus, the start-

Example Pay Communication

EXHIBIT A-2
Adding value at work.

Does Often	Need to Do	Activity	Action Plan
_____	_____	High quantity of work	_____
_____	_____	High quality of work	_____
_____	_____	Good team player	_____
_____	_____	Strong leadership	_____
_____	_____	Good citizen	_____
_____	_____	Innovative ideas	_____
_____	_____	Efficient at work	_____
_____	_____	Strong customer service	_____

Instructions. Check off your effort in each activity. Develop a plan of action to work on those activities not performed regularly.

ing point for bringing your performance to the attention of the organization is to have written performance standards for your job. These standards should be very concrete, specific, and measurable, so that the organization will recognize when you have met or exceeded them. Moreover, since these goals must be viewed as important to the organization, they must meet the approval of those making pay raise decisions. Many people don't get the pay raise they deserve because standards are nonexistent, forgotten, or not viewed as important.

Be sure to review the standards of your job often with your boss. Conditions change and the standards once viewed as attainable may not be because of conditions outside your control. For example, sales may drop due not to a lack of effort on your part but to a downturn in the economy. Other conditions outside your control may include new governmental regulations or legal requirements governing your products and services; a reorganization, merger, or buyout of your company; and new leadership and company strategy that affect your job. If conditions change, make sure that the standards are changed to ensure that you are held accountable for those events under your control.

Example Pay Communication

In order to get the pay raise you deserve, setting standards for your job is not enough. You must also have documentation of your accomplishments relative to these standards. It is a big mistake to rely upon the fallible memory of your boss to remember exactly what you have accomplished for up to a year at a time. Build a file your boss can review, including letters of commendation, completed significant projects, new and innovative ideas, and projects led or completed under time and budget. Whenever possible, copy your boss on significant pieces of work you have accomplished.

In most organizations, performance is reviewed on annual basis. While completing reviews on an annual rather than more frequent basis makes it easier on the boss, it does not help you get the pay raise you really deserve. To get that pay raise, the more frequent the review the better. By having frequent reviews, your accomplishments are more likely to stand out in your boss's mind when pay raise decisions are made. Frequent reviews also make it easier to alter performance standards that may have moved beyond your control. Most important of all, frequent performance reviews allow you to correct your actions if they are seen by the boss as straying from the target. In the absence of frequent reviews, you may end up in a position in which it is impossible for you to alter your course of action in time for a favorable pay raise decision. Steps to make sure your performance is recognized are:

1. Develop concrete, specific, and measurable performance standards
2. Document your accomplishments relative to the performance standards
3. Set up more frequent reviews of your performance standards and accomplishments

Boundaries on What Employers Can Pay for Performance

Two conditions may limit the pay raise that you receive even when your performance is exceptional: your salary and the budget. Don't fret about these issues, however, as steps can be taken to overcome these boundaries, as will be described.

Maximum Salary Ranges

The first threat to a performance-based pay raise is the size of your salary. In any job there is a maximum amount that the employer is willing to pay someone who holds the job. A maximum salary is established so that costs do not become too large for the company to earn a profit. Even if your performance is exceptional, many organizations will not give you the pay raise you really deserve because the pay raise would cause your salary to exceed the maximum salary allowed for your job. A way to get around this barrier is to ask your boss for a pay raise in the form of a *cash bonus rather than a salary increase*. Because the cash bonus is not made a permanent part of your salary, your pay raise will not make you exceed the allowable maximum.

Budget Limitations

A second threat to a performance-based pay raise is the size of the budget for pay raises. The raise budget is usually determined by the organization's ability to pay, which in turn is related to the successfulness of the business. During prosperous economic times, there may be a large enough pool of money to fund double-digit pay raises. During harsh times for the organization, there may be no money to fund any pay raises.

If the budget is too small for you to receive the pay raise that you really deserve based on your performance, then work with your boss to make cost reductions or revenue generation as standards of performance for your job. Obviously, increased revenues or decreased costs that you are responsible for will help the business. This puts you in a good position to negotiate with the boss for a portion of the profits to go to you for your accomplishments. In other words, you have funded your increase by your ability to cut costs or increase revenues. Not only do you benefit, but the organization does as well if you share a portion of the profits with the company. Hence, you have created a situation in which both you and the boss can win by focusing your standards on cost containment and revenue enhancement above the normal expectation for your job.

Raises Based on the Value of the Job You Hold

One of the best-kept secrets in organizations is a process known as job evaluation, in which the value of your job to the organization is established. This process takes place so infrequently that people in organizations sometimes assume that only their performance is evaluated. Although it is not frequently done, job evaluation is another leverage point in the organization to get the pay raise you really deserve. In order to receive the raise, you will have to show that your job adds more value to the organization than it is given credit for. To do so, you need to demonstrate that the scope of your job has been significantly increased beyond its initial level of value.

How Job Value Is Established

The starting point for determining the value of jobs in the organization is a job description. The job description details the duties and responsibilities of the job; the requirements needed to perform the job, such as education and experience; and the environmental and physical conditions under which work is performed. Each job description in the organization is evaluated to establish the relative value of each job to the organization. A hierarchy of jobs is arranged from the most valuable to the least valuable in the organization. Differences in pay reflect these differences in value.

The evaluation of jobs is usually conducted by a committee consisting of someone from the human resources department, an executive who oversees work in that area, and a member of an oversight panel, which is responsible for coordinating and approving the value of jobs in the organization. Once an initial determination of job value is established by this committee, it will not meet again until there is evidence that the scope of your job has been significantly altered such that it needs to be reevaluated. Unless you bring these changes in your job to the attention of the committee, your job may never be reevaluated and you may never be able to take advantage of this leverage point in getting the pay raise you really deserve.

Job Evaluation Procedures

Written standards are usually used by the committee to systematically review the value of jobs to the organization. These standards can be thought of as scorecards used to grade the relative worth of each job to the organization. The written standards are known as factors; points are assigned to the levels for each factor. The greater the points allocated to a job, the greater the value of the job.

Not all organizations use the same factors in evaluating jobs, but there is a great deal of commonality, so it is possible to have a general idea of what factors will be applied to your job. A brief review of these common factors follows.

The first factor commonly applied is the *level of education* required to perform the job successfully. The level of education required refers to the *minimum* level needed to perform the job duties competently in the job description. Thus, for example, even though someone with a Ph.D. could perform a secretarial position, the minimum requirement is usually a high school degree or a GED.

A second factor often used is *experience*. This factor refers to the *minimum* amount of experience needed to perform certain duties. Having experience with these duties is a prerequisite for performing the duties of the current job.

A third factor is the *complexity* of the duties performed on the job. More complex duties require more judgment on the part of the jobholder to complete these duties successfully. More complex duties also require a greater level of job knowledge to complete the duties. Highly technical jobs or those requiring supervisory responsibilities usually receive high scores on complexity.

A fourth factor is *accountability*. This factor refers to how much discretion the person has in performing the duties of the job. Jobs with low discretion receive a great deal of direct supervision, while jobs with high accountability have very little direct supervision; holders of high-accountability jobs make decisions themselves that have significant consequences for the company.

A fifth factor is *interpersonal contacts*. This factor refers to the number, types, and levels of contacts. Jobs that interface with the customer usually score more points, as do jobs that require the job holder to interact with high-level executives.

A sixth factor is *working conditions,* which refers to the conditions under which the job holder is required to work. The harsher the physical conditions, the more value the job has. Working conditions include physical effort required, such as lifting; environmental conditions, such as noise and heat; and psychological conditions, such as travel and stress.

Making Job Evaluation Work for You

One way to make job evaluation work for you is to evaluate your own job and see if there have been any significant changes in your current job from what was required when you started and what is required now (see Exhibit A-3). Remember, these changes refer to what is actually required of you by the organization, not a "wish list" of what you hope the job would require. If you do note that significant changes have been required of you in your job along the lines of the factors described, then you should bring

EXHIBIT A-3
Changes in job scope.

Factor	Start	Now
Education	_____	_____
Experience	_____	_____
Complexity	_____	_____
Accountability	_____	_____
Interpersonal Contacts	_____	_____
Working Conditions	_____	_____

it to the attention of your boss for purposes of upgrading your job to a higher category of pay.

Upgrading Your Current Job

Even if your job has not significantly changed since you started, you can still make job evaluation work for you. To do so requires you to take action to enlarge the scope of your current job. The first step is to show your boss that you are exceeding all expectations in performing your current job. By performing at a high level, it shows that you are ready to take on higher levels of responsibility worth more to the organization.

The second step is to help redesign your current job so that the duties and requirements are significantly upgraded. One way to do this is to talk with your boss about what things you can do in your job to add more value to the organization. Another way is to talk to the people you interface with in your work, especially customers, and see what additional responsibilities you could take on to help them in their jobs.

Lastly, you could consult job descriptions of others in similar jobs to see what else they may be doing to add value. An excellent starting point is the *Dictionary of Occupational Titles*, which has descriptions of work for thousands of jobs. It is published by the U.S. Department of Labor. Summarized below are steps to upgrade your current job:

1. Evaluate the value of your current job
2. Expand the scope of your current job
3. Consult job description reference guides

Raises Based on Market Adjustments

Like job evaluations, another less well-known way to get the pay raise you deserve is on the basis of a market adjustment. In order for employers to retain talent in the organization, they benchmark pay rates against the pay rates their competitors are paying for similar jobs. Pay raises, known as market adjustments, are sometimes allocated to make sure that talented individuals keep up with the market average. Some organizations are very good at gathering data in the market; others are not. To be sure that your salary is competitive with the market, you should gather your own data. This is especially true if your performance is consistently high and you have never received a market adjustment.

How Market Surveys Work

Why would employers tell one another what they pay their employees? Because by doing so, they are told what other employers are paying and can be sure that they remain competitive. A condition of receiving market data for employers is that they participate in the survey. If they don't participate, then they will not be able to keep up with the market because they won't know what the market is paying.

In conducting surveys, data are not gathered for all jobs. To do so would be too time-consuming a task. Instead, certain jobs are targeted for survey efforts. If your job is a targeted one, there is a large amount of data available for you to review. If your job is not targeted, then you may have to conduct your own survey. Both of these options will now be discussed.

Gathering and Using Existing Data

If your job is well known and employs a large number of people, then chances are there will be pay survey data available for you to use. Much of the data are available for no cost and some are available at cost. Sources of data available to you include the government, professional and trade associations, and consulting firms.

Government Data

The Bureau of Labor Statistics in the U.S. Department of Labor is the branch of the federal government that collects wage and salary data for the U.S. Government. These findings are available in area and industry wage surveys as well as in the publications *Monthly Labor Review* and *Occupational Outlook Quarterly*. Libraries often have these reports, but if they don't, they are available in the Bureau of Labor Statistics' nine regional offices.

Not only does the federal government collect pay rates, but so do state and local governments. At the state level, the personnel department will know where to find these data. At the local level, these data may be available from the chamber of commerce.

Two limitations should be noted with the use of these data. One is that the data may be somewhat dated. Second, the data are more likely to be available for nonexempt than exempt jobs. Hence, the data are a good source of information on low-level jobs in which pay rates may not change rapidly.

Professional and Trade Associations

There are thousands of professional and trade associations in the United States. If you are unsure of whether your profession or trade has such an association, there are several directories of these associations that you can consult at your local library. Associations such as these are sometimes a much better source of pay rates for exempt jobs than the government. Also, they tend to be more current than are government data. People in professional and managerial jobs in which the market shifts often are advised to start here. Often these data require a fee to be accessed.

Consulting Firms

There are many consulting firms that specialize in conducting market surveys, including Hay and Associates, Watson-Wyatt, and Mercer. These firms also do compensation consulting, and their databases contain the pay rates of their client firms. Of all the sources of data, these tend to be the most current, comprehensive, and expensive to use. Usually they have data on all levels of jobs.

Reviewing the Data

Regardless of which source of data is used, care must be taken in interpreting market survey data. In particular, care must be used to ensure that a fair comparison is made and that the correct figures are used. If not, your employer is very likely not to be convinced that you need a market adjustment. For a fair comparison, you need to carefully match the description of your job with the description of the job in the survey. Titles in and of themselves can be very misleading. Also, pay rates for the same job vary by industry and geographic area. Hence, the data you use should be from the industries and geographic areas from which your employer recruits. To find this out, all you need to do is look at the background of recent hires who also hold your job.

In terms of gathering accurate data from the survey, you also need to review the data carefully. The data presented are usually averages. When averages are reported, the larger the number of firms used to calculate the average, the more accurate the data. Also, the average is usually reported with a mean or median statistic. The median statistic is a more accurate measure of the market average for your job because it is less likely to be influenced by extreme values, which may distort the average.

Conducting Your Own Survey

Some people are in jobs in which there is not much existing data in summary form. When this is the case, you may need to do your own survey. One way to do so is to search for advertisements in newspapers and trade publications. Sometimes, they list pay rates. Unfortunately, most often they do not list these rates, so you need to contact people directly who hold these positions. Conducting your own survey requires the following steps:

1. *Develop a list of names.* Based on your knowledge of your industry, as well as professional and trade publications, list the companies that your employer competes against. Use professional directories and trade directories to locate a person in each organization in a position similar to your own.
2. *Contact people directly.* Use the telephone to contact people initially to see if they would be willing to participate in the survey. The answer is much more likely to be "yes" if you promise to tabulate the results in an anonymous fashion and send the results to them.
3. *Fax the survey.* Faxes are more likely than letters to be responded to and responded to in a timely manner. Be absolutely sure to include a brief job description to verify that the person you are surveying

is in a job similar to your own. Remember, job titles in and of themselves can be very misleading.
4. *Tabulate the results.* Calculate the median value and report the anonymous results back to the survey participants, along with a thank-you note.

Cost of Living

In terms of having leverage with your employer, market survey results are the most persuasive factor in getting a market adjustment because of how competitors' pay rates relate directly to the business. Cost of living, although a less effective method, is another indicator that can point out the need for a market adjustment. The argument can be made that as the cost of goods and services rises, it becomes more expensive to live in an area and to remain with the employer. The cost of living is indexed by the U.S. Government using an index known as the Consumer Price Index (CPI), which tracks changes in the cost of living over time. CPI data can be collected and shown to the employer along with actual survey data. Summarized below are ways to make the market work for you:

1. Read employment advertisements. Has your pay slipped below advertised rates? If yes, then go to steps 2, 3, and 4.
2. Gather data from secondary survey sources, including the government, trade and professional associations, and consulting firms.
3. If you cannot find market data for your job from secondary sources, then conduct your own survey.
4. Supplement your survey findings with data on the cost of living from the Consumer Price Index.

Outside Offers

A final method to show your market value is to go out and get a job offer elsewhere. Although this can be seen as strong evidence of your market value, it is a very risky strategy. For ethical reasons, you should look for another job only if you are genuinely interested in another job. You should not seek another job simply for purposes of obtaining a pay increase from your current employer. Organizations spend a lot of time and energy recruiting, and it is not fair to have applicants who are not genuinely interested. Getting an outside offer is also risky because it may backfire on you. Rather than being given a counter by your organization, you may be told

"Congratulations, we hope you enjoy your new job." Finally, outside offers are also risky because the word may get out among employers that you are not really interested in going to work for a new employer but simply looking to get a raise. This message can be devastating to you in the future should you ever be genuinely interested in a job outside your current organization.

If you are genuinely interested in a job at a different company, visit the organization and receive an offer. However, after a thorough review, if you decide the job is not for you, then submit this offer to your current employer for consideration. Note: Be extremely careful here, too. Your employer may view the offer as evidence of a strong chance that you will leave should the "right" offer come along. In this case, there is little incentive to provide a pay raise. In short, be very careful with outside offers as evidence of market value.

Raises Based on Promotions

An unwritten rule in many current organizations is that you need to engage in continuous learning in order to get ahead. No longer is it enough to simply earn a degree, attend an occasional company-sponsored training class, and put in your time on the job to get a promotion. In order to move ahead and get the pay raise you deserve in today's organization, you must take the initiative to upgrade your skills continuously in order to be flexible enough to adapt to the changing needs of your employer. The cycle time to bring new products and services has been drastically reduced in this country. In order to help develop and service new products and services, constantly evolving skill sets are required.

Career Lattices: More than Upward Mobility

An important point of leverage in getting the pay raise you really deserve is taking on new jobs. Traditionally, this has meant upward mobility in organizations in the form of promotions. While pay raises based on promotions still do happen in work organizations, they are much less common. Organizations have been downsizing, and this has resulted in far fewer managerial and staff positions. The upward mobility track has been replaced by much more flexible career paths in organizations. To get the pay raise you really deserve, it is essential that you move about jobs in nontraditional ways. Moreover, career paths are no longer clearly spelled out, and it is up to you to learn about what the flexible career paths look like in your organization. Increasingly, these career paths are lattices in which individuals receive lateral and downward promotions, along with upward ones.

You may be wondering how a lateral or downward promotion could lead to anything but a pay *decrease!* The reason you can still advance monetarily with these new lattice career paths is that the type of movement that is rewarded is the one that adds value to the organization. By taking a lateral move you may be gaining valuable experience, as in an international assignment in a company with global growth aspirations. By taking a downward move you may gain valuable technical experience that will be needed later, such as when you supervise people with that technical expertise.

Upgrade Your Capabilities to Be Mobile

Take every opportunity you can to learn about your business and to develop the appropriate skills. Take the opportunity to attend all company-sponsored training made available to you. Moreover, it is wise to set up an educational savings account in an effort to upgrade your most valuable asset—you! Plan to save 1 to 2 percent of your income to educate yourself further outside the company. Ways to invest in yourself include:

1. Obtain an advanced degree
2. Get certified or accredited
3. Become computer literate and keep up-to-date with the latest software
4. Maintain currency on your certificate or accreditation
5. Become familiar with general management and specialty areas outside your own
6. Learn a second language
7. Learn about the culture of other countries

Volunteer to work on special projects, especially those that involve working in teams that are cross-functional in orientation. That is, work on projects that span your area of the business and others with which you are less familiar. Usually, these teams are formed to come up with better and more efficient ways to deliver the product or service. By taking advantage of working on special projects in the organization, you will improve your knowledge of other areas of the business, improve your teamwork skills,

Example Pay Communication

and, perhaps most important of all, improve your visibility to those in power to make pay raise decisions.

Criteria Used to Assess Your Potential

In moving people about the organization into positions deserving of a pay raise, organizations rely upon many criteria, including the following:

- *Performance.* It is not enough to have just knowledge and skills. You must deliver on your potential to be considered a good risk for further advancement.
- *Willingness.* If you are hesitant to make changes, reluctant to take risks, unwilling to move or try new experiences, then you are likely to be bypassed in favor of those who are open and willing to embrace change.
- *Knowledge.* The knowledge earned through a degree becomes obsolete much more rapidly than in years past. A premium is paid to subject matter experts. To be one, you must be on the cutting edge in your field through further education, training, or professional involvement.
- *Skills.* Knowing about something is not enough. You must also be able to apply it to specific functions in the organization. Also, technical skills alone are not sufficient. You must also have sound people skills to be a team player, manager, and leader when the situation requires performing these roles.

How to Influence Promotion Outcomes

As shown earlier, there are steps that you can take to make sure that you develop the competencies needed to be eligible for promotion. These steps are designed to ensure that you have the competencies needed to match up with the advancement criteria being applied by organizations. However, it is also helpful to influence the decision makers who will apply these criteria.

One way to influence decision makers is to build a portfolio of your competencies. In some organizations, this is part of the annual performance review process. In other organizations, competencies are not formally monitored. Even in those organizations that involve a formal system of tracking competencies, records are often haphazardly maintained. Hence, it is wise to maintain your own portfolio of developmental experiences that have enhanced your competencies and made you a better "fit" in other parts of the organization. Not only should you keep a portfolio, but it should also be periodically reviewed with your boss. This will help keep him or her up-to-date on your capabilities and able to mention your name when advancement opportunities arise. Moreover, your boss can give you guidance on where further development is needed. Another possibility is to select a senior person to be your mentor and have that person review your portfolio for further development needs based upon his or her experiences for advancing in the organization.

In addition to reviewing your portfolio with your boss and mentor, it is also wise to review your portfolio with your peers. Increasingly in organizations, peers as well as supervisors are being consulted in advancement decisions. This is consistent with the notion of pushing decision making down in organizations to the level where the knowledge resides. Peers have day-to-day contact with you and are very conscious of your strengths and weaknesses. Thus, they need to be consulted as well. The following list summarizes how you can create your own developmental review team:

1. Develop a portfolio of your developmental activities
2. Select a senior-level executive to be your mentor
3. Select a close business associate to be your peer
4. Review your file at least yearly with your boss, mentor, and peer
5. Map out a plan of action to further upgrade your capabilities

Making Your Case to the Boss

Knowing how to get the pay raise you really deserve not only requires that you know the rules of the game, but also that you know how to use these rules to your advantage. Although it may happen from time to time, pay raises usually do not result from trickery, emotion, or need. In fact, trying to trick the boss, playing on the boss's emotions rather than logic, or being viewed as desperate will probably backfire—not only leading to no raise this time, but also tainting your chances of a raise in the future. For example, research has shown that using flattery or ingratiating behavior as a tactic to win a pay raise does backfire because the boss perceives flattery as a signal that you really like working for him or her and are thus likely to stay with the organization even if you *don't* get a pay raise. Tactical issues that do help get the pay raise you really deserve include knowing when to negotiate a pay raise, knowing what to present when asking for a pay raise, and knowing how to ask for a pay raise.

When to Ask for a Pay Raise

In some organizations, the timing of pay increases is limited by policy to certain time periods. Performance-based bonuses, for example, may be on a quarterly or yearly basis. Other types of raises, such as market adjustments, job upgrades, and promotions, may be on an as-needed basis. It is extremely important that you get to know the people and the policies in your human resources department and find out timing issues. Sometimes such issues as the timing of market adjustments are not made public through a policy manual or the like.

Another important issue in knowing when to ask for a pay raise is awareness of the budget cycle. It is better to ask for a raise as the budget is being prepared than to wait until after the budget is completed. This is especially true if your contributions will warrant a large raise. Your boss may be planning for average raises and needs to plan ahead for an unusually large raise. Also, it is better to ask for a raise immediately after the budget has been approved rather than just before the budget expires. Budgets can be overspent, and there may be less cash available for raises at the end of the budget cycle.

Closely related to knowledge of the budget cycle is the performance of the organization. During harsh economic times for the organization there may be no money in the pay raise budget. If organizational performance is poor, this may create an opportunity to be rewarded for good performance. You can ask your boss to consider a raise when organizational performance improves. Or suggest other rewards, such as flexible working hours or a chance to set up an incentive plan under which you are rewarded for cost savings or revenue generating activities that actually lead to an improvement in organizational performance. When organizational performance is good, as reflected in strong financial numbers, you may be more likely to earn a larger-than-average raise, especially to the extent that you can show your contribution to the strong figures.

A final issue that can affect your pay raise is how well received your boss is in the organization. A boss who is a strong performer and functions at a high level in the organization is more likely to be able to deliver larger raises. Similarly, bosses who are well connected politically in the organization are likely to deliver larger raises. The list below summarizes favorable times to ask for a raise:

- During the pay raise period spelled out in policy (e.g., anniversary dates or annual review dates)
- During the budget planning phase
- When organizational performance (e.g., profits) is strong
- When your boss is well respected and well connected

What to Ask for in a Pay Raise

To most of us, a raise implies more money, and usually it is. But a raise can be more than just money and may have to be something other than money when the organization is not doing well financially. There are several other important dimensions to pay increases to consider.

One dimension to consider is the permanence of your increase. An increase can be in the form of a permanent addition to your wage or salary. For example, your salary may go from $60,000 to $65,000 per year. In general, it is advantageous for you to get your increase made a permanent addition to your salary because of the compounding effects over time. The longer you stay with the organization, the greater the value of a pay raise. Remember, raises are usually granted once a year based on a review of your performance. It is possible, however, to ask for a more frequent review of your performance and pay raise. If you are doing really well at work, you can be put on a nine-month rather than twelve-month review cycle.

If a salary increase is not possible, another form of pay raise is a bonus—a one-time cash payment for outstanding work done. Although not as desirable as a salary increase, it is certainly better than no raise in a particular year. During difficult financial times for an employer, a bonus may be a practical alternative to a permanent salary increase.

Another dimension to consider in asking for a raise is rewards other than pay. Examples here include additional time off, flexible work schedules, benefits such as child care, and company stock. If you have a very busy schedule or a time-consuming family life, additional time off, a flexible schedule, or child-care assistance may have more value to you than a cash pay raise. If you can afford to take some risk and you anticipate that your organization will do well in the future, you may consider stock as a payment. Pay raises other than cash include:

Company stock
Child care

Time off
Flexible schedule
Company car
More frequent reviews
Company product purchase discounts
Office space
Use of company plane

How to Ask for a Pay Raise

In general it is best *not* to ask for a pay raise. Instead, present the data about your value to the organization and let the data sell your value. Throughout this section, the importance of documentation has been stressed. This documentation contains the data you should present to your boss. Present the data first, talk about the raise second. If the data are strong, your boss will come to you to discuss the raise issue. Psychologically, it is better to have your boss approach you about a raise than for you to approach your boss—this indicates that your boss believes that you have *earned* it. When you go to the boss, the perception is that you *need* a raise. Your contribution to the organization speaks louder than your need for money.

As has been stressed throughout the appendix, you should also present a strong record of your contributions to your boss. Going to the boss prematurely may signal that you are desperate, which may work against you not only now but later, when you truly do have a strong case. If you are unsure of your record, check with your peers and human resources department. If you have been doing a good job keeping your boss appraised of your record, then chances are the boss will bring up your review and possible pay raise.

Once in a while you may have a boss who is unwilling to review your case. The boss may, for example, feel threatened by your successes. Don't despair in this situation. After giving the boss ample time to review your record, ask about the possibility of a raise. If the answer is unacceptable to you, then you can approach your human resources department. Also, you may discuss the situation with your boss's boss, but only if you don't have reason to be fearful of reprisals. Or you can simply wait until you have a new boss. Strong cases are not forgotten for long, especially with sound documentation. Situations involving poor supervision are typically rectified monetarily in work organizations. Sometimes it just takes time to do so. The most important thing is to avoid allowing emotions and accusations to jeopardize your chances of getting the pay raise you deserve. Let the data talk for themselves once again.

A response to anticipate when asking for a pay raise is that while the employer would like to do something to reward your good performance, it cannot do so. Reasons given might include a limited budget this year, poor financial performance by the organization, or your salary bumping up against the maximum of your pay range. If this is the case, now is the time to help your boss see that there are some alternatives. Not all bosses are willing to share these alternatives, in the hope that you will be unaware of them. In any event, you can bring up the possibility of types of rewards other than cash or the possibility of further review of your accomplishments when rewards are more plentiful. Because bosses come and go, it is always wise to get the results of your discussion put in writing so that the pact is not forgotten by the current boss or overlooked by a future one.

Conclusion

In today's fiercely competitive marketplace, the rules of pay and promotion have changed. Whether entry-level or executive level, you are probably dealing with restructurings and cost reductions, while working harder than ever before. Some of the reasons for this are increased competition, changing regulations, emerging new technologies, and the changing needs of customers. All this change means people need to do some things differently. Change offers an opportunity for something new, something better.

In this appendix, a simple roadmap including four major leverage points shows you how employers make pay raise decisions and how you can influence them. By following all four steps in the pay raise model—elevating your performance, upgrading your current job, assessing your market value, and upgrading your capabilities—you have the tools to attain power over your pay. The last step is up to you. Create a new "you"—when you are excelling at your job and doing good work, your job will be worth more to you. Go ahead and lay the groundwork for success. Embrace the fast speed of today's business. Only you can earn the pay you really deserve.

Index

associations, 99–100, 109
attitudes measurement, 46, 253–255, 257–264
attraction pay philosophy, 26

balanced-scorecard strategy, 18
   compensation policy in, 145–146
   compensation strategy in, 36
   individual evaluation in, 163
   pay design in, 229
   pay implementation in, 244–245
   pay structures in, 141–142
   performance standards in, 162, 209, 210
   reward types for, 203–204, 205, 212–213
   work evaluation for, 83–84, 85–88
base pay systems
   determinants of, 8, 166, 204
   work analysis, 45–70
   work evaluation, 71–93
   see also broad pay bands; narrow pay bands
behavior as performance standard, 161–162, 168, 178
behavior-based compensation strategy, 27, 253–255
beliefs, measurement of, 46

benchmark jobs, 96, 98, 109, 121–126, 131–136, 144
benefits, 106, 115–116, 205, 213, 219
bonuses, 166–167, 205, 213
bottom-line results, 12
broad pay bands, 10, 11, 12, 30–31, 109, 142–143, 147, 244
Bureau of Labor Statistics, 99, 109
business processes, 6, 8, 34
business strategies
   cascading goals in, 20
   checklist for, 275–292
   context for, 5–6
   contingency factors in, 34, 35
   do's and don'ts for, 269–270
   example communication on, 293–316
   formulation of, 15, 20–21
   market surveys customized by, 96
   model for, 6–13
   sources of, 18–19
   types of, 15–18
   work evaluation and, 75–79
   see also specific types
Business Week, as data source, 100

case studies
   appliance maker, 105–109

Index

case studies (*continued*)
  cable television company, 8–11
  compensation decision making, 8–13
  compensation strategies, 34, 36–38
  computer maker, 11–13
  computer storage products company, 204–205, 233, 244
  county children services agency, 106, 109–115, 151–153
  county engineers office, 70, 89–93, 115–126, 150–151, 168–178, 232
  education agency, 84–88, 178–198
  educational distributor, 64, 68–69, 79–83, 116, *126–136*, 149–150, 231–232
  flight simulation company, 257–264
  gourmet products maker, 214, 218–219, 241–243
  gourmet rice meal maker, 38
  human resources provider, 211–214
  implement dealer, 37–38
  individual rewards, 168–198
  large retailer, 83–84
  law firm, 36
  lawn care products maker, 244–253
  market surveys, 105–136
  pay design, 231–233
  pay evaluation, 257–264
  pay implementation, 240–252
  questionnaire usage, 64, 68–69
  reward systems, 168–198, 204–205, 211–220
  work evaluation systems, 79–93
chambers of commerce, 99
Chief Learning Officer, 17
classification systems for work evaluation, 72–73, 75–76
client development as performance strategy, 36
closed compensation systems, 31–32
commissions, 226
communications for pay implementation, 238, *293–316*
community involvement as performance strategy, 36
compensation director, 11

compensation strategies
  checklist for, *25*
  context for, 5–6
  contingency factors in, 34, *35*
  do's and don'ts for, 269–270
  example communication on, 293–316
  forces influencing, 22, *23*
  market surveys customized by, 96
  model for, 6–13
  pay assessment in, 26–28
  pay form in, 28–29
  pay philosophy in, 22–26, 201
  segments in, *24*
  work evaluation and, 72, 75–79
  see also specific types
competencies
  development of, 9, 167–168
  measurement of, 46–48, 101, 162–163
  types of, 77–79
competency systems, for work evaluation, 74–79, 83–84, 239
consulting firms, 99, 228, 229
context as work analysis component, 48–50
controller as evaluator, 210–211
cost-driven strategy, 12, 17
  checklist for, 285–287
  compensation strategy in, 27
  compensation system in, 32
  core values and, 37–38
  job analysis emphasis for, 49
  labor market for, 98, 99
  market pricing in, 144
  pay bands in, 30, 31, 143, 147, 148
  pay design in, 228
  pay evaluation in, 255
  pay philosophy in, 24, 26, 145
  pay plan design in, 32, 33
  pay structures in, 141
  pay systems in, 29, 37–38
  performance standards in, 160, 161, 162, 163, 200
  rewards emphasis in, 29, 38
  reward types for, 166, 167, 202, 226–227

318

Index

work evaluation systems for, 75–76, 77, *78*, 200
critical success factors lists, 19
culture, organizational, 6, 8, 34
customer appreciation, 11
customer contact, 16, 38, 164, 205
customer service, 16, 18
customer service-based strategy, 10, 16
   checklist for, 275–277
   compensation strategy in, 27, 38
   individual evaluation in, 163–164
   job analysis emphasis for, 49
   network analysis in, 49
   organizational evaluation in, 211
   pay bands in, 143, 147, 148
   pay design in, 228–229
   pay evaluation in, 254
   pay philosophy in, 24, 26
   pay plan design in, 32, 33
   pay systems in, 29–30
   performance standards in, 161–162, 162, 200, 209
   rewards emphasis in, 29
   reward types for, 167, 202, 212–213, 227
   work evaluation systems for, 76, *77, 78*, 85–88, 201

data analysis, 101–105, 255–264
data collection techniques, 51, 100–101
data sources, 50, 99–100, 109
discrimination issues, 71–72
documents as work analysis sources, 50

economic downturn issues, 208, 209
economic modeling, 256–257
economic value-added (EVA) model, 17–18, *209*
education
   pay increase and, 31, 140, 162
   as reward, 167–168, 263
employee attitudes
   alignment with corporation, 5
   job descriptions and, 46

   pay design and, 228, 253–255
   survey of, 11, 257–264
   toward reward systems, 239
   toward traits as performance standards, 161
   work evaluation and, 71
employee empowerment, 9–10
   evaluation of managers, 164
   example pay communication for, 293–316
   in market surveys, 116
   in pay design, 229–230, 232
   in pay plan design, 32
   in quality-based business, 16
   reward allocation, 201, 211
   self-evaluation, 163
   team member participation, 201
external equity pay philosophy, 22–24, 95, 116, 129, 204

factor systems, for work evaluation, 73–74, 76, *77*, 79–83, 85–93
feedback, 13, 48, 160, 161
finance-driven strategy, 17–18
   checklist for, 287–289
   compensation strategy in, 27
   job analysis emphasis for, 49
   labor market for, 99
   pay bands in, 30, 31
   pay philosophy in, 24, 26
   pay plan design in, 32, 33
   pay systems in, 29
   performance standards in, 160, 161, 162, 163, 209
   rewards emphasis in, 29
   reward types for, 214, 218–220
   work evaluation systems for, 76
financial performance standards, 208–209, 253–255
firm management as performance strategy, 36
fixed pay systems, 29–30
focus groups, 11, 51, 262, 264
"free riding," 208, 209

General Electric, 17
"glass ceiling," 71

Index

goals, company, 5, 20
greenfield start-ups, 76, 142

hazardous situations, 48, 49
HRIS, use of, 240
human capital-based strategy, 18
  checklist for, 289–292
  compensation strategy in, 27, 38
  compensation system in, 32
  job analysis emphasis for, 49, 50
  labor market for, 99
  market surveys and, 95
  pay bands in, 30–31, 31, 148–149
  pay design in, 228–229
  pay evaluation in, 255
  pay philosophy in, 26
  pay plan design in, 32, 33
  pay systems in, 29
  performance standards in, 200
  rewards emphasis in, 29
  reward types for, 201, 202, 203, 219, 227
  work evaluation systems for, 77, 78, 201
human resources department, 6, 8, 34, 230–231

IBM, 72
incentive systems, 8, 106–107
individual rewards, 30
  case studies of, 168–198
  do's and don'ts for, 272
  evaluators for, 163–164
  performance standards for, 159–163, 215–218
  productivity gains and, 209–210
  by strategy type, 276, 279, 281–282, 284, 286–287, 289, 291
  types of, 165–168
  weighting of, 165, 166
innovation-based strategy, 9–10, 13, 16–17
  checklist for, 280–283
  compensation strategy in, 27
  individual evaluation in, 163, 164
  job analysis emphasis for, 49, 50
  labor market for, 99

market pricing in, 144
  pay bands in, 30–31, 143, 147, 148
  pay design in, 228–229
  pay evaluation in, 254
  pay implementation in, 244–245
  pay philosophy in, 24, 26, 145
  pay plan design in, 32, 33
  pay structures in, 142
  pay systems in, 29
  performance standards in, 161, 162, 200, 210
  rewards emphasis in, 29
  reward types for, 167, 201, 202, 203, 212–213, 218, 227
  work analysis in, 68
  work evaluation systems for, 76, 77, 78, 201
input, 17, 48
internal equity pay philosophy, 22–24
interviews, for work analysis, 51

job, as work analysis component, 48
job analysis, *see* work analysis
job analysts, 50, 70
job-based compensation strategy, 27, 101
job classification assessment, 27
job descriptions, 27, 45–46, 48, 64, 65–68, 96
job evaluation, *see* work evaluation
job incumbent, as work analysis source, 50
job titles, 12, 45–46, 47, 95–96

knowledge
  as factor, 82, 87, 92
  institutionalization of, 17
  transfer system for, 17
  see also education

labor, *see* human capital
labor market characteristics, 98–99, 109
lag compensation strategy, 33
lag market pay philosophy, 25–26, 37, 144–146

Index

laws and legal issues
   compensation policy and, 6, 8, 34
   equal employment, 46
   pay design and, 230
   performance standards issues, 161, 162
   work evaluation and, 71
layoffs, 37–38
lead compensation strategy, 33, 241
lead market pay philosophy, 25–26, 99, 105, 144–146, 213
line-of-sight issues, 208–209, 219–220
locked step pay structure, 141–142, 150

management by objectives, 5, 13
market surveys
   case studies of, 105–136
   discrimination issues in, 72
   do's and don'ts for, 271
   external equity strategy assessment by, 24–25
   job titles in, 46
   response rate of, 101
   sampling error in, 95–96
   steps in, 96, 97, 98–105
   use of, 95–96
"mass customization," 33
match market pay philosophy, 25–26, 105–106, 143–146, 151, 213, 219, 244
merit pay, 11, 12–13, 29, 150, 167, 204, 239–240
mission statement, 19, 20–21, 263
monetary rewards, 28–29, 166–167, 202
multi-rater assessment process, 163

narrow pay bands, 10, 12, 30, 142, 147
National Association of Social Workers, 109
National Labor Relations Act, 34
network analysis, 48
nonmonetary rewards, 28–29, 38, 219
nonprofit organizations, 29–30

observation as data collection technique, 51
open book issues, 208, 209
open compensation systems, 31–32, 38
operational performance standards, 207, 209, 253–255
operational plans, 19, 21
organizational flexibility, 12, 27
organizational learning strategy, *see* innovation-based strategy
organizational rewards, 245
   case studies for, 211–220
   do's and don'ts for, 273
   evaluators for, 210–211
   performance standards for, 207–210
   personnel excluded from, 226–227
   by strategy type, 277, 279–280, 282, 284–285, 287, 289, 291
   weighting of, 211, *212–214*
organizational structure, and compensation policy, 6, 8, 34
output, 17, 48

pay assessment
   by strategy type, 275, 277–278, 280, 283, 285, 287, 289–290
   types of, 26–28
pay bands
   narrow vs. broad, 30–31
   number of, 148, 151
   overlap in, 31, 109, 148–149
   ranges in, 139–140
   single-rate, 138–139
pay delivery
   by strategy type, 275, 278, 280–281, 283, 285–286, 288, 290
   types of, 30–32
pay design
   case studies of, 231–233
   consultant's role in, 229
   do's and don'ts for, 273
   employees' role in, 229–230
   human resources role in, 230–231
   management role in, 228–229
   objectives of, 225–227
   standards for, 227

pay design (*continued*)
  by strategy type, 277, 280, 282, 285, 287, 289, 291–292
  team for, 228
  union's role in, 230
pay evaluation
  benchmarks in, 256
  case study of, 257–264
  design factors in, 255–256
  do's and don'ts for, 274
  economic modeling in, 256–257
  measures in, 253–255, 259–262
  by strategy type, 277, 280, 282, 285, 287, 289, 292
pay forms
  by strategy type, 275, 278, 280, 283, 285, 288, 290
  types of, 28–30
pay grades, *see* pay bands
pay implementation
  alignment of, 235–239
  case studies of, 240–252
  do's and don'ts for, 273–274
  integration of, 239–240
pay philosophies
  by strategy type, 275, 277, 280, 282–283, 285, 287, 289
  types of, 22–26
pay plan design
  by strategy type, 276, 278, 281, 283, 286, 288, 290
  types of, 32–33
pay ranges, 139–140, 146–151
payroll system, 240
pay structures
  case studies of, 149–153
  do's and don'ts for, 272
  formation of, 137
  policy issues, 144–149
  by strategy type, 276, 279, 281, 284, 286, 288, 291
  types of, 137–144
pay system administration, 11, 13
  pay design, 225–233
  pay implementation, 235–252
peer evaluation, 164, 200–201, 205, 211

pensions, 240
performance-based compensation strategy, 27–28, 34, 106, 109, 139, 219, 259–262
performance standards
  for individuals, 159–163
  for organizations, 207–210
  for teams, 199–200
periodicals as data sources, 100
person, as work analysis component, 46–48
person-based compensation strategy, 27, 101, 239–240
"price warfare," 17
process reengineering, 16
productivity-based strategy, 17, 30–31
  checklist for, 282–285
  compensation strategy in, 27
  individual evaluation in, 163, 164
  job analysis emphasis for, 49
  pay bands in, 31, 143, 147, 148
  pay design in, 228–229
  pay evaluation in, 254
  pay implementation in, 244–245
  pay philosophy in, 24, 26
  pay plan design in, 32, 33
  pay systems in, 29
  performance standards in, 162, 200, 209
  rewards emphasis in, 29
  reward types for, 167, 227
  work analysis in, 68
  work evaluation systems for, 76, 77, 78, 201
professional development as performance strategy, 36
profit-sharing plans, 36, 38, 205, 213, 262
promotional opportunities, pay grades and, 147, 148
public-sector organizations, 29–30, 106, 109, 115, 141

quality-based strategy, 16
  checklist for, 277–280
  compensation strategy in, 27, 38
  individual evaluation in, 163, 164

Index

job analysis emphasis for, 49, 50
pay bands in, 31, 143, 147, 148
pay design in, 228–229
pay evaluation in, 254
pay implementation in, 244–245
pay philosophy in, 24, 26
pay plan design in, 32, 33, 34
pay systems in, 29
performance standards in, 162, 200, 209, 210
rewards emphasis in, 29
reward types for, 167, 201, 202, 214, 218–220, 227
work analysis in, 68
work evaluation systems for, 76, 77, 78, 201
questionnaires, for work analysis, 51, 52–63

recognition as reward, 28, 167, 202–203
research and development strategy, 10, 13
responsibility summary method, 51, 52–63, 64–70
results, as performance standards, 162, 178, 200
results-based compensation strategy, 10, 12, 27
retention pay philosophy, 26
reward systems, 5, 10–13
   cost-driven strategy and, 145
   goal-sharing plan, 10
   individual, 159–198
   team, 199–205
   types of, 28–29, 165–168, 201–204

sampling techniques for work analysis, 51
Sears, 18
seniority-based compensation strategy, 10, 27–28, 34, 105, 139, 150, 219, 258
senior management
   evaluation errors by, 238
   as organization evaluator, 210
   role in pay design, 228–229, 232
   as team evaluator, 201, 205
   training for pay implementation, 236, 238
single-rate pay structure, 138–139
skill-set development, 11, 12
   pay increase and, 140, 143, 149, 162, 239
   as reward, 167–168
skill-set development business strategy, 10, 31, 38, 263
statistical process control, 16
Stern Stewart consulting firm, 17
stock options, 203–204, 205
subordinates, evaluation by, 164
supervisors
   as reward evaluator, 163
   role in pay design, 229
   as work analysis sources, 50, 70
SWOT analysis, 20–21

task forces, 11
team leader, 10, 200
team rewards, 30, 245
   case study of, 204–205
   do's and don'ts for, 272–273
   employee attitudes toward, 239
   evaluators for, 200–201, 205
   performance standards for, 199–200
   personnel excluded from, 226–227
   by strategy type, 277, 279, 282, 284, 287, 289, 291
   types of, 201–204
   weighting of, 201, 202
teams, 10
   cross-functional, 17, 68, 69
   performance standards for, 199–200
   reward evaluation in, 163
   self-directed, 30, 47, 200
teamwork as performance strategy, 36, 244
360-degree assessment process, 163
throughput, 48
time off as reward, 167, 202
time to market strategy, *see* innovation-based strategy
timing of pay implementation, 238–239

total quality management program (TQM), 16, 26, 69, 143
training programs for pay implementation, 235–239, 241–252
traits as performance standards, 161
travel as work context component, 48
tuition reimbursement, 38, 167–168

unions
  business relations with, 70
  cost-driven firms and, 99, 105
  as data sources, 100, 116
  negotiations with, 106, 116
  role in pay design, 230, 232
  seniority-based systems and, 150
  single-rate grades viewed by, 139
U.S. Department of Labor, 71, 99

values, measurement of, 46
values statement, 19
variable pay systems, 29–30, 37–38
vertical integration, 68, 83
vision statement, 19, 20

work analysis
  components of, 46–50
  data collection techniques for, 51–64, 69, 70
  data sources for, 50
  do's and don'ts for, 270–271
  layers of, 47
  market surveys and, 96
  measurement of, 50–51
  need for, 45–46
  by strategy type, 276, 279, 281, 284, 286, 288, 291
work evaluation
  case studies of, 79–83
  do's and don'ts for, 271
  links to compensation and business strategies, 75–79, 151
  manual for, 85–88
  need for, 71–72
  pay assessment by, 27
  pay rates and, 138–139
  by strategy type, 276, 278–279, 281, 284, 286, 288, 290–291
  by supervisor, 12
  types of systems, 72–75
working conditions, 48, 90–91
work process flow, 48, 49

About the Author

Rob Heneman is a professor of management and human resources and director of graduate programs in labor and human resources in the Max M. Fisher College of Business at the Ohio State University. Rob has a Ph.D. in labor and industrial relations from Michigan State University, an M.A. in labor and industrial relations from the University of Illinois at Urbana-Champaign, and a B.A. in economics and psychology from Lake Forest College. Prior to joining the Ohio State University, Rob worked as a human resources specialist for the Pacific Gas and Electric Company. Rob's primary areas of research, teaching, and consulting are in performance management, compensation, staffing, and work design. He has received more than $1 million in funds for his research from the Work in America Institute, the AT&T Foundation, the Ford Motor Company, the American Compensation Association, the State of Ohio, the Consortium for Alternative Rewards Strategies Research, the Hay Group, and the Kauffman Center for Entrepreneurial Leadership.

Rob is the founder and editor of the *International Journal of Human Resources Management Education*. He is on the editorial boards of *Human Resource Management Journal*, *Human Resource Management Review*, *Human Resource Planning*, *Compensation and Benefits Review*, and *SAM Advanced Management Journal*. He has been awarded the "Outstanding Teacher Award" in the Masters in Labor and Human Resources program numerous times by the students at the Ohio State University. He has written four previous books including *Merit Pay: Linking Pay Increases to Performance Ratings*, and *Staffing Organization, 3rd Edition*, as well as numerous other publications. Currently, he is editing a new book, *Human Resource Management in Virtual Organizations*, and is writing a new book, *Human Resource Strategies for High Growth Entrepreneurial Firms*.

About the Author

Rob Heneman has consulted with more than sixty public and private sector organizations including IBM, Owens-Corning, BancOne, Time Warner, American Electric Power, Whirlpool, Quantum, AFL-CIO, Nationwide Insurance, the Limited, Borden, ABB, POSCO, U.S. Government Office of Personnel Management, and the states of Ohio and Michigan. He is past division chair, program chair, and executive committee member for the Human Resources Division of the Academy of Management. He is also a member of the certification program faculty of World at Work (formerly the American Compensation Association) and has served on the association's research, education, and academic partnership network advisory boards. He has made more than fifty presentations to universities, professional associations, and civic organizations. Rob has worked with business organizations and universities in North America, Europe, Russia, Asia, and Africa. His work has been reported in *The Wall Street Journal*, *USA Today*, *Money Magazine*, and ABCNEWS.com, and is listed in *Who's Who in the World*, *Who's Who in America*, *Who's Who in American Education*, and *Outstanding People in the 20th Century*.